King Arthur
and Robin Hood
on the Radio

King Arthur and Robin Hood on the Radio

Adaptations for American Listeners

KATHERINE BARNES ECHOLS

McFarland & Company, Inc., Publishers
Jefferson, North Carolina

Portions of this book originally appeared in Katherine Echols,
"Radio Adaptations of Robin Hood's Legend during the Golden Age
of Radio," *Journal of Radio & Audio Media* (2013),
reprinted by permission of Taylor and Francis LLC
(http://www.tandfonline.com).

LIBRARY OF CONGRESS CATALOGUING-IN-PUBLICATION DATA

Names: Echols, Katherine Barnes, 1966– author.
Title: King Arthur and Robin Hood on the radio : adaptations for
American listeners / Katherine Barnes Echols.
Description: Jefferson, North Carolina : McFarland & Company, Inc.,
Publishers, 2017 | Includes bibliographical references and index.
Identifiers: LCCN 2017032324 | ISBN 9781476667041
(softcover : acid free paper) ∞
Subjects: LCSH: Radio adaptations. | Robin Hood (Legendary
character) | Arthur, King.
Classification: LCC PN6120.R2 E34 2017 | DDC 808.82/22—dc23
LC record available at https://lccn.loc.gov/2017032324

BRITISH LIBRARY CATALOGUING DATA ARE AVAILABLE

ISBN (print) 978-1-4766-6704-1
ISBN (ebook) 978-1-4766-3000-7

© 2017 Katherine Barnes Echols. All rights reserved

*No part of this book may be reproduced or transmitted in any form
or by any means, electronic or mechanical, including photocopying
or recording, or by any information storage and retrieval system,
without permission in writing from the publisher.*

Front cover: King Arthur from *The Story of King
Arthur and His Knights* (© 2017 Old Book Art);
Robin Hood (© 2017 duncan1890/iStock);
1930s radio (© 2017 ideabug/iStock)

Printed in the United States of America

McFarland & Company, Inc., Publishers
Box 611, Jefferson, North Carolina 28640
www.mcfarlandpub.com

To my family and colleagues
for keeping the faith that this project would see
the light of day and for patiently listening
to me go on and on about radio:
my husband Robert,
my children Peyton, Austin, and Dylan,
my daughter-in-law Cassie
and my parents Wayne and Katherine Barnes.
With love to my granddaughter Annabelle
for bringing me joy.
Special thanks to my writers' group and colleagues,
JoAnn DiGeorgio-Lutz and Carol Bunch Davis,
for helping me navigate this process.

Table of Contents

Introduction	1
Prologue: When Radio Filled the Ether with "Winged Words"	11
1. Radio and the Formation of the Imagined Community	27
2. Adapting King Arthur and Robin Hood's Legend for Radio	35
3. What Is Radio Medievalism?	56
4. Adapting Malory's *Le Morte Darthur* for Radio	85
5. The Chivalric Ethos of the Comic Hero: Superman and Prince Valiant	116
6. White Knight of the Range: The Arthurian Knight in the Radio Western	134
7. Radio Adaptations of Robin Hood	146
8. Lighthearted Adaptations	178
Chapter Notes	189
Bibliography	192
Index	201

Introduction

Before the Internet, social media, and even television, newspapers and radio were the primary means of information and entertainment. Television began to replace radio in the 1940s, but for thirty years, the aural medium ruled the airwaves. Radio was unique in that it encouraged listeners to use their imaginations and to become participants in the story whatever their age, gender, race, or economic distinction. However, on radio, men were men, women were women, and white middle-class culture reigned. Radio programs did feature episodes that dramatized "minority-group life" (Barnouw, *A Tower*, 274), but African American characters were for the most part played by white actors. Two white vaudeville actors, Southerner Freeman Fisher Gosden and Midwesterner Charles J. Corell, played the parts of Amos and Andy on *Amos 'n' Andy*, one of radio's most important and influential programs. Other nationalities and ethnicities were portrayed on radio in programs such as Gertrude Berg's *The Goldbergs*, first broadcast as a radio drama and then as a television series. White middle-class American culture dominated the airwaves. Radio had a significant impact on American life and culture during its "Golden Age," from about the 1930s until the 1950s, but is now pretty much forgotten by most Americans except for "old time radio" enthusiasts.

Americans began embracing radio in the 1920s. Radio soon evolved from a hobby to a necessity, and the medium's cultural impact became clear. Radio was expected be a transmitter of high culture. To achieve this lofty goal of improving their American radio audience, radio networks were expected to align programming with a standardized broadcasting code. Children's programming especially was expected to promote American democratic values: morality, good citizenship, and patriotism. While radio networks did their best to meet this goal, radio advertising was at the same time encouraging consumerism; radio programs were endorsing race and gender stereotypes; and the aural format was becoming a useful platform for delivering hate speech, especially during the tumultuous 1930s and 1940s. Just as the twenty-first century today struggles with the challenges of the Internet and social media, in the early days of radio, alarmists worried that radio would have a potentially negative impact on American culture. This new and exciting technology was recognized as a powerful force that provided both new opportunities and unique challenges.

The radio generation grew up listening to all sorts of radio programs—educational and entertaining. Radio dramas, Westerns, detective programs, horror and science fiction programs, children's programs, situation comedies, and variety shows filled the airwaves. Material for these programs came from original scripts and adaptations of classic novels, short stories, plays, poetry, folk tales, legends, and movie scripts, such as adaptations of the works of Guy de Maupassant, James Fenimore Cooper, Louisa May Alcott, Ernest Hemingway, to the legends of King Arthur and Robin Hood and the Bible.

This book focuses on American radio adaptations of Arthurian romance and Robin Hood's legend, and it considers how these episodes illustrate the medieval British ideal of chivalric knighthood and embrace this ideal as a standard of *American* morality and masculinity. This study also situates these radio adaptations within a social and historical context in order to illustrate how, as examples of twentieth-century medievalism, these radio adaptations reflected American cultural anxieties. For example, radio scriptwriters in the 1940s engaged with medievalism when they incorporated into radio adaptations of Arthurian romance and Robin Hood's legend the themes of post-war world hunger and the rising threat of fascism. The scope of this project is limited to the decades that most fully experienced the medium of radio as a cultural force in America.

Thirty-three radio adaptations and/or appropriations of the legends of King Arthur and Robin Hood are considered here from all genres—children's programs, dramas, mysteries, comedies, musicals, and variety shows that aired between the 1930s and mid–1950s, with two additional programs from the 1970s. Taking radio's social and cultural influence into account, radio scriptwriters adapting these legends produced storylines that clearly defined the difference between "good" and "bad" conduct by stressing a character's chivalric qualities. For instance, storylines written for *Popeye the Sailor, Smilin' Ed's Buster Brown Gang, Family Theater, Let's Pretend, The Adventures of Superman, Prince Valiant, Escape, The*

Cisco Kid, *Wild Bill Hickok*, and *Gunsmoke* fulfilled this expectation that radio would be an active participant in the development of the auditor's moral behavior. Sources for these radio adaptations of the legends of King Arthur and Robin Hood were Thomas Malory's voluminous fifteenth-century *Le Morte Darthur*, Howard Pyle's nineteenth-century Arthuriad and collection of Robin Hood tales, *The Merry Adventures of Robin Hood*, and medieval Robin Hood ballad collections, all of which were adapted and compressed sometimes into fifteen-minute or thirty-minute radio formats for juvenile and adult programming.

Medieval chivalry was a gender-specific behavioral code intended to restrain a knight's behavior on and off the battlefield, but the medieval chivalric code also played a substantial role in the standardization of male, and to some extent female, conduct. During the nineteenth-century chivalric revival in Britain and America, chivalric literature and youth groups molded boys and girls into modern knights modeled on King Arthur, Sir Lancelot, Sir Gawain, the Lady Elaine, and even Robin Hood: men and women who modeled chivalry—virtue, honor, courtesy, bravery, and a sense of justice. Queen Guinevere as King Arthur's wife rarely made the list of virtuous women because of her affair with Sir Lancelot. The legends of King Arthur and Robin Hood were brought to American radio likely because their stories were already familiar to listeners and easy to adapt to an aural format. Because of time constraints, adaptations were based on only the most familiar scenes in the legends and highlighted personal and social morality as important character traits.

On radio the Middle Ages was reproduced through vivid descriptions of setting and costume while chivalry was demonstrated through a character's words and deeds. Arthurian legend, in particular, proved to be an especially pliable source for radio. The radio audience recognized a chivalric hero when they heard one. Scriptwriters couched modern anxieties in a medieval context and reinvented the knight errant as an American cowboy, a superhero, or a soldier. The chivalric knight, and we include among his number Robin Hood for obvious reasons, was not a character reserved solely for storylines set in the Middle Ages. He morphed into modern-day American heroes of the pulps, comics, movies, television, and radio. The modern knight was the "caped crusader" Superman, the "champion of justice " known as the Lone Ranger, and other knight–Robin Hood figures like the Cisco Kid, Britt Ponset the Six Shooter, Simon Templar, and the Saint, all men of character with a moral sense of right who upheld the law and protected the underdog. The cowboy was the white knight of the range who practiced a specific type of chivalry infused with *American* morality. Fans of the Western were encouraged to pledge to abide by the "cowboy code" promoted on radio and on screen in the 1930s by one of America's favorite cowboys of film and radio: Gene Autry. Autry's "cowboy commandments," similar to the Boy Scout code of honor and the Golden Rule, encouraged his fans to practice chivalric knighthood in their daily lives. Radio adaptations based on the legends of King Arthur and Robin Hood broadcast on family-friendly programs followed the same pattern.

One of the medium's primary responsibilities was to produce morally infused quality shows for radio's youngest listeners, so the majority of radio adaptations and appropriations of the legend reflect the chivalric values attributed to these medieval heroes. Chivalry as a model of behavior was reproduced on radio and debated in the newspapers into the 1950s and was still characterized by courtesy, kindness, and respect, especially for women, although modern women were expected to extend the same courtesies to men. For example, a Saturday morning round-table discussion on the topic of chivalry was broadcast on WDRC radio in Connecticut in 1952. High-school-aged boys and girls were invited to discuss the relevancy of chivalry in a modern world and asked whether the concept was already dead or dying. For this group of youngsters, chivalry was no longer attached to a medieval and outdated code but was illustrated in simple acts of kindness and courtesy ("Youth Panel Sees"). If chivalry was, in fact, dying by the 1950s, it was probably a good thing, according to another critic who considered it medieval—outdated and oppressive. Mary Hawthorn, writing for the *Washington Post*, blamed the "neurotic distress" of the era on the outdated ideas of chivalry and doubted whether anyone actually wanted to "return to the old ideology of masculine rule and female submission." According to Hawthorn, the neurosis plaguing men and women at the time was brought on by people trying to "adhere to cultural ideals of King Arthur's times, when the twentieth century situation seems to call for radically different behavior." She believed the time was long overdue for young people to be taught what "'real' masculinity" was about (Hawthorn), but more about this debate later.

Research for this project has made possible future lines of inquiry on a variety of topics related to radio and the radio generation, but this study did have its limitations. As radio is an ephemeral art form, one of the challenges was the unavailability of radio scripts. However, after reading the 1950s *Gunsmoke* script for the episode titled "Robin Hood" online in a script database, it became clear that printed scripts would not always have been beneficial. After all, radio is an aural medium that relies on dialogue and sound. As the focus of this research was how chivalry was conveyed on radio through a character's word and deed, the script would have little value other than clarifying dialogue. Scriptwriters were writing for the ear, not the eye. As suggested by the annotations on a copy of the *Gunsmoke* script, voice actors did not always speak their lines verbatim for many reasons. Despite these limitations, the nature of this project raised more questions than it answered about radio programming in the decades from the 1930s to the late 1950s, such as the following: the correlation between children's literature and other children's radio programming; the way in which the social and political climate influenced radio programming during and after wartime; patriotism as a theme in children's radio programming during wartime; and how radio representationed gender, race, and class.

Resources for this book spanned medieval and post-medieval sources and books and newspapers published beginning in the 1920s through today. Sources were comprised of books on American radio studies and radio histories, medieval history, and adaptation theory. Anthologies of radio programs and various studies of the history of radio abound, but particularly helpful were John Dunning's informative and often cited *On the Air: The Encyclopedia of Old-Time Radio* and J. Fred MacDonald's *Don't Touch That Dial! Radio Programming in American Life from 1920–1960*. Both are entertaining and insightful reads for radio scholars and enthusiasts alike. Neil Verma's *Theater of the Mind*, Susan J. Douglas's *Listening In: Radio and the American Imagination from Amos 'n' Andy and Edward R. Murrow to Wolfman Jack and Howard Stern*, and Michele Hilmes's *Radio Voices* and a number of additional texts offer in-depth studies of radio's influence on American culture. Also notable are Benedict Anderson's *Imagined Communities*, a study of the making of national identity, and the earliest study of radio's effect on the human psyche, *The Psychology of Radio* by Hadley Cantril and Gordon W. Allport (1935). Cantril and Allport were among the first to "map out" the "new mental world created by radio" and the power of the medium (Cantril and Allport, vii). Erik Barnouw's three-volume encyclopedic study on U.S. broadcasting history—*A Tower in Babel, The Golden Web*, and *The Image Empire*—traced the evolution and impact of emerging communication technologies that shaped the twentieth century: radio and television. Other useful sources were books published in the early twentieth century for emerging radio scriptwriters and broadcasters and collections of radio plays.

Benedict Anderson's study of how humans shape community identity explains how media can divide and unify a community and a nation. Marilyn Lawrence Boemer's *The Children's Hour: Radio Programs for Children, 1929–1956* explores the influence of some of radio's most popular children's radio programs. A significant part of this study is the process of adaptation, the transition of text "from one genre to another" to make dated material relevant to new audiences (Sanders 19). Linda Hutcheon's *A Theory of Adaptation* and Julie Sanders's *Adaptation and Appropriation* proved invaluable, especially when considering the process of adapting literature to film. Hutcheon's rubric for examining the adaptation process was also applicable to radio. Approximately a handful of books focus on literature adapted for radio, with the most informative written by Tim DeForest, *Radio by the Book: Adaptations of Literature and Fiction on the Airwaves* and *Storytelling in the Pulps, Comics, and Radio: How Technology Changed Popular Fiction in America*, two entertaining and informative reads. Books and articles written about the medium for the radio amateur and professional writers provided invaluable insight into a lost, and all but forgotten, craft. Radio truly ruled the ether.

This study is divided into sections that focus on the history and influence of American radio, the nature and process of adaptation, the chivalric revival and medievalism, background on Arthurian legend, a selection of radio adaptations of Arthurian legend, background on the history of the Western and the cowboy, a history of Robin Hood, and radio adaptations of Robin Hood's legend. By including such a broad overview, this author hopes to clarify how all of these pieces fit together through a general understanding of not only the role radio played in shaping American culture but how the legends of King Arthur and Robin Hood participated in this process.

Chapter 1, "Radio and the Formation of the Imagined Community," introduces readers to the phenomenon of radio in America from the 1930s and late 1950s, the medium's role in wartime and peacetime, its cultural influence, and the part radio played in the formation of national identity, class identity, gender roles, and ideas of race. This section includes a synopsis of the broadcasting code that standardized radio programs and the code instituted for children's programming, which was similar to the one that guided the publication of children's literature; this prologue also explores how scripts met the expectations established by such broadcasting codes. Because of these morality codes, children's radio programs were not only expected to entertain young listeners but to also mold their character. For instance, most radio adaptations produced for children's programs based on Arthurian legend and the legend of Robin Hood held up the knight and Robin Hood as chivalric heroes worthy of imitation.

Chapter 2, "Adapting King Arthur and Robin Hood's Legend for Radio," broadly defines "adaptation" and considers it in relation to historical and contemporary examples taken from literature, film, and radio, singling out three radio programs as examples of how a radio scriptwriter might approach writing an adaptation. Examples of radio episodes are drawn from *Family Theater, The Ford Theater*, and the situation comedy *The Life of Riley*. This chapter also discusses the controversy that can arise when a canonical work, such as Sir Thomas Malory's *Le Morte Darthur*, a fifteenth-century Arthurian romance, is adapted to an untraditional format. Radio and comic books were two mediums considered by some to be untraditional. As "low-brow" representations of American culture, adaptations of canonical works in these mediums were not without their critics. For instance, criticism arose when the works of British and American literary giants such as Sir Walter Scott, Charles Dickens, and Mark Twain were, like Malory, adapted for comic books produced by *Classic Illustrated* (1941–1971) and radio. This chapter considers the fidelity debate and analyzes three radio adaptations of Twain's *A Connecticut Yankee in King Arthur's Court* and a reaction to one of the modernizations of this book.

Chapter 3, "What Is Radio Medievalism?," picks up where the discussions of adaptation and medievalism left. This section provides an overview of the chivalric revival in America and Britain, discusses the various youth groups that were an outgrowth of this movement, and explores how chivalry became a standard or code of behavior for the ages. In particular, this section examines "radio medievalism" and the approaches medieval and post-medieval adapters took when they adapted these legends for different mediums. This section also takes a look at the history of both King Arthur and Robin Hood, suggests why they were adapted for British and American literature, and why they made it on the air. Radio is a uniquely aural medium that required the audience's full attention and engagement with the program. While the flexibility of these legends made it easy for the adapter to do his job, these tales were thought appropriate subjects and didactic fare for young listeners. With the emphasis on character-building programs in the 1930s and 1940s, it seems reasonable to assume that as chivalric heroes, both King Arthur and Robin Hood had something to teach young listeners through their chivalric deeds and dialogue. In addition to discussing the historical and post-medieval constructions of King Arthur and Robin Hood, this section looks at the medievalist impulse in adaptations of Arthurian romance and Robin Hood's legend and places these adaptations within an historical framework.

Chapter 4, "Adapting Malory's *Le Morte Darthur* for Radio," examines adaptations of Arthurian romance in radio programs on the air between the 1940s and late 1950s, a popular period for adaptations in all medium, across genres: the children's program, Westerns, dramas, and variety shows. Adaptations broadcast on family-friendly radio programs typically shied away from overtly violent scenes or adult content, in contrast to the adult drama *Crime Classics*. *Crime Classics* was promoted as a program that took for its content historical murder cases, but in an unusual move, this episode was inspired by the death of King Arthur in battle with his son Mordred. This storyline focused on Malory's "The Book of Sir Lancelot and Queen Guinevere" and "The Poisoned Apple" and provides an entertaining and engaging half hour tale of adultery, revenge, and murder. Two other quite different radio shows toyed with Arthurian romance. *Gunsmoke* produced an adaptation of Sir Walter Scott's "Lochinvar" and *Sealtest Variety Theater* reproduced the more tender scenes between Elaine and Lancelot. Of interest is how gender was constructed and chivalric knighthood conveyed for a wide audience made up children and adults listening to *The Land of the Lost*, *Let's Pretend*, *Family Theater*, and *Smilin' Ed's Buster Brown Gang*. One of the more chivalric females captured in a radio adaptation was the young Lady Elaine who gives succor and is a helpmate to Lancelot. Elaine in these radio productions stands in sharp contrast to the antagonistic Morgan le Fay, King Arthur's wicked step-sister, who attempts to usurp the throne and rule England. Unfortunately Queen Guinevere is unable distance herself from accusations of adultery, and if she is among the character line up in a radio program, her affair with Lancelot is alluded to and blamed for destroying King Arthur.

Chapter 5, "The Chivalric Ethos of the Comic Hero: Superman and Prince Valiant," looks at the radio adaptations featuring two of America's comic book heroes, Superman and Prince Valiant, and the radio programs *The Adventures of Superman*, and *Prince Valiant*. The discussion of the radio series *The Adventures of Superman* provides an overview of the social and historical context that informed a storyline with an agenda. The radio series took aim at the Ku Klux Klan in a series of three storylines broadcast in the 1940s that launched Operation Tolerance: "The Clan of the Fiery Cross," "The Hate Mongers Organization," and "Knights of the White Carnation." This last episode, "Knights of the White Carnation," is framed with an anti-bigotry message that warns of the dangers of hate speech ("Knights of"). This episode is indicative of how a scriptwriter adapted Arthurian tropes in order to grapple with the modern threat of fascism. Prince Valiant is an entertaining adaptation of Arthurian romance about the rise of a prince from squire to a knight of the Round Table.

Chapter 6, "White Knight of the Range: The Arthurian Knight in the Radio Western," juxtaposes the romanticized mythos of the medieval knight and the American cowboy and the influence of the Old West on American popular culture. The early western literature of writers such as James Fenimore Cooper, Bret Harte, Max Brand, Owen Wister, and Zane Grey was popular in the nineteenth century and presented "good guy" cowboys with the ethos of a knight who had Robin Hood's sense of social justice. The focus of this chapter is on two radio adaptations of Arthurian romance broadcast on the radio Westerns *Wild Bill Hickok* and *The Cisco Kid* in the 1950s, both which would have been heard by children. Of particular interest is a Christmastime episode of *Wild Bill Hickok* "Sir Tommy, the Silver Knight," which incorporates the medieval dream vision and allegorical figures to present a didactic tale about greed. In "Sir Cisco, Knight of the Round Table" the Cisco Kid and his companion Pancho encounter an old man who, like Don Quixote, believes he is a medieval knight. This storyline humorously explores how medievalism can go awry.

Chapter 7, "Radio Adaptations of Robin Hood," presents an overview of Robin Hood's legend in popular culture in the United States and Great Britain with an emphasis on radio adaptations. This section also analyzes adaptations produced for children and adults from the 1930s through the 1950s: *Popeye the Sailor*, *Smilin' Ed's Buster Brown Program*, *Family Theater*, and *Let's Pretend*, as well as two adult-themed dramas, *Casey Crime Photographer* and *Escape*. Discussed at length is Antony Ellis's "Robert of Huntingdon" broadcast on the radio drama *Escape* in the 1950s as an example of a radio program influenced by the paranoia many felt about Communism gaining influence in the United States. This section ties radio scripts to their possible sources, the ballads and collections such as *Gest of Robyn Hood*; Joseph Ritson's collection of ballads *Robin Hood: A Collection of All the Ancient Poems, Songs, and Ballads, Now Extant, Relative to That Celebrated English Outlaw: To Which Are Prefixed Historical Anecdotes of His Life in Two Volumes* (1795); and popular literature such

Howard Pyle's *The Merry Adventures of Robin Hood of Great Renown, in Nottinghamshire* (1883). Pyle's book was the source for early film adaptations of Robin Hood in the United States, such as Kinemacolor's *Robin Hood* released in 1913.

In this chapter, a section on Robin Hood and radio Westerns, traces the influence of chivalric knighthood and Robin Hood to the myth of the American cowboy. This section focuses on how post-medieval medievalism was less about the medieval period and more about the century or even the decade in which it was produced. The radio Western *Gunsmoke* adapted Robin Hood's persona for a 1950s storyline that presents a civics lesson on good citizenship and represents how radio scriptwriters engaged with medievalism. "Robin Hood" is about a bandit named Teddy Bluefisher who appropriates Robin Hood's reputation for stealing from the rich to give to the poor to gain the confidence of the residents of Dodge City in order to rob them. In the end, this *Gunsmoke* episode delivers a lesson on the necessity of respecting civic authority.

Chapter 8, "Lighthearted Adaptations," provides additional analyses of early and later radio adaptations of King Arthur and Robin Hood's legend. *Mickey Mouse Theater, Avalon Time, Abbott and Costello, Proudly We Hail, The Story Lady*, and *Crisis* created unique renderings of the legends and aired during different decades. These radio programs were included in this section for different reasons: they were unavailable for analysis, were simply a parody of the legends and, therefore, offered little more than entertainment, or aired after the 1950s. For whatever reason, these radio adaptations were worth mentioning to show that even after radio's golden years had ended, the legends of King Arthur and Robin Hood, the Middle Ages, and the trope of chivalric knighthood were all still being adapted for the medium.

Prologue
When Radio Filled the Ether with "Winged Words"

Radio was a fairly new medium when in 1929 one enthusiast was so awed by the power of this new technology that he waxed poetic, describing the transmission of radio sound waves as "fill[ing] the ether with [millions of] winged words ... darting around the world in the twinkle of a star" ("Winged"). To provide some sense of the power and popularity of radio in the twentieth century, we must look back at early perceptions of the new medium and its perceived influence. Between the 1920s and 1950s radio was as culturally important as the Internet and social media are today. The expectation was that radio broadcasting would serve the good of the people as a source of information, entertainment, education (college correspondence courses were available on radio) and culture. Great strides in radio technology and broadcasting by 1922 had amateur radio operators, commercial broadcasters, and the army and navy vying for the ether. Herbert Hoover, Secretary of the Department of Commerce, estimated that at least 600,000 to 1,000,000 people owned a wireless set and predicted that the country was "upon the threshold of a new means of widespread communication of intelligence" that would have a "profound" effect upon public education and welfare, and he saw the ether as "a great national asset" (qtd. in Loewenthal 10, 44, 46). Congress and the Department of Commerce had to consider the extent to which the government should be held responsible for the "moral and intellectual welfare of the people" (Loewenthal 50) while amateur and commercial broadcasters were at odds over the "equitable allocation of the airwaves" ("Radiotorial Comment" 9). Until legislation in the United States passed regulating the airwaves, broadcasters were encouraged to come to a "gentleman's agreement" and voluntarily comply with current licensing regulations while ensuring that even the youngest radio enthusiast could still access the airwaves ("Radiotorial Comment" 9).

Writing in 1946 at the height of radio's popularity, James Rowland Angell, the Public Service Counselor for National Broadcasting Company (NBC), described radio as "part theatre, part concert hall, part newspaper, part pulpit, part school, part forum," a "single medium [that] serves so many and so divergent purposes" with the potential to exercise a "tremendous ... influence upon the thought and feeling of millions of American" (qtd. in Waller viii). Hadley Cantril and Gordon W. Allport had drawn the same conclusion in 1935 in what was one of the earliest studies of the psychological impact of radio listening on the American public. Angell had, of course, experienced first-hand the effects of the medium in wartime. With the outbreak of war, radio had become the secret weapon of propaganda. Sherman Harvard Dryer evaluated radio's new role and looked to its "tremendous potential for building in a society an appreciation of the hazards and obligations of war and the ultimate peace" and recognized that it had awakened the public to current affairs (viii).

This was also a period of tremendous growth for research on the cultural and global implications of radio, the fifth estate, and the development of new technologies. The speed at which these new technologies developed would make it possible for business and politics to be conducted quickly, hopefully encourage women's active engagement in politics, and promote world unity by bringing world leaders together. People from all walks of life were fascinated with the possibilities of these new technologies. Radio had primarily been a means of transcontinental communication for the military and a hobby for almost everyone else. Soon radio clubs caught on: boys and girls learned how to build their own radio sets and read books about the adventures of amateur "radio boys and radio girls." Commercial and amateur radio stations continued to spring up nationwide, and young men were encouraged to train as radio technicians for what was becoming a promising profession.

Radio broadcast intermittently aired weather and market reports, news, music, sports, and "snake oil" advertising. Joining this usual fare of radio broadcasts were book reviews and book talks, musical events such as operas and symphonies, plays, and poetry recitations, a particular favorite of listeners with more literary tastes. When book review talks first aired on radio in 1924 in New York, the fear was that a program meant to supplement discussions about literature would replace the book sections in newspapers and magazines. Of course, this never happened. The understanding was that these quality programs had the potential to carry culture to the millions of listeners who lived in the "remotest parts of the country" ("Book Reviews"). Radio plays were "destined to be a greater dramatic art than the motion picture" that would "bring to its listeners what the motion picture never" could—"the literature of the theatre," with the understanding that it could never replace the traditional theater (Arliss qtd. in "Arliss Sees Radio").

Broadcasting was as "heavily fraught with potentialities as the discovery of printing," writes one optimistic individual in 1924:

> I suppose that at the end of the fifteenth century a number of people asked themselves what was going to happen to literature under the influence of the strange new monster that threatened individual expression. And certainly at the present moment many people are asking what will be the effect on literature of broadcasting. In a way, ... it is a return to the more primitive method of publicity when the bard stood up and recited his own epic. But it is a return with a difference: for, whereas formerly the audience was limited to a few hundred listeners, the audience of the contemporary bard may be several hundreds of thousands and within the next few years it may easily be several millions ["Book Reviews"].

Despite radio's role in acculturating the American public, nay-sayers doubted the medium could produce anything new that was worthy of the designation of "art."

Before watching television and surfing the "net" became American pastimes, people listened to the radio, tuning their dials to news and entertainment, listening to comedies, variety shows, horror and science fiction programs, Westerns, crime dramas, serials, film adaptations, and juvenile and educational programs, all simultaneously competing for the airwaves. The airwaves carried to listeners the works of William Shakespeare, Thomas Malory, Sir Walter Scott, Mary Shelley, Robert Lewis Stevenson, Herman Melville, Edgar Allan Poe, Dr. Seuss, and adaptations of fairy tales and legends featuring King Arthur and Robin Hood, along with adaptations of newly released films. Radio was a new forum for the author, the poet, and the dramatist.

Radio did become a permanent cultural and informational mainstay, for a while. The medium created a sense of national unity and sense of safety in the United States and abroad in both peacetime and wartime. By the 1930s, the radio was a standard feature in cars and on motorcycles. In wartime radio kept Americans current on war news, kept their spirits high with patriotic programs and messages, and provided a brief respite from the worries of the day. Radio programs addressed social anxieties, transmitted cultural values, reinforced cultural hierarchies, and "emphasized ... uniquely 'American' character" (Hilmes 1, 4). Americans listened to on-the-spot broadcasts of radio newsmen Edward R. Murrow and William L. Shirer and others reporting from Vienna and London as they followed Adolf Hitler's invasion of Austria. They listened with dread to Hitler's boast in 1939 that it was only a matter of time before Germany invaded Czechoslovakia.

Despite radio's rising popularity in the 1920s and 1930s, owning a radio set was not economically feasible for many Americans, especially during the Great Depression. Using data collected from the U.S. Census of 1930, 1940, and 1950, Steve Craig analyzes the rate at which Americans purchased radio sets during that time. Craig points to the differences between purchases of radios in the geographic regions of the United States and finds that only nine percent of southern rural households owned a radio set in the 1930s compared to radio ownership by fifty percent of urban populations living in the northeast, north central, and western parts of the United States (179, 182). As the economy slowly recovered after the Depression, radio sets became more affordable and Americans had more disposable income with which to purchase them. By 1945 the majority of American homes would have at least one radio set, according to a study conducted by the United States Office of War. The *American Handbook* published by the department reported that in 1945 alone more than 59 million Americans owned a radio, while approximately 90 million people listened to their radios on a daily basis (477). The Federal Communications Commission (FCC) began licensing television stations in 1939, but not until after World War II did the new medium become as significant as radio. By the 1950s, television had nudged radio to the sidelines and dominated the market. Radio networks were forced to adjust their format. During this transitional period, many radio programs were cancelled, adapted for television, or, like the popular Westerns *Gunsmoke* and *The Lone Ranger*, aired simultaneously on radio and television for a time.

With the growth of the radio industry came new problems. In the early days of radio broadcasting, idealists and skeptics alike reflected on the potential and the power of this developing technology. Predictions that radio would become a cultural force rang true. Many people expressed their high expectations for the medium. Radio could bridge the cultural divide, enlighten and entertain the masses, and even strengthen the family bond; in fact, the same predictions were made about television. The emerging technologies of radio and television could promote world peace and unity and be used as tools of democracy. Radio opened the world to listeners and exposed them to different cultures, religions, and political views and, many hoped, would encourage tolerance. Radio would "homogenize" the country, promote the ideas of "national uniformity," good citizenship, class cohesion, and a standardized English language (McLuhan qtd. in Douglas 25; Verma; Cantril and Allport 27–35, 26).

Early scholars studying the influence of radio upon listeners "hailed radio as a powerful medium of improvement" and praised the medium for "fulfilling ... optimistic cultural hopes" (Lazarsfeld 6). Still others worried that the "real" problem was radio's psychological grip (Cantril and Allport 3). Similar to the concerns raised today over the influence of the Internet upon human interaction and children, critics of the medium, parents, and civic leaders worried that listening to the radio would lead to "group think" and that the auditory pleasure one got from listening to radio would have a detrimental effect on social interaction and younger, more sensitive listeners (Cantril and Allport 4). Social psychologists in the 1930s predicted that in a world unaccustomed to the possibilities offered by radio, the reality was that it could also be used as a powerful tool of propaganda with the potential to "make mischief" (Cantril and Allport 32). Moreover, the timely publication of research that identified the potentially harmful effects of film content on youth did not do much to help the industry, either (Ellis 197).

This was also a period of territorial dispute between newspapers and radio stations over the broadcast of news. Loose self-regulation had left the door open for abuse and accusations that radio advertisers were responsible for deceptive advertising and used unsavory marketing strategies in children's programs. Children's programs were believed to play a role in the "emotional, intellectual, and social development of the child's personality" (Waller 246). Network executives and watchdog groups, such as the Radio Council on Children's Programs and the Women's National Radio Committee, which lobbied for educational and cultural programming, were comprised of community leaders, educators, and parents who voiced their concerns about the potentially negative influence radio could have on listeners, especially children. In an editorial written by The Women's National Radio Committee chairwoman, the organization shared concerns over the quality of radio programming and standards of advertising with members calling for the "improvement in the character of all programs" but stopped short of laying "sex delinqueny and moral perversion at the feet of the industry" (Milligan). The radio industry reacted in the same fashion as the motion picture industry had in response to the same sort of criticism of film content following World War I (Ellis 197). Thus far radio networks had self-regulated content, but this caused radio networks to react by enforcing a more strident "self-policing" policy when faced with the threat of future state or even federal censorship. The Federal Trade Commission and the FCC joined forces with radio networks with the expectation that only appropriate content and truthful advertising would make it on air.

A decade before this standard for broadcasting was written, WGY, a radio station in New York City, had anticipated potential on-air problems with questionable content. The station warned participants in its Radio Drama Prize Competition to keep "PLOTS ... CLEAN with no attempt at questionable situations," and, most important, that "No 'sex dramas' be considered" (qtd. in Barnouw, *A Tower* 137). The National Association of Broadcasters created the broadcasting code in the 1930s in reaction to public criticism of radio content and to avoid government censorship. Juvenile radio programs especially were to promote "democracy, equality, freedom, ... individualism, and the ... law," values that could also be easily "link[ed] ... with the anti-fascist cause" (MacDonald 63). This last expectation was especially important in wartime broadcasts when radio joined the war effort. The Motion Picture Production Code, or the Hays Act, adopted in 1930, regulated depictions of profanity, violence, crime, sexuality, and a host of other taboo topics. Despite or because of this effort to appeal to a variety of listeners, radio networks continued to be scrutinized, debated, and critiqued.

With regard to children's programming, radio content continued to be held to a similar standard established at the turn of the century by the book industry governing children's literature, a point discussed shortly. According to the broadcasting code, children's radio programs were expected to impart the same prescribed *American* values taught in children's books. This "children's code" banned the following from juvenile radio programs: the "unfair exploitation of others"; "exalting, as modern heroes, of gangsters, criminals, and racketeers"; "overt violence and horror [and] references to kidnapping"; as well as advertising appeals that urged children to participate in contests by promising to keep programs on the air or to keep radio heroes and heroines out of trouble (Callahan 369, 374). Despite efforts to control radio advertising, premiums and contests were slyly incorporated into the programs and were quite popular with listeners. According to guidelines for radio scriptwriters of children's programming, children's shows were expected to convey American morality and the qualities reflected in the juvenile radio program *Jack Armstrong, the All-American Boy*, which were to have "respect for the law" and parental authority, and to encourage the chivalric qualities of "clean living, high morals, ... fair play, and honorable behavior" (Callahan 369, Waller 241). Scriptwriters creating content for children's programs were cautioned not to "talk down" to children and were encouraged to write scripts that "contain[ed] wonder: including chivalry and adventure; ... built of image-provoking words and sentences" and that engaged the imagination (Callahan 414). Moreover, scriptwriters should "transmit the mood and particular excitement of the story" ("Acting").

In addition to following the standards outlined in the radio broadcasting code, children's radio programs had to meet a list of criteria to stay on the air. For example, fantasy and fairy-tale radio programs were to identify the "fantastic and imaginative" as "unreal" while the problems encountered during childhood "involving friendship, gang loyalty, and respect for one's equals" were to be "frequently and honestly portrayed" (Waller 246). Times had changed. The radio generation had outgrown simple fairy tales and had traded Jack the Giant Killer for Superman. Children had experienced war and were living in "an age filled with every kind of thrill and adventure" (Waller 243–244). Naturally they preferred exciting thrillers. If parents had their way, children would only listen to classic tales like "*Treasure Island, Huckleberry Finn*, Robin Hood, Hans Christian Andersen's stories, Grimms' Fairy Tales," despite the violence woven into the fabric of such stories (Waller 239). As Judith Waller, an executive with NBC radio in the 1940s pointed out, they had forgotten the level of violence that played out in classic fairy tales. With this being said, many of these classics were adapted for radio.

The legends of King Arthur and Robin Hood were ideal content for radio programs listened to by a mixed audience. Not only were these medieval heroes familiar to a twentieth-century radio audience who knew of these tales through various media, but the flexibility of the legends, the ease with which they could be adapted to an aural medium, and the values the characters imparted were ideal for an aural format and mixed audience. Even though they were iconic British figures, the adventures of Robin Hood or King Arthur and his Knights of the Round Table had always been popular with American readers. Even Benjamin Franklin was familiar with Robin Hood but grumbled that American colonists preferred reading Robin Hood ballads to reading scripture. The Middle Ages remain visible in American popular culture. King Arthur and Robin Hood continue to be merchandised for toys, board games, Halloween costumes, and all manner of collectibles. Theme parks and festivals are organized around Robin Hood and the Middle Ages. King Arthur and Robin Hood appear in operas, plays, books, comic books and comic strips, television series, films, and radio plays. Though they are British national heroes, Robin Hood and King Arthur have been adopted worldwide. In the United States their images are politicized and linked to presidential candidates and tax proposals and have been used to drive cultural and moral agendas. King Arthur and Robin Hood are identified with the chivalric qualities necessary to a civilized society—bravery, loyalty, courtesy, truthfulness, and a sense of protection toward the oppressed.

According to Ralph Rose, a director and adapter writing for radio interviewed in the 1940s, the classic adventures of King Arthur and Robin Hood were adaptable to radio primarily because they appealed to a wide audience. For Rose and his fellow adapters, writing for radio was challenging because it required radio scriptwriters to emphasize the plot of a "complicated adventure yarn," think of Malory's complex *Le Morte Darthur*, and Robin Hood's *Gest*, while still "transmit[ting] the mood and particular excitement of the story" ("Acting"). Moreover, children needed "genuine characters of truly heroic proportions as imaginary playmates and models to imitate and with which to identify" themselves (Waller 264). What source or sources were used for most of these radio adaptations is unclear since literary and film adaptations of these legends number in the thousands. What is clear is that the scriptwriter stuck to the more familiar storylines already adapted, and sometimes modernized, by others.

The radio scriptwriter had unlimited source material for his adaptations, such as Professor Eugene Vinaver's collection of Malory's works based on a fifteenth-century manuscript discovered in 1934 in the Fellows Library of Winchester College. Vinaver edited Malory's sprawling romance *Le Morte Darthur*, the *Death of Arthur*, divided it into eight parts comprised of forty-two books and tales, and published it in 1945.[1] This has become the standard edition of *Le Morte Darthur*. Howard Pyle's three-volume Athuriad and collection of Robin Hood tales, along with a host of other medieval and post-medieval adaptations and modernizations of both legends, also provided plenty of material for radio. On radio Arthurian legend and the tales of Robin Hood exhibited tight writing, fast-paced action, lively dialogue, and complex sound effects that transported the audience back to the Middle Ages.

King Arthur and Robin Hood Come to Radio

Before Arthurian romance and Robin Hood's legend could be adapted for children's radio programs, the more violent and salacious episodes had to be expunged. For instance, among the episodes in Malory that never made it on radio were King Arthur's killing of the Mont St. Michel Giant, a cannibalistic monster wearing a cape bordered with the beards of fifteen kings, who dined on Christian children and raped and murdered maidens, as well as King Arthur's effort to protect his throne by ordering the extermination on May Day of male children born to nobles. Likewise, the more violent episodes in the ballads of Robin Hood are either glossed over or missing from radio adaptations of Robin Hood's legend, such as Robin Hood's killing of Guy of Gisbornne and the Sheriff of Nottingham, and the yeoman's death caused by the prioress of the Kirklees nunnery. In one radio adaptation in particular, Robin Hood fights and kills the bounty hunter Guy of Gisbornne, but his death is described for the radio audience as an act of self-defense.

Saddened by the turn children's radio programming had taken by 1942, *New York Times* columnist Richard Match shared with readers his disappointment that in wartime younger listeners of the radio generation preferred a superhero's radio adventure to the "time-hallowed fairy tale":

> Young ears listen avidly [to the adventures of the new heroes] Captain Midnight and five or six other modern Jack-the-Giant-Killers ... [while] ... [t]he old fantastic two-headed giant has been replaced by master spies and supercriminals. The fair damsel in distress is now a stolen airplane design.... The hero, man or boy, is a simple, modest fellow, all courage, all virtue. His opponent, very often a "master criminal," bent on control of the world or the destruction of the United States, is the epitome of evil and low trickery.

Match had no cause to be disheartened. Superheroes and cowboys had become Arthurian knights and heroes who by example taught children to hate criminals and traitors, to live by the honor code, and above all to be brave and live a clean life. Contrary to Match's estimation of children's programs, quite good adaptations of tales and legends were airing on some of radio's most popular and highly rated family-friendly programs such as *Let's Pretend* and *Family Theater*. These radio versions were likely loosely based on Malory's *Le Morte Darthur,* itself an adaptation of English and French Arthuriana, Howard Pyle's early twentieth-century adaptations of Arthurian legend, and Robin Hood tales published for young readers, or any number of modernizations or interpretations of the legends. Tracking down the penultimate source for these radio adaptations is all but impossible.

Sections of Malory's *Hoole Book* and medieval and post-medieval Robin Hood ballads were produced for *Buster Brown, Popeye the Sailor, The Adventures of Superman, Prince Valiant, The Cisco Kid,* and *Wild Bill Hickok,* and the adult programs *Escape, Crime Classics,* and *Gunsmoke.* Depending on a listener's taste, many of these radio adaptations would probably fail the litmus test for "high art," but most of them were highly entertaining, even for twenty-first century "old time radio" enthusiasts. Arthurian legend and the legend of Robin Hood, both adapted for various mediums in American popular culture, continue to perpetuate the romantic illusion of the Middle Ages as a time of chivalric medieval knights, peace, and orderliness. This modern perception considers the Middle Ages as a medieval model for a political utopia that celebrates the "grandeur" of the period (Eco 70). As Umberto Eco explains, "Our return to the Middle Ages is a "quest for our roots, ... for a 'reliable Middle Ages,' not for romance and fantasy, ... though frequently this wish is misunderstood and, moved by a vague impulse ... [and/or] escapism" (65). Nostalgia for an imagined innocent, bygone age of knights in shining armor, damsels in distress, and displaced noblemen fighting for justice features in many of the radio adaptations.

American popular culture continues to embrace the Middle Ages. Medieval images are used to sell the unlikeliest products and services, such as the lovable and memorable Vikings featured in anachronistic Capital One advertisements hawking banking services or the medieval court and king promoting the Texas Lottery. Theme parks or festivals inspired by medievalism encourage interest in the medieval period among the general public: examples include the Austin, Texas, Robin Hood–inspired Sherwood Forest Faire, or the Houston Renaissance Festival (a mix of medieval renaissance—and cyber punk—costumed participants). Medievalism is also promoted by social groups made up of like-minded enthusiasts dedicated to recreating all aspects of the Middle Ages or Renaissance periods, such as the Society for Creative Anachronism, an international organization. As mentioned, American culture and politics have equally appropriated the British king and yeoman. King Arthur and Robin Hood have been linked to crime fighters, criminals, and cowboys in popular culture and, in politics, with twentieth-century American political figures and ideologies. In her now famous interview with *Life* magazine following the assassination of President John F. Kennedy in 1963, the widowed

Jacqueline Kennedy described the thousand days of her husband administration as "one brief shining moment [when] there was Camelot" (qtd. in Lupack, *King* 277). The 1950s was a particularly prolific period for adaptations of the legends of King Arthur and Robin Hood in literature, film, and on radio. Tom Henthorne provides one explanation for this 1950s medievalism in his study of the representation of masculinity in cinematic medievalism in his article, "Boys to Men: Medievalism and Masculinity in *Star Wars* and *E. T.: The Extra-Terrestrial*." Henthorne theorizes that the popularity of the Middle Ages at the time was a reaction to an imagined threat to traditional values following a world war. As Henthorne explains, whether these adaptations were historically accurate or not, the medieval period in film and on radio was idealized as a time of "peace and order" and one that promoted "faith, loyalty, courage, and for women, at least, chastity"; further, film reduced "complex narratives ... to simpler tales about knights in shining armor and damsels in distress" (73–74). Even more important, "war brought out strong political emphases. Motifs of invasion and national betrayal were common. Nearly all new versions [adaptations of medieval texts] stressed the need for supreme power to be used firmly by a central government against its enemies, without and within, to guarantee peace and unity" (Lynch 28). Medievalism then is an expression of enthusiasm for the Middle Ages or an engagement with aspects of the medieval period transferred "into any current idiom of political, social, or cultural self definition" (Boldrini 44). Put simply, medievalism "encompasses all manner of interaction with the Middle Ages" in any medium (Kaufman, "Medieval" 1).

Although post-medieval writers often considered and referred to their retellings as "translations," another way of defining the changes they made to original medieval narratives to better suit the interests and reflect the cultural concerns of their audiences was "adaptation." Post-medieval writers practiced medievalism by adapting the chivalric tales of King Arthur and his Knights of the Round Table or Robin Hood and his Merry Men and adopting those characters' chivalric ethos for modern masculine conduct. Radio scriptwriters also put a modern twist on many productions featuring the Arthurian knight and Robin Hood by writing adaptations that incorporated contemporary social issues to analyze modern problems or address modern themes, such as war and general social problems. Most of the radio versions of the legends discussed here aired in the 1940s and 1950s and illustrate how radio scriptwriters engaged with medievalism. For instance, a number of wartime radio adaptations of King Arthur and

Robin Hood's legend explore the wartime themes of personal sacrifice, fascism, prejudice, and post-war hunger.

A 1940s episode of *Smilin' Ed's Buster Brown Gang* is one example of radio's perceived influence upon an audience, especially younger listeners, when the narrator of the children's program, "Smilin'" Ed, encourages children to avoid waste and to join the "Clean Your Plate Club." Robin Hood is also a cultural icon and chivalric figure through whom contemporary political issues also have been examined. Robin Hood scholar Stephen Knight has followed the evolution of Robin Hood from the first mention of the character's name in *Piers Plowman* to present-day Hollywood. According to Knight, Hollywood has continued to politicize Robin Hood by making him "a political figure with concerns much broader than the local and regional significance of the late medieval figure" whose "impact transcends the English national significance that he developed in the nineteenth century" (*Robin Hood: A Mythic* 156). Robin Hood continues to be an adaptable representative for socially and politically motivated groups, but at the same time is criticized when he is adopted as a champion of the oppressed. In the 1950s Robin Hood was accused of trading in his green tights for red ones when his reputation for re-distributing the wealth came under scrutiny. Mrs. White, a local school board member who lobbied against Robin Hood, called for his stories to be banned from Indianapolis school textbooks because they promoted robbing "'the rich to give to the poor'" which, she believed, promoted Communism ("Exploits"). The *Chicago Daily Tribune* ran the front page story reporting Pravda was jubilant "that American censors [had] placed Robin Hood on the subversive list although the outlaw and his merry men flourished 600 years before Karl Marx" ("Exploits"). A Moscow-based spokesman for the party considered the scandal a joke ("Governor"). Even so, Robin Hood's persona would be adapted for radio in the 1950s into storylines addressing economic disparity and Cold War era tensions.

Medieval and post-medieval literature presents the Middle Ages in nostalgic tones and posits chivalry as an ideal. Britain's Edward I and Edward III established ties to the Round Table and identified themselves with the Arthurian ethos. In a display of nationalism, Edward I associated himself with the warrior Arthur while his grandson Edward III in 1349 established the Order of the Garter to promote chivalry as a code for the nobility. Just as their medieval counterparts had done before, modern adapters treated King Arthur's court as "an ideal society" that existed in "a vanished, golden age ... worthy of imitation" and adopted chivalric literature as a handbook for medieval society (Leyerle 131). Beginning with the chivalric revival in the fifteenth century in the courts of Spain and England, writers of medieval romance embraced an idealized vision of the Middle Ages and associated the medieval knight with the tradition of courtly love, a version of the period American audiences were probably most familiar. Radio adaptations, like their filmic cousins, show the Arthurian knights and Robin Hood practicing medieval values. With few exceptions, radio adaptations, like chivalric literature, gilded the medieval period and treated the Arthurian knight and Sherwood outlaw as civilized chivalric knights. In most cases, radio adaptations show these iconic heroes in a positive light who through their deeds and words practice a chivalric code that stressed loyalty, honor, faith, and charity. In fact, they shared with their radio audience the same "morals" identified "with the ethical ideals ... of American life" (Callahan 369).

Malory, and later his editor and printer William Caxton, practiced medievalism in the fifteenth century when they recast a thirteenth-century French version of Arthurian knighthood for an English audience reading his *Le Morte Darthur*. For Malory the present stood in sharp contrast to the past, a period when chivalry and virtuous love prevailed, unlike

> nowadayes men can nat love sevennyght but they muste have all their desyres. That love may nat endure by reson, for where they bethe sone accorded and hasty, heete sone keelyth. And ryght so faryth the love nowadays, sone hote sone colde. Thy ys no stabylyté. But the olde love was nat so. For men and women coude love togydirs seven yersys, and no lycoures lustis was betwyxte them, and than was love trouthe and faythefulnes. And so lyke wyse was used such love in kynge Arthurs dayes.
>
> [Now days men cannot love seven nights but they must have all their desires. That love may not endure by reason, for where they are both soon accorded and hasty, soon hot, soon cold. There was no stability. But the old love was not so. For men and women could love together seven years, [with no] lecherous lust between them, and then love was truth and faithfulness. And so likewise was such love used in King Arthur's days] [649].

Here Malory pines for something that never was. In the moralizing Preface included in Vinaver's *The Works of Sir Thomas Malory*, Caxton also shares his hope that the book's English audience would follow by example Malory's characters.

Perhaps the radio listener, like the earlier medieval audience of Malory's book, was expected to pay close attention to what Caxton describes as the "noble actes of chyvalrye, the jentyl and virtuous dedes that somme knyghtes used in tho days, by whyche they came to honour, and how they that were vycious were punysshed and ofte put to shame and rebuke [noble acts of chivalry, the gentle and virtuous deeds that some knights used in those days, by which they came to honor, and how they that were vicious were punished and often put to shame and rebuke]" (Caxton xiii). Here Caxton, an early editor of Malory, imposes judgment on the moral values of King Arthur's Round Table brotherhood despite notable violent acts performed by individual knights, such as Sir Gawain's beheading of a damsel in distress and his affair with his fellow knight's lady.

Malory's Gawain is not the mythic Gawain and legendary Celtic hero whose power waxes and wanes with the time of day, the flower of chivalry and courtly romance, or the virtuous Christian of *Sir Gawain and the Green Knight,* a knight who truly exhibits *gentilesse,* courtliness and refinement. Malory's Gawain is impulsive and impatient, a knight whose decisions often result in violence. When a damsel in distress visits King Arthur's court during his wedding feast, Gawain eagerly volunteers to follow the quest for the white hart. However, Gawain's hotheadedness causes the death of a knight, the knight's greyhounds, and the beheading of the same damsel. Following a skirmish with the knight, the damsel throws herself upon his corpse. Gawain impulsively reacts and mistakenly "smote of hir hede by myssefortune [smote off her head by misfortune]"; for this "fowle [foul] deed," he was duly punished and ordered to ride back to Camelot wearing the damsel's severed head around his neck, and to confess his actions to King Arthur (Malory, *Works* 68). Gawain was also accused of being a false knight when he breached the chivalric code of honor and was found in bed with Ettarde, Sir Pelleas's lady. Pelleas's request was that he only mediate their relationship, not engage in a liaison. Malory presents a much different version of Gawain than the chaste knight capable of holding off the sexual advances of an amorous hostess in *Sir Gawain and the Green Knight.* Despite his failings, Gawain was chivalric when he defended Queen Guinevere against a charge of adultery.

Clearly, in this editorial move, which provided further evidence of Caxton's engagement with medievalism, the printer/editor was prefacing his presentation of King Arthur's life story by instructing Malory's potential readers, specifically the *English* nobility, about which behaviors by King Arthur's knights they should imitate and which they should ignore. Insufficient evidence exists that can identify with certainty Malory's intended audience. However, his audience is thought to have "consisted of the wealthier middle class, the gentry, and nobility, ... people rich enough to acquire books, and literate and leisured enough to read them"

(Coleman 49). In fact, adapters for radio did something similar when they were writing storylines for a juvenile audience.

From the sixteenth century onward, chivalry was received as a code of conduct associated with the medieval knight that later became a behavioral model that guided the English gentleman. Post-medieval writers continued to debate and to redefine the chivalric code while medieval ideas of chivalry were "absorbed into contemporary manners" as one way to refine modern male conduct (Girouard 17). Geoffroi de Charny, a fourteenth-century knight considered to be the quintessential knight of the Middle Ages, wrote three works on chivalry. *A Knight's Own Book of Chivalry* is a manual establishing the rules governing a knight's conduct. For Charny, knighthood was a valiant vocation in which "piety and chivalry [were] inseparable" (Kaueper 35). He expected men-at-arms to exhibit prowess in battle, to show restraint, to exhibit "no desire to engage in any evil undertaking," and to express courtesy towards others (Charny 47–48). Ramon Lull and Christine de Pizan, also writers in the Middle Ages, traced chivalry to "auncynet tyme[s] [ancient times]" the Trojan and Roman models of soldiering and the noble acts of King Arthur and the fellowship of the Round Table Knights (Lull 99).

Particularly during the British and American chivalric revivals during the late nineteenth and early twentieth centuries, chivalry became the standard behavior illustrated in children's literature and taught in Arthurian-themed youth organizations. This turn-of-the-century medieval revival, an example of medievalism, took root in Britain and fully flowered in America at the same time. Out of this enthusiasm and nostalgia for the Middle Ages in America emerged social clubs for boys and girls such as the Boy Scouts and Queens of Avalon, respectively: chivalric literature, art, film, and even radio programs elevated chivalry as a positive quality.

As this analysis of radio programs broadcasts from the 1930s through the 1950s demonstrates, the legends of King Arthur and Robin Hood were successfully adapted and transmitted to the aural medium of radio as entertaining and action-packed adventures that appealed to a wide audience but also taught chivalric values through a character's words and deeds. Radio scriptwriters took advantage of the culturally elastic legends of King Arthur and Robin Hood and produced didactic stories that entertained and educated the radio audience. In radio adaptations, the Arthurian knight—usually identified as King Arthur, Lancelot, or the yeoman outlaw Robin Hood—validated through their deeds and words the chivalric traits of truth, honor, justice, courtesy, and bravery. Thus, medieval *British* ideals of chivalry became standards of *American* morality and masculinity as illustrated in print and on radio.

The following chapters discuss concepts such as the social and cultural impact of radio in the United States, adaptation, medievalism, the cultural influence of King Arthur and Robin Hood; the book concludes with an overview and analysis of these radio adaptations broadcast during radio's "golden age." This study does not judge the fidelity of adaptations but rather considers the adapter's approach to bringing these tales to radio.

1

Radio and the Formation of the Imagined Community

The power of radio was most significant during the 1930s and 1940s, when individuals took advantage of the aural medium to promote and to condemn fascism and to call a nation to war. Because the act of listening to the radio invited the outside world into the private space of the listener's living room, critics and supporters of radio equally recognized the medium's potential to manipulate audiences and play the part of "an agent of change" (Cooney 98). According to one study published in the 1930s, in the early days of radio, the medium was already recognized as having the ability to reach a mass audience, a power that could and would have far-reaching consequences. In their book *The Psychology of Radio* (1935), a study of radio's influence on American audiences, Hadley Cantril and Gordon Allport pointed out that "the radio, more than any other medium of communication, [was] capable of forming a crowd mind among individuals who are physically separated from one another" (21).

Audience reception of two particularly sophisticated radio dramas in the 1930s illustrated radio's ability to create a huge impact upon a large number of listeners. Orson Welles was a writer, actor, producer, and director of films and radio.[1] Welles' radio adaptation of H. G. Wells's science fiction novel *The War of the Worlds* (1898) was broadcast in 1938 on CBS's *The Mercury Theater on the Air* during a politically and socially turbulent time. Welles and writer John Houseman adapted a number of literary classics for the series, including Bram Stoker's *Dracula* (1897), Robert Lewis Stevenson's *Treasure Island* (1883), Alexander Dumas's *The Count of Monte Cristo* (1844), and William Shakespeare's plays and original novels. *Mercury Theater*, renamed *The Campbell Playhouse*, aired from 1938 through 1946. Welles always had a starring role in his adaptations. As an interesting side note, Peter Conrad writes in his biography of Welles's career that Welles's favorite novel was T. H. White's "Arthurian epic" and is quoted as saying that he "believed very strongly in the quality of chivalry" and "put great value on being chivalrous in [his] interpretation" of a character (313). Welles's convincing portrayal of a hysterical radio newsman reporting a Martian landing in Grovers Mill, New Jersey, and the sophisticated technical effects to create the reality of this imagined invasion, panicked an already fearful nation anticipating the possibility of war. Although Welles claimed his radio play was only a "Halloween 'trick,'" for "millions of listeners fantasy had become a reality" (MacDonald 53). *The War of the Worlds* aired one month after the Munich crisis, unnerving many listeners who thought the report too real not to be true. Americans were listening to radio reports of Hitler's movements in Europe, causing many to believe an invasion was actually taking place that Halloween eve. The mass hysteria created by the radio broadcast's first-person narrator provides some insight into the power and influence of radio and the medium's role in creating an imagined community.

The invention of paper and Johann Gutenberg's development of the printing press not only created the "primary medium of human communication" (Cook 8) but "became a communication root for disseminating the concept of nationalism" (McLuhan qtd. in Cook 8). The aural medium of radio was also another form of communication that transmitted cultural values, spread nationalism, and formed communities. According to Benedict Anderson, when individuals in a radio audience, living perhaps miles apart, simultaneously tuned their radio dials to hear a favorite scheduled program, they shared an identical listening experience and thus became an imagined community (35–36). Cantril and Allport anticipated this theory but applied it to the aural medium of radio about forty-five years earlier. They suggested that "when millions of people listen to the same thing at the same time—and they themselves are aware of the fact," then the medium becomes a powerful tool of democracy that erases class distinctions (Douglas 24; Cantril and Allport 20). Radio networks also recognized that they catered to a heterogeneous audience. Moreover, since people preferred "individuality to uniformity," the radio broadcaster attempted to appeal to a majority of listeners by steering the "middle course" and "aiming at the average intelligence" of his audience (Cantril and Allport 21).

Setting Standards for American Children's Literature and Radio Programs

Radio's power of influence had far-reaching consequences. Because the "mind of any child is fertile soil for the seeds of suggestion, and the radio is an ideal means of planting these seeds ... the techniques used in ... children's programs [proved] amazingly effective" (Cantril and Allport 236). Radio was treated as a "supplementary teaching device" praised for "psychologically cement[ing] the family circle at a time when an evening at home for the whole family was almost unheard of" (Bartlett 9) and for its social role as an arbiter of "cultural improvement" (Hilmes 17). Skeptics had their reservations. Although radio broadcasting was on the air by the 1920s,[2] children's radio programming was not a mainstay of those broadcasts until 1931. As children's programs gained popularity, so too did criticism of the radio industry and radio programming. Educators, parents, civic leaders, sociologists, and psychologists, like Cantril and Allport, scrutinized and criticized radio's influence upon American audiences. At the same time, parents were encouraged to monitor their children's listening habits and to teach good listening skills that were vital to producing responsible radio listeners (Smith).

Networks were also expected to enforce a standard for juvenile programming. Radio networks had no choice but to respond to the protests of parents and educators concerned about the content of children's programs. While many radio programs such as *The Adventures of Superman* and *Jack Armstrong, the All-American Boy* might have encouraged morality, good citizenship, and patriotism, they also encouraged consumerism, promoted stereotypes, and spread messages of hate. Watchdogs blamed radio and comic books for juvenile delinquency, for giving children nightmares, and for filling their heads with drivel. However, these fears may have been exaggerated, as the president of the National Congress of Parents and Teachers suggested during the time controversy over the content of children's programming was heating up: "The folk tale, with its dragons breathing fire, its child-eating ogre, and its bloody conflicts, is as old as language. Children and childish adults have been frightened into being good by threats of the bogey man or the policeman. These tales have served ... to stimulate and engergize many a flagging spirit" (Langworthy qtd. in Waller 239). Racial inequality, juvenile delinquency, fears of communism, and concerns over immigration and perceived race problems influenced radio content, especially in the 1950s. Juvenile delinquency in the 1950s was blamed on family instability and a lack of parental influence caused by working mothers and absentee fathers, especially during the war years.

As Jacqueline Foertsch points out in her book, *American Culture in the 1940s*, J. Edgar Hoover, the director of the FBI, "associated 'crime' and 'perversion' with a working mother's neglect of children" (29). Moreover, worries over the increasing number of immigrants coming to the United States were causing unrest. Velma Bourgeois Richmond blames these concerns on the "population growth in the United States and Canada [that] contributed to Saxon numerical inferiority because other races dominated in emigration and birth rate," demographics that caused anxiety among the decreasing representatives of "Anglo-Saxon" stock (23). As the country moved toward the Cold War era in the twentieth century, there was a widespread fear that Communism was rampant. McCarythism shook not only the Hollywood film industry but also the television and radio industries.

Beginning in the 1930s, and especially during wartime, juvenile delinquency and other societal ills were linked to radio crime dramas. Parents and educators in Scarsdale, California, campaigned in 1933 against nationally syndicated radio programs, in particular crime programs, which they considered too exciting and too violent for their children. The National Association of Broadcasters code, created in 1934 by NBC, CBS, and Mutual radio networks, was a preventative measure to protect children from mature content. As a Milwaukee juvenile court judge noted in a 1938 interview, parents could say "no" to paying for the price of a movie ticket, "but the radio is always handy and free, and the potential influences for not only bad, but good, are greater" ("Curb"). Such comments drew nationwide attention to crime radio programs in particular and prompted calls for stricter legislation. Radio programs were criticized for not only giving children nightmares, but also for exciting "impressionable youngsters, creat[ing] negative, destructive thoughts, and turn[ing] attention to crime instead of normal constructive activity, and [for] lead[ing] boys to make crime a part of their play" ("Curb"). These fears may have been exaggerated, however. When in 1946 a student was asked about his taste in radio programs, and particularly about the possible influence of crime programs, he remarked that any influence was down to the individual: "It can affect you if you have an open mind toward a crime … but the majority just listen for adventure" ("Pupils"). Children's radio programming and children's books seemed to have equally shared the responsibility of guiding

1. Radio and the Formation of the Imagined Community 31

young listeners down a moral path with scriptwriters following similar guidelines.

Radio adaptations of medieval legends were presumably safe and, therefore, ideal material for a medium struggling to satisfy its critics. Radio scriptwriters writing content for children's programs likely followed the example of turn-of-the-century children's books that encouraged virtuous and rational behavior. The conviction that children's books, and in some respect children's radio programs, should promote *American* values is important as it might explain why the legends of King Arthur and Robin Hood made it on radio and how they were presented to a mixed audience. Anne Scott MacLeod explains that this thinking was a product of "the dominant Protestant, middle-class culture of the early United States [that] took it as a given that self-regulated citizens formed the basis of social order ... a commitment to the work ethic, and a reasonable concern for the good of the community" (*American* 112–113). Children's literature was prohibited from containing adult themes and the taboo subjects of "divorce, mental breakdown, alcoholism, rape, drug dependence, suicide, prostitution, sexual deviance," and violent crime (MacLeod, *American* 180); this prohibition was guided by an "implicit code of values ... observed virtually unbroken in thousands of children's books published between 1900 to 1965" (179). Radio programs were held to the same high expectations.

Scriptwriters and sound artists were well trained in their arts. Universities encouraged the same high standards in future radio scriptwriters, who would be tasked with writing material for children's programs. Radio writing handbooks were part of the curriculum at colleges and universities offering certificates and degrees in all aspects of radio. Future scriptwriters learned the fundamentals of how to bring a story to radio and were cautioned to remember that a listener's "aural memory [was] not as strong as his visual memory, [that] important material and significant events—items which must be" remembered and recalled—"must be firmly fixed so they will" have the desired effect "when their time comes" (Wylie 179). Scriptwriters were also to avoid being condescending, which could create resentment in children, and were encouraged to speak directly to their youngest listeners. In particular the adapter writing a radio script was to only invent material that he deemed both "useful" and "economical" (Wylie 179).

Before the invention of the sound effects machine used in radio, sound engineers relied on human ingenuity to simulate real world and otherworldly sounds, therefore lending believability to radio programs.

Radio was "sound [and] sound alone" that required scriptwriters to write specifically for the "ears of the people" (Weaver 15, 21). When they were incorporating sound effects into children's programs especially, scriptwriters and sound effects artists were tasked with creating sound effects and music that were both familiar and convincing to the child and that clearly "communicate[d] emotions, mood, and feelings" (Waller 247). Columbia Workshop, a production of Columbia Broadcasting, experimented with music to replace sound effects and to create character and mood. "Music turned over the pages of" a radio adaptation of a newly released Dr. Seuss book, *And to Think That I Saw It on Mulberry Street* ("And to Think"). Theodore Geisel's entertaining tale is about an imaginative boy named Marco and his imaginary encounter with a parade of animals on Mulberry Street in New York City. The radio adaptation's careful acoustic control recreates the various animals the boy in the story, and that the listener imagines he also sees marching down the street. Creating a sense of illusion was the job of the radio sound artist, who had to make a story believable. In his textbook for radio scriptwriters, Max Wylie describes radio sound effects as the "pulse of the radio bloodstream" with the power to "tease the imagination into an acceptance of illusions" not otherwise possible (39).

Sound effects were live or pre-recorded and were often the result of mixing various sounds, referred to as "sound patterns" (Maltin 103). For example, consider radio's famous creaking door, the signature sound effect that introduced the popular horror program *Inner Sanctum*: the creaking door actually existed and was the sound made by an in-studio creaking door. Conversely, striking a metal sheet with a hammer provided the artificial sound of rolling thunder. Sound also came from the unlikeliest sources: coconut shells or a sound technician beating on his chest to simulate hoof beats. Hoofbeats and the sound of steel striking steel to simulate swordplay were often used as sound effects in storylines set in the Middle Ages.

For Orson Welles, producing radio drama was an art. Welles reportedly wanted to "create" for his radio audience "the illusion of the story" (qtd. in Hilmes 220–221). Welles, a consummate professional on radio, stage, and screen, adapted a number of literary works for radio's *Columbia Workshop*, producing exceptional adaptations of Bram Stoker's classic horror novel *Dracula*, Robert Louis Stevenson's *Treasure Island*, William Shakespeare's *Hamlet*, and many other literary classics. The scriptwriter's primary duty was to make the story clear and memorable. CBS's *Columbia Workshop* was the pioneer of sophisticated radio sound effects, and it paved the way for radio drama by producing literary adaptations, adaptations of films, and exceptionally well-written original scripts (Godfrey 86; Dunning 170).

On April 11, 1937, a timely broadcast of "The Fall of the City," a radio play broadcast from WABC in New York, sealed *Columbia Workshop*'s reputation for quality programming (Godfrey 86; Verma 17). Broadcast at a politically and socially turbulent time, similar to the broadcast of *War of the Worlds*, Archibald MacLeish's verse play was a contemporary tale of a city blindly welcoming a conqueror. This intense drama was the "first outright attack on fascism" (Weaver 92) and offered a chilling foretelling of the terrors of Hitler, Francisco Franco, and Benito Mussolini. *Columbia Workshop*'s ambitious production of *The Fall of the City* is still regarded as a radio play that "moderniz[ed] and invigorat[ed] radio broadcasting aesthetics and extend[ed] highbrow culture to the masses" (Verma 18).

Nine years later, and only one year after the end of the Second World War, another American student who was asked about radio's influence on young listeners surprisingly recognized radio's power to control and to manipulate its audience. She remembered Hitler's successful use of radio "'to turn the youth of that country against us [Americans]'" (qtd. in "Pupils"). This book's discussion of *The Adventures of Superman* illustrates just how much of an influence radio network executives, their producers, and scriptwriters believed the aural medium had on audiences.

Standardizing Radio English

Radio content was not a radio watchdog's only concern. The way the English language was spoken on the air was hotly debated as well. Dialogue placed characters in a particular locale, indicated time, and suggested the overall mood of the storyline. Writing for radio was recognized as an art form requiring a skilled, delicate craftsman who could mold the "English language to the audience's thought" simply because the "spoken word is long remembered in the mind" (Weaver 3, 4). Scriptwriters, like poets, were thought to work "with [individual] words, not with clauses, sentences or paragraphs," so each word was to be selected based on its individual value (Weaver 11). Geoffrey Chaucer's handling of the pilgrims' conversation in the late-fourteenth-century poem *The Canterbury Tales*, especially his ability to make his characters believable and their conversations memorable, was a model for radio scriptwriters. Ideally they would follow

Chaucer's lead and use "[s]hort, concise Anglo-Saxon monosyllables" to ensure that scripts were easy on the ear—"easy to listen to [and] easy to understand" and vividly memorable (Weaver 3).

Critics of radio defended the standardization of English on air, especially in children's programs, and decried nonstandard English as inappropriate and the stuff of comedy; for instance, "malapropisms, wrong pronunciations, overly thick regional accents, and dialects marked the speaker, rightly or wrongly, as ignorant, stupid, and low-class" (Douglas 103). Colloquialisms were saved for "dialogue and characters" (Weaver 415). Writers and actors also were to "differentiate among characters ... sharply" for a better "contrast in voices" and to keep class differences obvious (Weaver 94). Radio adaptations of King Arthur and Robin Hood's legend incorporated an Americanized British accent intended to lend an air of authenticity; perhaps in some way this addition was also thought to culturally improve the audience. By politicizing the English language, radio held a power of influence and "cultural authority" over its American audience (Hilmes 33).

In his pioneering work *Novels into Film* (1957), George Bluestone—who overlooks radio adaptations but does recognize the medium of radio as culturally important a medium as film, literature, theater, television, and even the comic strip—regards radio as heavily involved in the process of "building up a whole new American folklore" (44). Radio "is an ephemeral art form" that "exists in the moment of its produced performance" (Cook 7) just as radio content is a product of the times. As an art form, radio was a "literary drama for the ears" (Huwiler, "Engaging" 133), a blending and layering of sound effects, music, and words. Combined, these elements manipulated a listener's imagination and elicited an emotional reaction to the program. As Douglas suggests, "[d]ramas, plays, soap operas, and many radio comedies tapped into and reshaped story listening, a pleasurable mode of listening that requires concentration on language, wordplay, verbal imagery, and sound effects" (34). Moreover, when writing dialogue for children's program, scriptwriters were also cautioned not to over-narrate or to provide too much detail that could interfere with the "imaginative processes by which the listening child lives the story" (Waller 247). In other words, dialogue should not do the work of the child's imagination. Imaginative play was to be encouraged.

2

Adapting King Arthur and Robin Hood's Legend for Radio

Most radio programs were musical and informational in the 1920s, with a smattering of dramas introduced as the decade progressed. In 1922 the General Electric Company founded WGY, Schenectady, and introduced the WGY Players, who introduced drama to radio. The WGY Players treated listeners to adaptations of literary classics, such as the balcony scene of William Shakespeare's *Romeo and Juliet,* as well as original scripts. Cincinnati's station WLW soon followed with dramatic broadcasts. The first children's radio program was broadcast in 1922 by Carnegie Library of Pittsburgh through KDKA. Radio scriptwriters wrote original scripts, adapted Hollywood film scripts, and turned to the works of classic literature, adapting poems, short stories, novels, and plays. Many good radio dramatizations were also adaptations of folk tales, fairy tales, and legends.

In addition to reading adaptations of Arthurian romance and stories about Robin Hood, or watching these exciting cinematic adventures unfold on-screen, by the mid–1930s children were also *listening* to the these tales adapted for radio. In particular, the flexibility of the legends of King Arthur and Robin Hood permitted radio scriptwriters of the 1930s through the 1950s to deliver lessons in personal and social morality via family-friendly programs. As already mentioned, the adventures of King Arthur, his Knights of the Round Table, and Robin Hood and his Merry Men all probably made it to radio because they were familiar to listeners of all ages and were easily adaptable to a restrictive format. The length of a radio program could be anywhere between fifteen minutes, thirty minutes, or an hour long, and the only way to engage the listener was through aurally sparking his imagination with dialogue, description of the action, and sound effects. As they had in chivalric literature, on radio the Arthurian knight and yeoman outlaw embodied timeless values, conveying through their words and deeds strong leadership, courage in the face of danger, and loyalty to others. As positive chivalric models, the Arthurian knight and Robin Hood illustrated a code of ethics acceptable and practical for everyone. Adaptations fixed in the listener's mind the Arthurian knight and yeoman outlaw as chivalric figures as examples of ideal masculinity, who reinforced a standardized code of specific *American* morality adaptable to a modern world. For instance, the *Family Theater* adaptation of "Fifty-first Dragon" focuses on the importance of faith. According to Gawaine's sad outcome in Heywood Broun's humorous short story, without faith, the individual is lost. This adaptation uses humor to encourage listeners to believe that faith in oneself is important, but faith in God is how one achieves true happiness.

1. *Family Theater,* "Fifty-First Dragon"

Family Theater produced thirty-minute family-friendly, quality radio programs from original scripts or adaptations of classic tales, a variety of which we will look at later. Another entertaining and family-friendly story brought to the airwaves by Father Patrick Peyton, a Catholic priest and producer of *Family Theater,* was an adaptation of Heywood Broun's short story "Fifty-First Dragon," broadcast on April 12, 1950. This entertaining and well-acted play closely follows the short story included in Broun's *Seeing Things at Night,* published in 1921. Jane Wyatt hosts this episode and Charles Davis plays Gawaine. "Fifty-First Dragon" does not present the character of a knight protagonist who, through his actions, proves to be an exemplar of chivalry. Broun plays with the concept of the medieval chivalric knight and presents a post-medieval rendering of knighthood. Broun shows Gawaine to be a parody of the medieval knight who lacks two important chivalric qualities—courage and faith. Faith was a chivalric quality and the medieval knight, above all, was the warrior of mother church.

Gawaine le Cœur-Hardy shares his name with Sir Gawain, a popular knight in Arthurian legend known for his superhuman strength in the *Le Morte Darthur*; in *Sir Gawain and the Green Knight,* Gawain is the virtuous knight who adorns himself with a jeweled set of armor and shield and who prays to the Virgin Mary. However, Broun's young knight lacks superhuman strength and faith. Rather he is known for his poor memory and lack of confidence, though he is brawny enough to "lick his way through dragons." Broun's Gawaine suffers from melancholy because he fails to live up to his potential as a knight, until he is tricked into believing he can slay dragons with a "magic word." "Fifty-First Dragon" is set in Northern England in the "days before the flower of knighthood whithered on the vine," when knights errant "clank[ed] around" and the land was populated by "a huffing, puffing, blowtorch type of dragon" (Heckert). This narrator, saddened by the loss of an ideal medieval world, shares Malory's nostalgia for bygone days when stability, truth, and faithfulness supposedly existed.

Following a series of failures in his studies to become a knight, Gawaine's professor gives him a "magic word" to improve his prowess at dragon slaying. Gawaine performs bravely, slicing the heads and tails off every dragon he encounters. This wins Gawaine the admiration of his professors and peers, until he discovers the magic word was not magic at all. Gawaine then loses his confidence and his battle with the fifty-first dragon—the tale ends with Gawaine's disappearance, although he is fondly remembered as the "greatest man England ever had" (Heckert).

The Language of Adaptation

What did Shakespeare and a radio scriptwriter share in common? Technique. A sixteenth-century playwright and twentieth-century radio writer both knew their source material well, "depend[ed] on the spoken word to set the scene, explain[ed] the characters, and start[ed] the action moving" (Wylie 128). On stage or on the air, the opening scene introduces characters and creates atmosphere, establishes time and place—all through dialogue. Wylie suggests that "like Shakespeare, the radio writer has no printed program to explain these things to his audience, and he is playing, so to speak, upon a bare stage without scenery, exactly as Shakespeared did in the old Globe Theatre" (129). Radio's format restrictions did require scriptwriters to make significant changes to source material in order to adapt these legends, such as severely compressing for brevity the scope of the tales, especially when drawing from Malory, or eliminating material thought inappropriate for a mixed audience. Scriptwriters were likely working from a broad range of specific sources and from their own familiarity with the legends, which permitted some degree of flexibility.

In his guide for prospective radio writers published in 1939, Wylie defines adaptation as the "transplantation from one medium to another of a series of sympathies and antipathies already established in the original," though both the original work and the adaptation were equally "sacred" and always belonged to the "first writer" of the work (178). For Wylie, adaptation was a privilege and responsibility for the adapter, the "protector of the author's interests and the custodian of his literary valuables," so he sternly warns scriptwriters that in the process of adapting a work for radio they must avoid "tamper[ing] with the feelings or the prejudices of the original or with those of any characters created by the author" because doing so is "literary grave-robbing" (179). He presses the point that a scriptwriter's responsibility is to clearly convey radio content.

Adapters first interpret and then create a work: the process of adaptation is the result of adjusting, altering, interpreting, appropriating or salvaging a text (Fischlin and Fortier qtd. in Hutcheon 9, 18). According to Daniel Fischlin and Mark Fortier, adaptation "includes almost any alteration performed upon specific cultural works of the past and dovetails with a general process of cultural recreation" (qtd. in Hutcheon 9). Linda Hutcheon, in *A Theory of Adaptation*, describes adaptation as both "process" and "product," a "transcoding" or shifting of mediums—the adaption of a novel to film is therefore seen as a "creative *and* an interpretative act of appropriation/salvaging" a work (8).

Although *The Story Lady* aired in the 1960s, this radio program is an example of one adapter's approach to bringing to life the legends of King Arthur and Robin Hood. As the Story Lady, Joan Gerber presented short radio adaptations intended primarily for an adult audience. Her long list of funny radio adaptations included *The Wizard of Oz, The Picture of Dorian Gray*, and *Lolita*. Gerber's radio adaptations "King Arthur" and "Robin Hood," discussed in the conclusion, ran one minute and twenty seconds and focused on a familiar scene with each story ending in a strange twist. For "King Arthur," Gerber borrowed the sword in the anvil scene in which Arthur becomes the rightful ruler of Britain and the archery contest in Robin Hood's legend. Because of time constraints, Gerber compressed and summarized events, did away with character dialogue, made a few minor changes to details. For example in "King Arthur," the anvil is a stone, the archbishop is Merlin, and an alternate ending is provided: King Arthur ends up in the hospital needing a hernia operation. In

"Robin Hood" Gerber disguised Robin Hood as Errol Flynn, who wins the contest and, in the surprise ending, shoots his opponent with a misguided arrow that causes the man to bleed to death.

Pascal Nicklas and Oliver Lindner interpret the adaptation or appropriation of a source as a symbiotic relationship and creative process that results in "new cultural capital" (6). With each retelling, the story may change, but it remains essentially recognizable despite alterations to the source that might include changes to plot, character, point of view, time, or the conclusion (Hutcheon 10–12, 18), as evident in Gerber's short adaptations. Radio scriptwriters were forced to work against the clock. To adapt the legends of King Arthur and Robin Hood to radio, these sprawling tales had to be compressed into fifteen- and thirty-minute formats, or in Gerber's case under five minutes, and would depend upon a limited number of scenes with which the listener would be most familiar.

Radio adaptations of King Arthur and Robin Hood's legend are part of the long tradition of translation and adaptation that goes back hundreds of years. Like their literary predecessors, the adaptations produced between the 1930s and 1950s were products of their times as aural retellings and modernizations of medieval legends sometimes coded with contemporary concerns. They negotiated the past and the present, addressing aspects of the past that were relevant to their adapter's immediate cultural situation. For Elke Huwiler, whose primary interest is the literary radio drama broadcast in German-speaking countries and the pedagogical possibilities offered by the study of radio, "an adapted radio play is a work of art different from the literary piece used as source material" (144). Huwiler divides radio adaptations into two categories: "the literary text as source material [used] to create a new work of art; and ... the literary text as the main basis for storytelling" (139).

As Hutcheon explains, "when a change of medium does occur in an adaptation, it inevitably invokes that long history of debate about the formal specificity of the arts—and thus of media" (34). Authorial motivation and audience expectation influenced the final product, whether the story was repackaged for radio, stage, or screen (Cooney 33). Scriptwriters had some flexibility when adapting prose, poetry, or drama to radio, but the adaptation had to maintain the integrity of the source and "truthfully translate to radio the importance, the flavor, and the purpose of the original in its fullest" (Wylie 178). Criticism of an adaptation is usually an argument of fidelity, especially when a "canonical" text is transformed into a different medium such as a radio play or comic book. People who find pleasure in the "recognition and remembrance ... of experiencing an adaptation" may be disappointed if the new version fails to meet their expectations and could judge the outcome as derivative or even "'culturally inferior'" to the original (Hutcheon 2, 4).

This was certainly the case when school children were asked their opinion of an author's reworking of Robin Hood's legend for a radio adaptation. *The Merry Adventures of Robin Hood* was adapted for the radio series *Tales from Far and Near*, which was broadcast in schools between 1939 and 1940. In all probability, adaptations of Robin Hood were derived from American illustrator and writer Howard Pyle's popular 1883 collection of Robin Hood stories titled *The Merry Adventures of Robin Hood*, which was read in schools. Perhaps expecting Pyle's more familiar version, the program's juvenile audience was disappointed that *Tales from Far and Near* rewrote the "whole story," making significant changes to what they were anticipating (O'Brien 110). More than likely because of time constraints, the adapter was forced to excise content and to gloss over the more exciting and violent scenes.

A radio adaptation of Twain's *A Connecticut Yankee in King Arthur's Court* (1889) also received a cool response from one radio critic following its broadcast on the first night of *The Ford Theater* radio program in 1947. Twain's satire about a nineteenth-century Connecticut Yankee transported to sixth-century England illuminates injustices in Victorian England and Twain's America. *A Connecticut Yankee in King Arthur's Court* has been adapted for movies, musicals, and radio: radio adaptations include productions in 1947 for *The Ford Theater*, two in 1950 on *The Railroad Hour* and *Favorite Story*, and in 1976 on *CBS Mystery Theater*, which is discussed later. In addition to the obvious influence of Twain's book, the radio adaptations of the 1940s and 1950s were based on Herbert Fields's popular Broadway musical comedy, *A Connecticut Yankee*, staged in 1927 and revived in 1943. Subsequent discussion considers the various approaches adapters took when bringing Twain's satire to radio. Most of these adaptations borrowed from the more comedic scenes in the novel, such as the Yankee's reaction to waking in Arthur's England, his "magic trick" that makes the moon disappear (a timely lunar eclipse), and his besting of Sir Sagramore during the tournament. Only one adaptation presents the final violent scene of death and dying, in which Hank's war planes mow down the knights, thus dispensing with chivalry altogether. Inventions of the nineteenth and twentieth centuries converge in all of these radio adaptations: Hank's bicycle is replaced by the motor car, the telegraph by the telephone, and the sandwich board by radio advertising.

2. *The Ford Theater,* "A Connecticut Yankee in King Arthur's Court"

Barbara and Alan Lupack describe Twain's *A Connecticut Yankee in King Arthur's Court* as a "central text in American Arthuriana" written in reaction to Tennyson's medievalism that actually works against nineteenth-century romantic notions of the Middle Ages. According to the Lupacks, the text does this "by reject[ing] the notion of the knights of Camelot as models of virtue ... and ... deliberately deflat[ing] ... the literary and moral pretensions of the *Idylls of the King*; at the same time, however, he recognizes ... that there can indeed be some nobility—not of birth but of character—even in the people he mocks" (*King Arthur*, 35). According to Elizabeth S. Sklar's study of Twain's *A Connecticut Yankee in King Arthur's Court* as adapted for children, Twain's book is "arguably the single most visible and widely disseminated individual text in the entire neo-Arthurian canon," and is one that has been "reedited, reduced, amputated, spun-off, ripped-off, and in the extreme reaches of textual bad manners, mauled" (73). If, as Sklar notes, "Twain's quirkly rhetorical play, with its zany mélange of excerpts from Malory, pseudo-medieval dialogue, and nineteenth century colloquialisms, combined with moments of purposefully rambling and long-winded prose, makes for an impotable stylistic beverage for most readers" (77), then transforming the book into a radio script proved to be a challenge for the radio scriptwriter. Part of the adapter's difficulty in transforming Twain's book into a thirty-minute radio script was deciding which elements should be retained or redacted and how to present the material to a mixed radio audience of children and adults.

In his review of *A Connecticut Yankee in King Arthur's Court* as broadcast on *The Ford Theater*, Jack Gould, a reviewer for the *New York Times*, comes close to charging Lillian Schoen, the adapter of Twain's book, with mauling the original text. Schoen's adaptation was written for the initial broadcast of *The Ford Theater* on October 5, 1947, on NBC. *The Ford Theatre* remained on the air until 1949 and was billed as "the highest-budgeted program of its kind" (Dunning 257). According to Dunning, the cast originally consisted of New York radio performers who were replaced by national radio and film stars when the show changed networks to CBS (257). The cast of *A Connecticut Yankee in King Arthur's Court* included Mason Adams as the Yankee, Karlen Swenson as King Arthur, Charita Bauer as Sandy, James Monks as Clarence, and Santos Ortega as Merlin. Howard Lindsay was the announcer.

Twain says that in writing *A Connecticut Yankee in King Arthur's Court*, he "dipped into old Sir Thomas Malory's enchanting book and fed at its rich feast of prodigies and adventures, breathed-in the fragrance of its obsolete names, and dreamed again" of Camelot ("A Word" 5). Twain delivers a lively satire that brings to light the worst qualities of human nature exposed by Hank Morgan, a nineteenth-century time traveler, transported back to the not-so-chivalric sixth-century in Camelot. The radio play keeps the plot and the main characters—the Yankee, Clarency, Sandy, Merlin, and Sir Sagramore—and sticks to a few familiar scenes from the novel, but provides an addition to the ending. In the program's closing remarks, Howard Lindsay addresses the spirit of Mark Twain in what sounds almost like an apology when he says, "to Mark Twain on his star" that he hopes this adaptation "followed you in spirit, if not always in letter," but noted that at the end of this nineteenth-century tale was "add[ed] a twentieth-century moral: 'Freedom, which is greater than gadgets, must be learned and guarded, still'" (Schoen).

Gould, however, accuses Schoen of "subject[ing]" Twain's book "to a soap-opera rewrite" and a free marketing opportunity for *The Ford Theater's* sponsor, the Ford Motor Company, in its "allusion to the Model T and Lincoln automobiles," which it was. Radio listeners were also treated to a plug by Henry Ford II. According to Gould, Schoen played too loose with Twain's language and the actions of his protagonist. Gould writes that Shoen's "inventiveness of the Yankee was enlarged to such a degree that Twain's original characterization was all but hopelessly lost" with Hank Morgan no better than a "comic-book hero." In this radio adaptation, the Yankee is a well-read Navy SeaBee in the war, which explains his ability to accomplish so many modernizations in Camelot. The Yankee is transported to Camelot after he is punched and knocked unconscious by an Army engineer.

What seems to bother Gould the most about the radio adaptation, which is actually an entertaining hour of listening, was that Schoen modernized the "vernacular" of Twain's book. Gould also found the "most disconcerting void in the script" to be the "omission of any of Twain's restrained and inspired statements in affirmation of the freedom and dignity of the individual as opposed to oligarchy of the knights," which was replaced with "bombastic clichés long worn thin by their inherent ordinariness." Given the difficulties adapting this lengthy book for radio, the "telescoping" was done to the "extreme," and "Merlin emerged as [a] burlesque buffoon" and a crafty politician while Arthur "was more a walk-on rather than a monarch of both stature and weakness" (Gould). King Arthur is a tertiary figure in the radio adaptations that focus on Sir Lancelot of the Lake.

In addition to Schoen's alterations to the characters, Gould accuses the writer of over embellishing Twain's "original work in the vernacular," though all Schoen is guilty of is inserting war slang, a move that does not significantly alter the story. Schoen's changes probably made the story more accessible and more enjoyable for the post-war audience. For instance, listeners were treated to colorful words and phrases categorized as war slang, such as "snafu," "hash is cooked," and "top secret operation" (Schoen). The Yankee also makes a passing a reference to the zoot suit, a style of suit for men popular during the 1940s. According to Gould, Schoen also paid too much attention to "the discordant jive talk and GI slang" which only detracted from the Yankee's "heroic qualities."

The flower of chivalry has been completely destroyed fifteen years into the Yankee's arrival in Camelot, when everyone now enjoys "freedom of speech" and "freedom of worship" (Schoen), until the final act when all is unraveled and King Arthur and his knights are wiped out in a civil war. Under the Yankee's influence, Camelot has become a city of half a million people, with a movie theater, schools, a university, and a ladies' club. Women in Camelot are emancipated but "hard to handle," as the narrator notes (Schoen). Nineteenth-century technology introduced by Twain has been replaced with twentieth-century modernizations. Camelot is fully electric. A radio blares an advertisement hawking the latest in armor, an invention King Arthur sees as a "mixed blessing," (Schoen). Office buildings have telephone, intercoms, and typewriters, and the Yankee's automobile assembly line pushes out the latest Model T, the knights' mode of transportation instead of the bicycle used in the novel. Another war reference and mode of transportation is the airplane. A squadron of planes flying in formation allow the knights to parachute in to save King Arthur from certain death. Gould experienced an adaptation that was a product of its time, and he did not care for the result. Gould represents this adaptation as a derivative work when, in fact, Schoen had only "(re)-interpreted and (re)-created," "appropriat[ed] and salvag[ed]" (Hutcheon 8) Twain's original text for a new audience.

3. *The Railroad Hour*, "A Connecticut Yankee in King Arthur's Court"

NBC's *The Railroad Hour*, sponsored by the Association of American Railroads, broadcast a thirty-minute musical adaptation of Twain's novel that was based on Herbert Fields's adaptation and Broadway hit, *A Connecticut Yankee*. The radio cast featured Gordon MacRae, Jimmy Simms, Katie Lee, and Ed Begley. Jerome Lawrence and Robert Lee adapted the script for radio and were also listed as the writers and producers of *Favorite Story*, discussed below. Lyrics were by Lorenz Hart and music was by Richard Rodgers.

The Railroad Hour's November 27, 1950, production is faithful to Fields's Broadway musical. The plot is driven by a love story, or love triangle, that involves Hank, Sandy, and Merlin. The action moves quickly and is punctuated by musical numbers and one-liners. Merlin is typecast as Malory's Mordred, who is infatuated with Queen Guinevere. In the radio production, Merlin loves Sandy with an obsession that borders on violence, though on radio the violence is all in good fun. How the Yankee ends up in Camelot is also changed. The radio play opens with Hank and Sandy caught kissing by Mervin, her fiancé, who also overhears Hank remind her that "this isn't the dark ages," and she is "supposed to follow [her] heart" (Lawrence and Lee), an obvious reference to the fate of many women through the centuries, not just in the Middle Ages. Mervin hits Hank over the head with a bottle and knocks him out. Hank awakens in Camelot to find himself among knights dressed in "tin tuxedoes" (Lawrence and Lee). In Fields's musical stage production, Fay Morgan (Malory's Morgan le Fay) catches Martin (Hank) with his former fiancée, Alice Carter, the night before their wedding and likewise knocks him over the head with a champagne bottle.

Hank awakens in Camelot, is named "Boss," and quickly brings Camelot into the twentieth century, inventing cars (the new Guinevere 6), the radio (tuned to MABC, the Middle Ages Broadcasting Corporation), and television. Sandy accuses him of neglecting her and wonders "with all these magical contrivances wilt thou ever have time for me?" (Lawrence and Lee). Merlin gives Sandy a magic love potion, but before it takes effect, she calls Sir Boss for help. He arrives by train in time to save her and threatens to "pulverize" Sir Sagamore with a "bazooka" if he interferes with the rescue. Sandy does drink the potion but has refused to open her eyes until she is sure the first man she sees is the one she really loves. Sure that Hank is nearby, she opens her eyes, but it is Hank who awakens in the twentieth century in the middle of his marriage ceremony, repeating the words "I do" (Lawrence and Lee). When a confused Hank wonders how that happened, she assures him he was unconscious but "said I do at the right times" to Sandy, "a paragon of cleverness" (Lawrence and Lee).

4. *Favorite Story*, "A Connecticut Yankee in King Arthur's Court"

Favorite Story aired a playful yet condensed version of Twain's book with an alternate ending. "A Connecticut Yankee in King Arthur's Court" was broadcast on October 11, 1947, six days after *The Ford Theater* aired its production of Twain's story. Ronald Colman, a popular radio and film star, hosted the program. *Favorite Story* is remembered for well-acted thirty-minute adaptations of classic literature. In addition to the work of Twain, the program aired adaptations of Charles Dickens' *Oliver Twist*, Emily Brontë's *Wuthering Heights*, and Mary Shelley's *Frankenstein*. The program remained on the air from 1946 to 1949 on KFI, a Los Angeles station, and was picked up nationally. The program's producers and writers were Jerome Lawrence and Robert E. Lee.

In the *Favorite Story* adaptation, Hank awakens in Camelot with no explanation as to how he arrived. The focus is on Hank's preparation for his "duel to the death," or trial by battle, with Sir Sagremor. Sound effects include a tournament announcer who sounds like a boxing match emcee, cheering crowds, clashing steel to mimic armored knights in battle, and the sound of a bicycle tire air pump. Hank announces that he has prepared a deadly grenade that will cause it "to rain Sir Sagremor," unleashes the "curse of the Turkish spirit with the hundred syllable name" with a string of nonsense words, "to enchant his hot-tempered opponent," and then blows Sagremor "to cinders" (Lawrence and Lee). Merlin's revenge for disturbing the inhabitants of Camelot with "strange magic" and for confusing them about the "day and age in which they were born" is to cast a spell over Hank. The last line is delivered by Clarence after Merlin "keels over" from shock that his magic actually "took" (Lawrence and Lee). Time constraints likely prevented Lawrence and Lee from doing anything more than focusing on this one comic scene: the fight between Sir Sagremor and Hank. This duel was also an opportunity for radio to do what it did best, which was to engage the listener's imagination through sound aesthetics.

As these radio adaptations of Twain's *A Connecticut Yankee in King Arthur's Court* illustrate, adaptation involves adjusting, altering, interpreting, appropriating and/or salvaging a source, or in this case, sources—adaptations of adaptations—in order to produce new material that will keep audiences engaged. The result, as we see here, is a "cultural revision" influenced by anyone who had a hand in the editing or publication process, including the reader and the audience who "reshape[d] the originating work to reflect their own desires for the text, themselves, [and] their culture" (Bryant 48). The matter of fidelity obviously accompanies most discussions of adaptations, especially film adaptations of literature. As Lawrence Venuti, a scholar of translation studies, explains, "in adaptation studies informed by the discourse of fidelity, the film is not compared directly to the literary text, but rather to a version of it mediated by an interpretation" (90). According to Brian McFarlane, "fidelity criticism depends on a notion of the text as having and rendering up to the (intelligent) reader a single, correct 'meaning' which the filmmaker has either adhered to or in some sense violated or tampered with" (8). However, an adaptation should be appreciated for what it is: an amalgamation of sources that include the original work and other outside influences, such as the adapter's intent. McFarlane describes this process as "intertextuality" (10), a term coined by Julia Kristeva, Mikhail M. Bakhtin, and Roland Barthes in the 1960s.

Building upon MacFarlane's idea, Christa Albrecht-Crane and Dennis Ray Cutchins suggest that "adaptation must adopt this richer notion of intertextuality in which the interpretive roles of writers, directors, screenwriters, producers, etc., play a more significant part" (19). More to the point, adaptation theory must "address *intentionality*" since an adaptation is created from another reworked source text; consequently, "adaptations are dialogues with other texts, including the texts upon which they are based, and those texts are in dialogue with other adaptations" (Albrecht-Crane and Cutchins 19).

Radio adaptations of Arthurian romance and Robin Hood's legend are part of the long tradition of translations and adaptations. As aural adaptations and modernizations, the legends of King Arthur and Robin Hood are intertextual and transcoded works. Like their literary predecessors, the radio adaptations produced between the 1930s and late 1950s were products of their times. They may be aural retellings and modernizations of medieval legend, but they were coded with contemporary concerns. Radio adaptations of medieval romance negotiated both the past and the present, finding aspects of the past that were relevant to listeners' present cultural situations.

Adaptation and the Comic Book Controversy

In addition to traditional media outlets such as literature and film, the comic book industry kept King Arthur and Robin Hood alive in American popular culture. The radio generation grew up reading collections of illustrated stories about the chivalric adventures of Saint George, King Arthur, Sir Lancelot, and even Robin Hood. Authors of these adaptations and appropriations, written by the likes of prolific author and illustrator Howard Pyle, historian Thomas Bulfinch, and a host of other writers, were eager to share their enthusiasm for the medieval period but were careful to create tales that combined *sentence* and *solaas*, Geoffrey Chaucer's renowned *Canterbury Tale* criteria. In other words, adapted tales needed to be both entertaining and amusing.

Critics of adaptation equally scorned adaptations of classic literature, whether produced for film, radio, and television, or comic books. Albert Kanter, the creator and publisher of *Classics Illustrated* (1941–1971) was criticized for adapting English canonical works for comic books. Kanter claimed that he intended his adaptations to "wean young readers from *Action Comics, Detective Comics*, and *Marvel Comics* [by] employing the same medium to win new adherents to the works of Dumas, Scott, Cooper, Melville, and Dickens" (Jones, W. *Classics* 6). The comic book controversy grew more heated and the industry continued to be scrutinized for producing material that many parents and educators considered too violent and too sensational for young readers, despite the publisher's adaptations of well-known classics such as Scott, Cooper, Dickens, and the legends of King Arthur and Robin Hood.

Rafael Astarita introduced King Arthur as a *New Comics* character in February 1936; a Robin Hood comic book series appeared in the 1940s and 1950s *Detective Comics* (*DC Comics*). Bob Krane introduced Robin, the "Boy Wonder" and Batman's youthful sidekick, a modernized Robin Hood, in 1940 as a *DC Comics* character, one year after Batman's inaugural appearance. In Volume 1, Issue 36 of the August-September 1946 edition, King Arthur and Robin Hood appeared in the *Batman* comic book titled "Sir Batman and Robin in King Arthur's Court." Both characters also appeared in "The Rescue of Robin Hood" in the October 1946 Batman *Detective Comics* series, Volume 1, Issue 116: Batman is drawn on the cover of this issue in Robin Hood fashion, armed with a bow and arrow preparing to shoot at a target. This is an adaptation of a scene in the ballad *Robin Hood and the Potter* dated to around 1500 AD, in which a disguised Robin Hood participates in and wins the Sheriff of Nottingham's archery contest. In 1941 Mort Weisinger introduced The Green Arrow, a *DC* character based on Robin Hood, and *Quality Comics* produced the short-lived comic book series *Robin Hood Tales* (1956–1958).

While children were reading about their favorite superhero in the comics or listening to the adventures of their comic book heroes play out on radio, their parents were being urged to turn their children's attention to reading classic literature (Jones, W., *Classics* 10). Much to their parents' dismay, children were so caught up in their comic books that the classics were a hard sell. To address this problem, *Parents' Magazine* produced a series of educational "wholesome, fact-filled comics" that were "designed to wean preadolescents" from those popular comic books (Jones, W., *Classics* 10). The outcome of this effort was a comic book series devoted to educational and inspirational topics. *Classics Illustrated* was creator Albert Kanter's idea to get children reading classic literature by using a format they already enjoyed. Despite his best intentions, the series had a rough start and was criticized for "pollut[ing] great literature and subvert[ing] culture" (Jones, W., *Classics* 6). Critics of the series—educators, parents, and anyone else who saw himself as a guardian of American culture—regarded the publication of adaptations of canonical literature as low-brow alternatives. As the quality of the adaptations written for the series improved, so did the publication's reputation. Published under the title *Classic Comics* until 1947, *Classics Illustrated* became "the most significant, successful, and influential publication of its kind," even surviving the "postwar anti-comics campaign" and "emerg[ing] as a juvenile-publication powerhouse in an international market" (Jones, W., *Classics* 4–5). Some of the early critics of the series who had doubted its literary value, or others who refused to consider the publications as part of the comic book genre, conceded that *Classics Illustrated* was one way to get children reading classic literature, instead of reading only the much maligned, but popular, comic books featuring superheroes and super villains.

After battling with his own son about the value of comic books and wishing the nine-year-old had chosen an edition of Robin Hood or Grimm's Fairy Tales over a comic book, one father writes in 1943 that whatever their "shortcomings," Captain Marvel and his ilk had become the "Robin Hood and King Arthur [of the] day. And through their actions a young boy was taught to hate gangsters, crooked politicians, and traitors. In their personal lives these heroes have the daring ruthlessness of Sir Launcelot joined to the moral cleanliness of Sir Galahad. Both directly and indirectly they preach a highly edifying way of life, but they preach it better than did the cloying, nice-nasty stories of two generations ago" (Davis). Although the writer of this article, Arthur Davis, had dismissed comic books and was, like many other parents in the 1940s, afraid that the villains and violent scenes would give his son nightmares, he had a change of heart. Comic books encouraged children to read, provided them an escape from their "dull," sometimes dreary, world, and three years into the Second World War, were perhaps preparing children for the future: a world of technological and scientific advances foreshadowed in the pages (Davis).

5. *The Life of Riley,* "Comic Books"

Radio also entered the comic book controversy in a *The Life of Riley* episode titled "Comic Books," broadcast on November 5, 1948. The episode opens with an expression of nostalgia for the books of childhood, a list that includes Robin Hood. Chester A. Riley, voiced by star William Bendix, is a family man and a riveter in a California aircraft plant, who despite his intentions to do the best for his family, usually ends up entangled in another "revoltin' development" of his making. *The Life of Riley* aired on NBC from 1944 until 1951. The situation comedy originated in a slightly different format on CBS three years earlier, starring Lionel Stander in the title role, and was later aired on the Blue Network/ABC from 1944 through 1945 (Dunning 396).

In "Comic Books" Riley attempts to rid the town of comic books, starting with his son Junior's collection. Thematically, this episode tackles three important issues for the period: the comic book controversy, juvenile delinquency, and censorship. This episode is indicative of Robin Hood's place in American culture and imagination, and, more importantly, how the medium addressed contemporary issues and expressed listeners' concerns. Announcer Ken Niles introduces this episode by engaging the reader's attention and encouraging recall of a shared childhood memory: "In the childhood of Chester A. Riley and perhaps yours as well[,] the boyhood dream was to follow the stirring adventures of the literary heroes of that time, Huck Finn, Tom Sawyer and Jim Hawkins of *Treasure Island*, Robin Hood, and other stalwarts of the printed page. Today the modern American boy is moved just as strongly by literature as was his father, only now his heroes behave a bit differently" ("Comic Books"). Riley is convinced that violent comic books will lead his son Junior, played by Tommy Cook, into a life of crime. Of course, the classic books read by Riley as a child—stories about Robin Hood and *Treasure Island*, as mentioned earlier, contained the same level of violence as the comic books read by children in the 1940s, an irony that was probably not lost on adults listening. Riley decides that as the "cultured bulldog guarding the American youth," he will enlist other like-minded parents in his crusade to burn all of the lowbrow, offensive comic books in town ("Comic Books"). A series of events leads Riley to reconsider his position, and by the end of "Comic Books," Junior's collection remains intact. As this *Life of Riley* episode demonstrates, radio programs reveal the cultural climates against which they were produced. Scriptwriters adapting medieval legend in the 1930s, 1940s, and 1950s approached Arthurian legend in much the same way as had adapters working with children's chivalric literature in the nineteenth century.

As we will see shortly, twentieth-century radio adaptations of King Arthur and Robin Hood's legend reinforced long-held gender constructs and a standard code of American morality that aligned with the chivalric code favored by British and American scriptwriters. As children, these scriptwriters may have been exposed to adaptations or modernizations of the legends, or they may have been members of an American Arthurian youth group or a scout troop. Especially when producing material for a children's radio program, scriptwriters ignored or alluded to the more salacious incidents in Malory, such as overt violence or sexuality, and instead favored the familiar: Arthur's drawing of the sword from the stone, his chivalric behavior toward his enemies, Morgan la Fay's treachery, and Lancelot and Guinevere's love affair.

For radio adaptations of Robin Hood, scriptwriters drew from Pyle's adaptations and Robin Hood ballads. Many radio adaptations focus on the mutual hostility between Robin Hood and the Sheriff of Nottingham, the way in which Robin Hood and his men merrily exact justice. In all but one radio adaptation, Robin Hood is a kind-hearted, chivalric figure whose primary joy comes from besting his opponents—the equally skilled and kind-hearted Little John or the querulous Sheriff. Unlike King Arthur, however, Robin Hood's persona on radio proved flexible: bandits in the Old West, cowboys, and gumshoe detectives appropriated his identity equally. As they had in literature and in film, on radio King Arthur and Robin Hood continued to convey "the spirit of chivalry and the spirit of adventure" (Weaver 416). Scriptwriters depended upon a limited number of themes and tropes of medieval romance such as disguise, which was borrowed for the majority of radio adaptations. These adaptations included "King Arthur and How He Won His Sword" on *Let's Pretend*, "Sir Cisco, Knight of the Round Table" on *The Cisco Kid*, another of McConnell's *Buster Brown* episodes titled "Robin Hood," and "Robert of Huntingdon" on an episode of *Escape*. Both the Arthurian knight and Robin Hood use disguise to challenge the hierarchy and aid an oppressed individual, both female and male, who then recovers lost property in the form of money or land.

Let's Pretend, on the air for twenty years, is an example of how a radio scriptwriter approached writing adaptations for children and an aural format. For Arthur Anderson, a former *Let's Pretend* cast member, many of this program's stories took place within the colorful aura of the Middle Ages. Both the setting and the magical and fantastical nature of stories were well suited to dramatic radio and the "theater of the imagination" or "theater of the mind." Nila Mack, the highly regarded director, producer, and adapter of the much-loved children's radio program *Let's Pretend* (1934–1954) and the "'fairy godmother of radio,'" was known for quality radio adaptations of fairy tales and legends and for "modif[ing] freely" or "changing ... the classics if the changes suited her notions of 'honor, service in a good cause, courtesy, and kindness'" (Dunning 392).

Anderson suggests that Mack never intended her stories to convey morality to her young listeners (36), and that instead it just happened that way. Mack's stories relied on the trope of the fairy tale, presenting "characters [who] were always courtly and respectful when addressing royalty ...

[who] traveled on horseback, or in carriages if they were royalty or of the nobility. People ... were poor but honest lived in humble cottages.... The good people, whether royalty or paupers, were completely and uncompromisingly good. And villains were completely evil ... and ... were either punished or in some way eliminated by the time each program ended" (Anderson 36). Listeners could count on Mack's episodes ending "happily ever after" and for conveying a positive, moral message. Contrary to Mack's highly regarded storylines, programs also promoted stereotypes, gender constructs, and class hierarchy.

Coded Language and Sound Cues in Radio Adaptations

Radio has been described as "'the tribal drum'" and as a medium that had the power to "homogenize" a nation through its "develop[ment] of national uniformity" with the ability to bind "together social classes" (McLuhan qtd. in Douglas 25; Verma 26). As the "modern analogue to the oral storyteller," radio forced the listener to use his imagination (DeForest, *Storytelling* 156). When the United States went to war, radio followed suit, airing patriotically infused programs of every genre to inspire patriotism and to motivate listeners to action.

Whether radio plays were set in modern or medieval times, narration, dialogue, sound, and music were equally important to a story and keeping the audience engaged. In the 1920s critics of radio predicted that radio listening would replace the practice of novel reading; sixteen years later, however, radio was praised for giving back the art of storytelling and narration. Radio was "where story-telling ... belongs.... The best story-telling was, and is, oral. The best tales are told tales, designed for immediate effect, where the voice readily does what written style accomplishes with such difficulty, and is so sure to be ineffective unless a master hand molds the diction (*Saturday Review of Literature* qtd. in "Radio as Modern Story-Teller").

The narrator was an important part of radio. Using vivid word images, the narrator—a role played by men and women—summarized the plot, described scenes, settings, and characters as the action unfolded, chronologically or chronologically with flashbacks, and, hopefully, always kept the listener in mind. The narrator urged his listener to "listen" and to "see" and to imagine he too was a part of the action. Yet a narrator's interruption could also destroy the illusion of the story. Other imperfections plagued radio: radio waves often failed "to carry the human voice in all its intonations," a male voice was preferred over a female voice, and the listener did not have the benefit of seeing the actor's facial expression (*Saturday Review of Literature* qtd. in "Radio as Modern").

Storylines and characters were intentionally "structured representations of ethnicity, race, gender, and other ... social and cultural norms—all through language, dialect and carefully selected aural context" (Hilmes 21). McFarlane suggests the language code in film can be "read" as a "response to particular accents or tones of voice" and may even have social meaning for the audience; the writer, whether he is adapting for film or radio, assumes the audience already "know[s] the codes" (29). McFarlane's theory is applicable to radio. On radio, language, sound codes, and description encouraged a particular response to a given situation or character. Radio plays depended upon a limited number of distinct character voices to avoid confusing the audience and employed musical bridges and varied transitional devices—narration, atmospherically through music, the voice-fade, and pause or cut-off (Wylie 73–74)—to indicate scene changes.

Sound already used or fixed in a scene was familiar and recognizable to the listener (Wylie 73). Complex sound effects were also incorporated into the radio play to better reflect mood and to better indicate the temporality of the piece. Scenography, created through auxiliary sounds—birds, wind, background noise—also helped create "background sounds linked with certain locales ... [to] draw on cultural memory to counterfeit cliché sets" (Verma 33). Music was also used to indicate mood and atmosphere and to add intensity. Sound effects in adaptations of King Arthur and Robin Hood's legend provided auditory time travel, transporting listeners back to the Middle Ages. Sound artists typically used a limited number of sound effects to create an aurally realistic Middle Ages that the audience had come to expect. For example, for descriptions of a medieval village or forest, sound artists relied on characters who spoke with an Americanized British accent to lend an air of believability; the early English folk tune "Greensleeves" and other "folksy" tunes musically set the mood; the musical notes of a trumpet signaled the opening of a medieval tale or a jousting tournament; an ethereal sound suggested magic; the "clash" of steel laid over the sound of galloping horses recreated a violent encounter between two armored knights; and the "natural" sounds of twittering birds and rustling trees transported auditors from their living rooms to Sherwood Forest.

Family Theater is an example of the level of sophistication and quality that a children's radio program could reach. Dagonet, King Arthur's jester in the episode "Sir Lancelot of the Lake" (1950), sets the tone of the episode in such a way that he transports listeners back in time so that they become part of the action. By speaking directly to listeners, he encourages imaginative play. Dagonet's good humor and jovial voice immediately engages the ear and piques the audience's curiosity. Additionally, his obvious excitement is infectious as he describes the sights and sounds of a medieval tournament set in Camelot. His voice urges the listener to imagine he has the "best view of the fray," watching the list of knights enter the field of battle: "Look there lords and ladies" at the "green field," see the "sheen of armor," and the "people of all degrees, knights and dames all moving toward a station" (*Family*, "Sir Lancelot"). Children's programs depended on this "look-see dialogue," as delivered in this episode, to make the action in the story clear to the audience by "carefully describ[ing] all visual incidents to a companion...." (Wells qtd. in Maltin 31–32).

Smilin' Ed McConnell in his 1949 half-hour episode on the Saturday morning children's radio series *Smilin' Ed's Buster Brown Gang*, broadcast on NBC (1944–1953), encourages his audience to participate in imaginative play, while also recognizing that he is in a unique position to influence a listeners' perception of a character. Arthurian romance and Robin Hood's legend intersect in this half-hour adaptation titled "Robin Hood." In this episode, Robin Hood aids displaced siblings cheated out of the family estate by a treacherous nobleman. The yeoman knight dressed in armor wins the jousting tournament and the prized property. McConnell glosses over Robin Hood's socialist tendencies in his adaptation of the legend for *Smilin' Ed's Buster Brown Gang*, and he introduces Robin Hood as a benevolent outlaw who "only took back the gold stolen from the poor people in the first place" but out of necessity kept part of the wealth for himself and his Merry Men ("Robin Hood"). Because Robin Hood is an adaptable representative for politically and socially motivated groups, his motivations are often criticized, especially his fondness for helping the oppressed. Drawing a parallel between the medieval Robin Hood and modern politician is nothing new. Eighty years ago the controversial figure Huey Long,[1] a senator and former governor of Louisiana, outlined a scheme that secured his image as a Gulf Coast Robin Hood. As a senator and a political opponent of Franklin D. Roosevelt and his New Deal in 1934, Long proposed his controversial and divisive "Share Our Wealth" proposal in a thirty-two page pamphlet titled "Share Our Wealth: Every Man a King."

2. King Arthur and Robin Hood's Legend for Radio

Long described wealth as "concentrated in the hands of a few" and emphasized the "need for spreading the wealth and work in America" (2). Long shared his proposal with the country in a thirty-minute radio address on February 23, 1934. His plan was to limit wealth, shorten the work day, provide for senior citizens and veterans, and lift American families out of poverty to make it possible for them to achieve the American dream of buying a home, a car, and a radio (Leuchtenburg 98). Both of these episodes will be explored in detail.

3

What Is Radio Medievalism?

Recovering the Middle Ages in popular culture is one way to come to terms with the present while analyzing contemporary social and political issues and anxieties, all camouflaged beneath a medieval plot and characters. Our modern understanding of the Middle Ages resides in the period's "themes and images—the quest, the secret, the adventure, the forest and the castle" that when "on the screen" is interpreted as a "projection of childhood" (Zink qtd. in Williams 2). Martha W. Driver suggests that medieval films "impose a conservative ideology on the present ... in depictions of ideal masculinity where whiteness, heterosexuality, youth, strength, and entitlement rule. Nevertheless, the medieval hero, both literally and filmic, has many facets that are sometimes contradictory—nobility, piety, and strength, but also rebelliousness, outlawry, and rakishness" (9). Nostalgia for the past is correlated with a specific enthusiasm for all things medieval, despite the obvious problems that result from recreating or reimagining the Middle Ages as a time of innocence and romance when it was actually a brutal, violent era. This desire to recoup an idealized past springs from a fascination with romanticized images of the period as a colorful, heroic time (Barczewski 26).

According to Stephanie Barczewski, medievalism implies an admiration for the medieval period's "unselfish chivalrous devotion—the constant and courageous sense of duty and of God—[and] a high disdain of all things churlish—[that are] the vital essence of the [medieval] tales" (91). Cultural and moral agendas are driven by British and American perceptions of the Middle Ages and a desire to reclaim a lost past. The Middle Ages are "envisioned as a time of chivalric high sentiment and beauty" where some individuals also "sought inspiration for national identity and schemes of religious reform" (Richmond 22). In the modern imagination, chivalry is understood to embody certain values associated with a code of conduct for "civilized society": bravery, loyalty, courtesy, truthfulness, and a sense of protection projected toward the oppressed and the weak, with this group particularly defined as female.

Though Victorian critics doubted whether chivalry was still relevant, by that era the chivalric code had already been absorbed into the contemporary manners of the post-medieval English gentleman (Girouard 17). The Medieval Revival greatly influenced American literary tastes and encouraged adult readers to discover the "'childhood of their race'" through novels of myth and romance (MacLeod, *American* 118). Radio adaptations of medieval romance likewise encouraged nostalgia for an innocent past. This nostalgia, in literature, and eventually in film and on radio, came from a desire to recover lost virtues, but in the process, these media "constructed a highly idealized (and highly inaccurate) idea of medieval society as simple and direct, childlike in its robust emotions and love of action" (MacLeod, *American* 118).

Robin Hood in the Cold War Era

Radio broadcasts of the 1940s and 1950s that brought the medieval adventures of King Arthur to radio were programs from all radio genres: *The Land of the Lost, Family Theater, Let's Pretend, Smilin' Ed's Buster Brown Gang, The Adventures of Superman, Prince Valiant,* and, strangely enough, the adult program *Crime Classics*. In one way or another, each of these programs projected onto the legends of King Arthur and Robin Hood contemporary concerns such as fascism, war, and even gender constructs. What was happening in the news headlines informed much of what was translated into radio dramas. Storylines tended to address very real fears about war and even Communism. As the country moved toward the Cold War era, many people continued to fear the threat of a communist influence that was thought to undermine American democracy. McCarthyism had upset the Hollywood film industry but also the television and radio industries: even Robin Hood's heroics were treated with suspicion. At the height of the Red Scare, an atmosphere of "paranoia and suspicion" prevailed (Chapman 281), while accusations that Robin Hood was a communist made the front page of national and international newspapers. As already mentioned, Robin Hood had made international headlines as a communist sympathizer in the fall of 1953 when a conservative member of the Indianapolis State Textbook Commission argued to ban the legend from school textbooks because of this alleged Communist sympathies and because he promoted wealth redistribution: a plan, ironically, that the anti–Communist Senator Huey Long had proposed some twenty years earlier. This paranoia was also captured in a television and radio adaptation of Robin Hood, *The Adventures of Robin Hood* (1955–1960), that aired in Britain and America, a program "notable for its broadly left-liberal politics and for its implicit critique of the institutions and ideologies of Cold War America" (Chapman 281, 284).

The themes explored in *The Adventures of Robin Hood* resonated with both American and British viewers. As James Chapman explains in his essay "*The Adventures of Robin Hood* and the Origins of the Swashbuckler on Television," for the British, Robin Hood "stands both for the Crown and for the people: he is a figure representing national unity and social consensus. In contrast the villains represent privilege and vested interests. To this extent *The Adventures of Robin Hood* was responding to the social changes occurring in Britain during and after the Second World War" (281). After she was blacklisted for alleged un–American activities, Hannah Weinstein, the producer of the television series and a "left-wing activist," assisted by Sidney Cole, recruited a group of fellow blacklisted Hollywood writers to write for their series under pseudonyms (Chapman 275). Emboldened to encode their adaptations with their own feelings of "paranoia and suspicion," these writers introduced into *The Adventures of Robin Hood* the "recurring motifs of tribunals, inquisitions, witch hunts[,] and informers that seem[ed] [to be] explicit commentary on HUAC and McCarthyism" (Chapman 281).

Communist paranoia is also detectable in a 1952 radio adaptation of Robin Hood's legend written for *Escape*, titled "Robert of Huntingdon." *Escape* was a sophisticated, highly entertaining, action-packed, tense radio drama written by Antony Ellis that aired on CBS from 1947 to 1954. Ellis created an atmosphere of paranoia for a tale in which Robin Hood meets his match in the Sheriff of Nottingham, a bully with a Russian accent, and Martin Greenleaf, a bounty hunter and spy who succeeds through subterfuge to become a member of Robin Hood's Merry Men. Aside from the radio play's obvious entertainment value, the plot warned listeners that spies were among them. If even Robin Hood could be deceived by the enemy, so could the audience, this radio adaptation implies. In the twenty-first century, presidential candidates and tax proposals have continued to be linked to Robin Hood, particularly when agendas focus on wealth redistribution. With its anti-communist tone, allusions to spying, and suggestive violence, "Robert of Huntingdon" must have caused the radio audience, by then firmly in the grip of McCarthyism, some measure of anxiety. Perhaps the storyline was written in reaction to the power wielded by the Republican Senator Joseph McCarthy and the House of Un-American Activities Committee (HUAC). Robin Hood's pranks at the sheriff's expense were often in good fun and ended with the Robin Hood besting the sheriff. In this engaging adult drama, the disembodied voice and subtle cartoonish Russian accent of the Sheriff might have resonated with postwar listeners accustomed to the negative Russian and German stereotypes perpetuated in American popular culture. The appropriate audience response to "Robert of Huntingdon" should have been a mix of fear and suspense. Much of the episode's action focused on corrupt civil authority and the abuse of power, as illustrated in the Sheriff's strong-arm tactics. Moreover, this radio drama resonated with the "paranoia and suspicion" in the air and was further captured in the Robin Hood—themed television series that aired around the same time (Chapman 281).

Similar to the 1950s radio episode "Robert of Huntingdon" and television series, a Superman storyline, which will be discussed at length, was another good example of medievalism on radio. Robert Maxwell, the writer and producer of the late 1940 juvenile radio adventure series *The Adventures of Superman*, adopted images of chivalric knighthood for a modern allegory about fascism. In the 1947 episode titled "Knights of the White Carnation," the twentieth-century comic book superhero Superman rights wrongs and fights racism bred by a secret organization calling itself the "Knights of the White Carnation," a fraternity mirroring medieval orders of chivalry such as the medieval "Knights of the Garter." However, Maxwell's covert American "Order" was really a version of the Ku Klux Klan. Maxwell incorporated Arthurian tropes into a radio episode about modern fascism to drive a moral agenda. Norman Corwin, a leading radio personality and the director of the influential dramatic anthology CBS's *Columbia Workshop*, was among a growing body of radio writers and producers who, like Maxwell, believed that the medium of radio should educate and warn the public about the dangers of fascism (Blue 20–21).

Medieval and Post-Medieval Understandings of Chivalry

Modern ideas of medieval chivalry are also attached to medievalism. Whatever form it takes on the air, on the screen, or in print, medievalism "brings the past and the present into a lively relationship" (Williams 25). Newspaper columns in the 1950s, published during a period that saw a significant number of adaptations of Arthurian romance and the legend of Robin Hood, project an antiquated notion of chivalry and gender. Chivalry, however, was not dead in the post-war twentieth century. According to at least one columnist writing for *The Christian Science Monitor* in January 1952, "the age of chivalry and of service to humanity is not limited to any one era" since nowadays American soldiers, here described as "gallant khaki-clad knights," gave "their all in the service of humanity" (Blaisdell). American radio adaptations of King Arthur and Robin Hood participated in this nostalgia by representing the Middle Ages as an idyllic era. King Arthur and Robin Hood conveyed "the spirit of chivalry and the spirit of adventure" (Weaver 416) and represented the "moral" and "ethical ideals ... of American life"—"respect ... law and order, clean living, ... fair play," and honor (Callahan 369). These same values were also demonstrated in turn-of-the-century children's chivalric literature, scout organizations, and Arthurian youth groups.

Children were being shaped by the values reflected in the chivalric knighthood of King Arthur, the Arthurian knight, and Robin Hood. The Boy Scouts and The Knighthood of Youth were character-building organizations that employed the chivalric code as a guide to exemplary qualities important to the development of the child into a responsible citizen. Illustrating such qualities were individuals that included medieval and modern heroes. America's founding fathers and presidents, both living and dead, joined the ranks of King Arthur, the Knights of the Round Table, and Robin Hood as individuals who shared common chivalric attributes that were believed to be still useful in daily life. The Knighthood of Youth organization, founded in the 1920s and promoted in the 1930s, was intended to prepare children to fulfill their destiny. This generation was being groomed to become the "citizens of tomorrow," who would oversee "as a sacred heritage," the "millions of souls, resources and matrial possessions" of the nation ("America of the Future").

From the sixteenth through the twentieth centuries, chivalry was recognized as a code of conduct associated with the knight of the Middle Ages, but chivalry was also deemed an appropriate behavioral model originally for English gentleman, and eventually, American boys and girls. Chivalry was a "blanket term ... applied both to the code and to its medieval trappings" (Girouard 16). Engravings and illustrations from as early as the sixteenth century depict the full flowering of knighthood, with medieval combatants splendidly dressed in plate armor, equipped with large swords or lances, and sitting astride equally impressive *destriers*: war horses costumed as elaborately as their knights, with ornamented trappers and decorated headdresses sporting crowns of large plumes. These images likely already resided in the minds of twentieth-century audiences listening to radio adaptations of Arthurian romance.

Adapters of medieval romance based their impressions of the Middle Ages on their preconceived ideas of the chivalric code, a medieval sociopolitical and cultural institution that evolved over a period of about four hundred years, from around the 1100s to the 1500s. The definition and cultural understanding of what was meant by "chivalry" was determined differently depending on the period in which the term was used. According to *A Concise Anglo-Saxon Dictionary*, "knight" is a Middle English word derived from the Old English *cniht* in reference to "a boy, lad, youth, servant, ... retainer, disciple," or a "man of an age to bear arms, a warrior." In Spanish he is a *caballero* and in French a *chevalier*. The Old French *chevalerie* is the equivalent of the English word "knighthood." The *Middle English Dictionary* defines *chevalrie* as associated with the nobility described as a group of "armored, mounted warriors or knights serving an overlord" who defended Christianity and the church (*MED*). Knighthood then was "a ceremonially conferred rank in the feudal social system" that demonstrated proven "prowess in warfare" or any "feat of arms" (*MED*). As an ethical code, chivalry was "compris[ed] of allegiance (honor), valor, generosity, courtly manners, or any one aspect of it" (*MED*). Beginning with the fifteenth-century chivalric revival in the courts of Spain and England, writers of medieval romance have tried to capture an idealized vision of the Middle Ages, as imagined in the representation of chivalric knighthood. Originally the chivalric code was tied to Christian ideals and was intended to govern military behavior. When chivalry was adopted as a courtly tradition, the chivalric code referred to courtesy, truth, generosity, honor, bravery, and the protection of a weaker individual—who was likely a woman—or followed a description similar to that of the Knyght in the General Prologue to Chaucer's fourteenth-century estates satire *The Canterbury Tales*.

Post-medieval British and American familiarity with the chivalric ethos or the chivalric code would have been more familiar with the depiction of chivalry and knighthood in Malory's *Le Morte Darthur* or any number of other earlier medieval Arthurian romances and later adaptations as literary texts, films, and radio plays. King Arthur gives voice to Malory's chivalric code when he instructs his Knights of the Round Table:

> ... bever to do outerage nothir mourthir, and allwayes to fle treson, and to gyff mercy unto hym that askith mercy ... an allwayes to do ladyes, damesels, and jantilwomen and wydowes [socour:], strengthe hem in hir ryghtes, and never to enforce them, uppon payne of dethe. Also, that no man take no batayles in a wrongefull quarrell, for no love ne for no worldis goodis.
>
> [... never to do outrage nor murder, and always to flee treason, and to give mercy unto him that asks for mercy ... and always to do ladies, damsels, and gentlewomen and widows [succor:], strength them in their rights, and never to enforce them, upon pain of death. Also, that no man takes to battle in a wrongful quarrel, for love nor for worldly goods.] [Malory, *Works* 75].

Malory's chivalry was based on the ceremonies performed by the Knights of the Order of the Bath. Robin Hood was not a medieval knight, though he does retain chivalric attributes that are highlighted in radio scripts. He championed women, the oppressed, and the downtrodden.

Although chivalry is associated with courtly love, it proved problematic because chivalry as an ideal was predominately restricted to and practiced by the ruling class. Medieval chivalry was "more than a code of manners in war and love. Chivalry was a moral system governing the whole of noble life," but during the Crusades they were guided by faith and Christian duty, at least until these champions of the oppressed themselves became the oppressors (Tuchman xix, 62, 64). Probably the best-known fictional chivalric knight is Chaucer's pilgrim "Knyght," a professional soldier, and a

> worthy man, / That fro the tyme that he first bigan / To riden out, he loved chivalrie, / ... / Ful worthy was he in his lords were, / And therto hadde he riden, no man ferre, / As wel in cristendom as in hethenesse, And evere honoured for his worthynesse
>
> [worthy man, / That from the time that he first began / To ride out, he loved chivalry, / ... / Full worthy was he in his lord's war, / And there too had he ridden, no man farther, / As well in Cristendom as in heathen lands, And ever honored for his worthiness] [li. 45–50].

From this description the reader recognizes Chaucer's knight as a soldier who is heavily invested in the business of warfare and who served in "many a noble armee [many a noble army]" and participated in at least fifteen battles for the sake of Christendom (li. 60–2). Despite this knight's obvious experience with the rigors, violence, and brutality of medieval warfare, he also was wise, faithful to his lord, and meek. Chaucer's pilgrim is a "verray, parfit gentil knyght [very, perfect, gentle knight]" who also loves "Trouthe and honour, fredom and curteisie [Truth and honor, freedom and courtesy]" (li. 24, 46, 24, 76).

Chivalry in the Middle Ages had been a gender specific behavioral code based on honor and was more likely attributed to men than women; however, facets of the chivalric code were prescribed for America girls who held membership in one of the popular Arthurian youth groups that were organized in the nineteenth century and promoted well into the twentieth century. Honor was an important attribute of chivalry, whether or not a man was engaging in conflict. Medieval and post-medieval writers would continue to refine chivalric knighthood as an ideal while the chivalric code remained virtually the same. Geoffroi de Charny, a fourteenth-century knight considered to be the quintessential knight of the Middle Ages, wrote three works on chivalry. *A Knight's Own Book of Chivalry* is a manual establishing the rules governing a knight's conduct. For de Charny, knighthood was a valiant vocation in which "piety and chivalry [were] inseparable" (Kaueper 35). He expected men-at-arms to exhibit prowess in battle, to show restraint and to exhibit "no desire to engage in any evil undertaking," and to express courtesy towards others (de Charny 47–48). Ramon Lull and Christine de Pizan, also writers in the Middle Ages, traced chivalry to "auncynet tyme[s] [ancient times]" and to the Trojan and Roman models of soldiering and the noble acts of King Arthur and the fellowship of the Round Table Knights (Lull 99).

For Lull, the knight was a worthy soldier of the church who showed restraint in all aspects of his life and who practiced the seven virtues: faith, hope, charity, justice, prudence, strength, and temperance. With this combination of religious practices and feudalism, Lull's knight was much like Gawain in the courtly romance *Sir Gawain and the Green Knight*. Additionally, Lull's treatise on knighthood, *The Book of the Ordre of Chyualry* (*Order of Chivalry*), produced in the late thirteenth century, had become the "standard handbook of chivalry" by the fifteenth century (Painter 77). A courtier at the court of James II of Aragon during the Crusades, Lull dedicated himself later in life to converting the Moslems to Christianity. Lull was stoned to death by the Saracens in 1315 and martyred. His writings were widely available in Latin, French, Scottish, and English translations and were familiar to Edward IV and Richard III, two English kings believed to exemplify chivalry. William Caxton printed and dedicated Lull's book to Richard III and interjected, as he did in Malory's *Le Morte Darthur*, his wish that his readers, preferably noble gentlemen, reinvigorate chivalric ideals. Lull's *Ordre of Chyualry* continued to be popular and was later reprinted by William Morris at the Kelmscott Press (1892) during the Victorian Medieval Revival in England and America. British and American writers during the chivalric revival of the nineteenth century would follow the examples of these experts on chivalry, publishing books and pamphlets devoted to chivalric knighthood written as guides for a male audience.

Caxton, Malory's editor and publisher, also translated and printed *The Book of Fayttes of Armes and of Chyvalrye* (*The Book of Feats of Arms and of Chivalry*) written by Christine de Pizan of France sometime around 1410. This treatise on the art of warfare is largely based on the work of the fourth-century Roman writer Vegetius, whose writings were also available through French translations in the Middle Ages (C. Willard 1). In addition to these texts, Caxton translated, edited, and printed *Historia Longobardica seu Lengda Sanctorum* [*The Golden Legend*], a collection of stories about the lives of saints written in the thirteenth century by the Dominican Jacobus de Voragine. Pizan's *Fayttes of Armes*, written as a guidebook for princes, established France's Charles V as the standard for chivalry. Pizan later wrote a biography of his life. For Pizan, true chivalry was Charles V, a man who illustrated "good fortune, good judgment, diligence, and strength" (C. Willard 4). Caxton, as an early editor of Malory's *Le Morte Darthur*, similar to Malory, imposed his own morality on the actions of Arthur's Round Table knights. Caxton's preface instructs Malory's potential readers, specifically the English nobility, about which behaviors by King Arthur's knights they should imitate and which they should ignore.

On radio, the narrator never explicitly directs the listener to look to King Arthur, the Arthurian knight, or Robin Hood as examples of chivalry or suggests that listeners perform chivalry in the same way. The narrator only coaxes the auditor to pay attention the temporal framework. The auditor must draw comparisons between what is deemed moral and immoral behavior based on a character's dialogue and actions.

Caxton, a practical businessman who also translated, edited, and printed the most popular books read during the Middle Ages, may have anticipated the eagerness with which his medieval audience read or heard these tales. Perhaps medieval readers even regarded Caxton's editorializing as good advice. The period saw the popularity of the "chivalric biography," tales modeling chivalry based on the "actual lives" of knights that were "embellished" for entertainment value (Leyerle 133). Again in the nineteenth and early twentieth centuries, chivalric literature became part of a character-building effort. Doubtless Caxton's work paid off. He must have anticipated that the "secular scripture of chivalry, like the divine scripture of the Bible, would sell briskly" (Leyerle 133).

Engravings and illustrations from as early as the sixteenth century depict the full flowering of knighthood: the knight dressed in plate armor, equipped with a sword or a lance, sits astride his elaborately rigged *destrier*. Medieval and post-medieval readers, including a radio audience listening to a radio play set in the Middle Ages, whether or not these storylines featured King Arthur, recognized chivalric knighthood based on their exposure to any number of chivalric romances and adaptations of Arthurian romance, including Malory's *Le Morte Darthur* and adaptations of Malory in various mediums, or images of knights. Moreover, they may even have been familiar with a version of the knight's oath recited by King Arthur. Even before Malory's adaptation of Arthurian romance became popular, nostalgia for the Middle Ages existed, although it ignored the brutality of what is still perceived to be a "Golden Age, a time when all the virtues of chivalry (but none of its vices) were practiced" (Eckhardt 120). This was the golden age of chivalry that resided in the imaginations of nineteenth- and twentieth-century readers and auditors when, in fact, the institution of chivalry was an "imperfect" "human system" that divided loyalties and reeked havoc with one's sense of justice "in times of crisis" (Girouard 270).

The British Chivalric Revival and Medievalism

British thinkers such as Edmund Burke, William Godwin, Bishop Richard Hurd, and Joseph Warton, who had romanticized notions about chivalry, believed that as an institution chivalry kept alive honor, gallantry, and virtue among the ruling class. Reclaiming the Middle Ages in the eighteenth century was an attempt to regain public and private virtue. Just as writers and historians held romantic notions about the Middle Ages and chivalry, cynics rejected any romantic idealization of the past. Burke, a sentimentalist, was so shaken by the revolution in France that, for him, this breakdown in traditional hierarchies was a clear indication that chivalry was dead. America of the 1950s would later feel much the same way, though chivalry's demise was not the result of a political revolution but a sexual revolution. In his *Reflections on the Revolution in France* (1790), Burke waxes nostalgic for the "old feudal and chivalrous spirit" that kept king and subject in their respective places (78). Furthermore, for Burke, the overthrow of the hierarchy in France was symptomatic of chivalry's demise because this leveling of society perverted and threatened what he perceived to be the natural order of things in Britain (49).

In Godwin's estimation, chivalry during the reign of Edward III and during Chaucer's lifetime was not solely intended as a behavioral code for knights to follow on and off the battlefield. According to Godwin, chivalry could specifically guide the behavior of the eighteenth-century *gentleman* toward "women of quality" (*Life*, Vol. 1, 396). As a radical thinker and critic of politics, political philosopher, and novelist, Godwin was at first critical of medieval chivalry in his novel *Things as They Are, or, The Adventures of Caleb Williams* (1794) published during the revolution in France; later, however, Godwin seemingly regained his admiration of the medieval institution. *Caleb Williams*, a novel based on Godwin's political writings in *An Inquiry Concerning Political Justice* (1791), called for an end to priests, kings, lords, government, and taxes, yet he expressed some regret over the absence of the medieval chivalric institution in his biography of Geoffrey Chaucer, *Life of Geoffrey Chaucer, the Early English Poet: Including Memoirs of His Near Friend and Kinsman, John of Gaunt, Duke of Lancaster: With Sketches of the Manners, Opinions, Arts and Literature of England in the Fourteenth Century* (1803).

Godwin's sentiments resided with the social structure of the medieval past and the chivalric institution most aligned with the ruling class. His medievalist impulse was to praise the institution of chivalry as a successful system that regulated conduct because it "assigned each sex its respective department" (*Life*, Vol. 2, 113). According to Godwin, chivalry during the reign of Edward III during Chaucer's lifetime was not solely intended as a behavioral code for knights on and off the battlefield. Chivalry was supposed to guide the behavior of eighteenth-century *gentleman* toward "women of quality" (*Life*, Vol. 1, 396). In the nineteenth and early twentieth centuries, chivalry was adapted for the same purpose. Reclaiming the Middle Ages in the eighteenth century was an attempt to regain what was thought to have been lost: public and private virtue. Just as writers and historians held romantic notions about the Middle Ages and chivalry, still others rejected any romantic idealization of the past. "Enlightened" thinkers like Burke, Hurd, and Godwin were nostalgic for the medieval past but were subjected to the "cultural consequences of the Enlightenment" (Duff 118) and, therefore, were unable to reconcile antiquated notions with a present society grounded in reason. Hurd's *Letters on Chivalry and Romance* (1762) introduced the idea of chivalry as an institution that was represented by the figure of the medieval knight. Hurd was of the same mind as Burke and Godwin. He too understood chivalry as a behavioral code meant for upper-class men.

General nostalgia for the past was correlated with a specific enthusiasm for all things medieval, though the medieval institution remained a paradox. While enthusiasts envisioned the Middle Ages as a period of innocence and beauty and the chivalric code became a part of the contemporary manners of the post-medieval English gentleman (Girouard 17), still others felt connected to the Middle Ages when they went looking for their own sense of national identity (Richmond 22).

The British Influence on the American Chivalric Revival and Symbolic Knighthood

Nineteenth-Century Chivalric Literature

American and British writers enthusiastically promoted the emerging movements of "literary medievalism" on both sides of the Atlantic (Bryden 18). Nineteenth-century British and American medievalism had mutually inspired and supported one another. Just as late medieval authors were nostalgic about the earlier Middle Ages, writers in the nineteenth and twentieth centuries were driven by a similar impulse. As Barbara and Alan Lupack point out in their study of American Arthurian children's literature, contributions to the genre of chivalric literature that modeled "moral knighthood that was influenced largely by Tennyson" were adopted by the American Arthurian youth group movement of the late nineteenth and early twentieth centuries (*Arthur* 75). This movement inspired similar organizations, such as the Boy Scouts and the Knighthood of Youth organization popular in the 1920s, 1930s, and 1940s, that were created to train America's children to become upstanding citizens of the future. Chivalric literature had already set the tone for this type of character-building.

As Sidney Lanier writes in his introduction to *The Boy's Froissart* (1878)—an adaptation for young male readers of the noted fourteenth-century chronicler Jean Froissart's *Chroniques*, an account of political and cultural events during the Hundred Years' War—nineteenth-century males continued to face significant moral struggles necessitating a chivalric code. Lanier's *Boy's Froissart* (1878) and its companion volume *The Boy's King Arthur* (1880, 1917) were meant to be accepted by readers as a record of the Middle Ages and "an illustration of nineteenth[-century] manners" (xxi). According to Lanier, men who aspired to "love and glory" were also called to pursue the "same qualities" of the "young" fourteenth-century knight (ix). In an attempt to authenticate his treatise, Lanier addressed his male readers directly and expressed his hope that they commit to the fellowship of the knights and "folowe [follow]" by example the "noble actes of chyvalrye [noble acts of chivalry]" performed by their medieval exemplars known for their "jentyl and virtuous dedes [gentle and virtuous deeds]" (xiii).

Twentieth-century American writers who turned to Arthurian legend for inspiration adapted medieval chivalric legends and figures to promote their version of chivalry as a character-building program for American males. American enthusiasm for Arthuriana adopted a "symbolic interpretation of knighthood" that was consistent with "national moral values" (Lupack, "Arthurian" 209) and, many hoped, one that would shape the nation's children. On both sides of the Atlantic, nineteenth-century medievalism inspired fiction and non-fiction books on medieval history and architecture, armor, and weaponry, and paintings by the Pre-Raphaelite Brotherhood depicted Arthurian romance. Medievalism as a theme drives an entertaining radio episode of *Cisco Kid*, one of radio's most popular Westerns set in the nineteenth century. In this particular episode, which is discussed at length, Cisco and Pancho are surprised to find a knight inhabiting a medieval castle on the frontier since the only point of reference for the Middle Ages these caballeros have comes from the art and literature to which they were previously exposed.

During the Victorian and Edwardian periods, "artists and patrons envisioned the Middle Ages as a time of chivalric high sentiment and beauty, others sought inspiration for national identity and schemes of religious reform to reclaim an early strength.... They recognized particular connections with the Middle Ages for their own seeking of national identity" (Richmond 22). According to Velma Bourgeois Richmond, a "proliferation of books of retold medieval narratives" entertaining and teaching children "lessons of courtesy, modest decorum, character, racial/national identity, service, bravery, integrity, and patriotism" (14). Tennyson's *Idylls of the King* (1859–1885) had attracted readers on both sides of the Atlantic and helped stimulate American enthusiasm for Arthurian romance, but it came to be associated with the same nationalist impulse felt in Britain at the time. Tennyson would also feature on radio.

In England, both the Romantic Movement and the Victorian Gothic Revival participated in a full blown literary medievalism. This was a period especially focused on both King Arthur and Robin Hood. Scott's *Ivanhoe* (1819), another work adapted across mediums, featured Robin Hood as a secondary character; additionally, Scott's other medieval historical "Waverley" romances (1814) were widely read, making him "a central figure in literary medievalism" and a major contributor to the century's Medieval Revival (Bryden 18). Also popular was the 1816 reprint of Joseph Warton's *Observations on the Faerie Queene of Spenser*, first printed in 1754, and Malory's *Le Morte Darthur*, available in print for the first time since 1634. By the mid–1830s, Americans were inspired by the same medievalist impulse that had swept through England. Tennyson's *Idylls*, a verse adaption of the *Le Morte Darthur* reflecting Victorian but not necessarily medieval values, was applauded and parodied. With the publication of *The Black Arrow* (1883), set during the fifteenth-century War of the Roses, Robert Louis Stevenson joined the ranks of British novelists writing pseudo-medieval historical romance during the medieval revival. Stevenson's novel was first serialized as "A Tale of Tunstall Forest" and published under the pseudonym Captain George North. *The Black Arrow* and Pyle's *Merry Adventures of Robin Hood* even shared a publication year: 1883. The nineteenth century was thus the era of Arthurian youth organizations, chivalric handbooks, and chivalric literature that borrowed and then transmitted the medieval code to a modern world.

Twentieth-Century Chivalric Literature

Anne Scott MacLeod describes Pyle's work as representative of "both the era's take on medieval life and a storytelling mode very popular during the turn of the century" while the popularity of these "and other, equally romanticized legends suggests the disquiet in American culture" ("Howard Pyle's Robin Hood" 45). Given the era during which the legends of Robin Hood and King Arthur and other tales of the distant past aired on radio, it stands to reason that these stories appealed to listeners in wartime for the same reason. Bulfinch, Pyle, and many others adopted the chivalric ethos as a code of conduct for American boys, claimed for Americans a medieval past, and promoted an American version of chivalry and knighthood tied to "national [American] moral values" (Lupack, "Arthurian" 209). In some respects these same values were also reflected in radio adaptations. The works of both Pyle and Tennyson were also adapted radio. Especially during times of war, the image of the knight and the chivalric code were adopted to inspire patriotism. Pyle, Sidney Lanier, and

Tennyson were among the most widely read American and British adaptations of Malory's *Le Morte Darthur*.

Writers like Thomas Bulfinch and Howard Pyle, who embraced the Middle Ages and chivalry, intentionally transmitted to readers the idea that chivalric qualities aligned well with the standard of American values. Nobility of character was an especially important quality in Pyle's characters and in the opinions of so many writers of chivalric stories for young readers reflected in many of the radio adaptations of medieval tales and the legends of King Arthur and Robin Hood. Pyle intentionally encouraged boys to identify with the morality of King Arthur and his knights in his Arthuriad, *The Story of King Arthur and His Knights* (1903), *The Story of the Champions of the Round Table* (1905) and *The Story of Sir Launcelot and His Companions* (1907). In his triad of books about King Arthur, Pyle, who was also an illustrator and adapter of Robin Hood's legend and a contributing illustrator in James Branch Cabell's collection of chivalric short stories *Chivalry* (1909), followed Arthur from his birth through his development as a youth, to the founding of the Round Table, all of which were identical themes favored by scriptwriters adapting the Arthurian legend for American radio. Along with many American adapters of Arthurian legend, Pyle arguably wanted to create an American national hero using as his examples British heroes such as King Arthur and his Knights of the Round Table, or Robin Hood and his Merry Men.

As British exemplars of chivalry, these characters defined for an American reader a sense of true leadership, duty, and integrity that could safely be tied to a Christian ethos. Pyle promotes the Round Table knights as the most "renowned in arms in all of Christendom" who were "never to be seen again in this world"; moreover, King Arthur was "the most honorable, gentle Knight who ever lived in all the world" and the "looking-glass of chivalry" (*The Story* v–vi, 97). Pyle's *The Story of King Arthur and His Knights* (1903) framed chivalry as an ideal model for masculine behavior, thus adding to the literature that made Arthurian legend compatible with American ideals. Because of these American authors and the various channels that transmitted chivalric ideas—literature, stage, film, and radio—the Arthurian knight and Robin Hood "entered into virtually everyone's consciousness" and became part of American culture (Fraser 12). In addition to Bulfinch, Pyle, Lanier, and Cabell, children and adults were reading collections of folk tales, myths, and legends written by Americans Hamilton Wright Mabie, Lawton Bryan Evans, and Rev. Louis Albert Banks. Other authors who produced works of nineteenth-century medievalism included Henry Wadsworth Longfellow—his posthumous collection of poetry *The Children's Longfellow* (1908) was written about medieval subjects—and Mark Twain, whose work was adapted for radio, television, film, and stage. In fact, giving equal time to Robin Hood, Twain's 1876 novel *The Adventures of Tom Sawyer* included an episode in which Tom Sawyer and Huckleberry Finn engaged in role-playing as Robin Hood and Little John, a scene briefly mentioned with a twinge of nostalgia in the 1948 episode of the situation comedy *Life of Riley* titled "Comic Books."

Hamilton Wright Mabie's *Heroes Every Children Should Know: Tales for Young People of the World's Heroes in all Ages* (1906) and Evans's *Old Time Tales* (1922) were collections based on real and fictional medieval figures such as King Arthur, Robin Hood, Alfred the Great, Saint George, William Tell, King Richard, Edward, and the Black Prince, as well as historical events such as the Hundred Years War.[1] American national heroes George Washington, Thomas Jefferson, Benjamin Franklin, Abraham Lincoln, Theodore Roosevelt, Woodrow Wilson, and Herbert Hoover would also be described in terms befitting chivalric knights. The Rev. Louis Albert Banks, a Methodist minister, writes in his *Twentieth Century Knighthood* (1900) that an American man's duty is to aspire to courage, simplicity, beauty, loyalty, purity, character, compassion, virtue, and temperance, thus including a number of character traits usually reserved for women (30). Lanier's *The Boy's Froissart* (1878) instructs young male readers to aspire to "love and glory" and to pursue the "same qualities" of the fourteenth-century knight (ix). *The Boy's Froissart* was an adaptation of fourteenth-century chronicler Jean Froissart's *Chroniques*, an account of political and cultural events during the Hundred Years War. Both *The Boy's Froissart* and its companion volume *The Boy's King Arthur* (1880, 1917) were presented as records of the Middle Ages that also reflected nineteenth-century manners (xxi). In an attempt to authenticate his work, Lanier writes in Middle English, expressing his hope to readers that they "folowe [follow]" the same "noble actes of chyvalrye ... and the jentyl and virtuous dedes [noble acts of chivalry ... and the gentle and virtuous deeds]" as had their medieval exemplars (xiii). King Arthur and Robin Hood would continue to play a "prominent role" in the "construction of a national identity based upon the purported [chivalric qualities of] sincerity, honesty, and courage" (Barczewski 28). Americans who idealized the Middle Ages believed that "the spirit of the pure chivalry of King Arthur and the Knights of the Round Table" illustrated the "best ideals for youth to be found in history" (Forbush 22). Though Robin Hood was absent from this list of "champions," he demonstrated the same chivalric qualities attributed to King Arthur and his Knights: "valor, courtesy, munificence, and justice" (Forbush, *The Boys'*), especially when he was adapted for children's literature of the period and later emerged in children's radio programming in the twentieth-century America.

The Arthurian Youth Group Movement

William Byron Forbush had an eye to the future. Forbush's personal quest was to standardize American morality and to encourage Christian values in American youth, who were ideally white and middle class. He would help inspire the Arthurian youth group movement in 1893. According to Forbush, chivalry should be woven into the fabric of life. Forbush was praised for teaching children chivalric values that had inspired the "origin of most of the modern ideals of the gentleman who is tender, generous, ... helpful, as well as brave" (*The Boys'* 22). Writing in 1911, Forbush estimated that, within fifteen years of starting the boys' organization the Knights of King Arthur, membership had grown to thirty thousand (*The Boys'* 16). With Frank Lincoln Masseck, Forbush co-authored *The Boys' Round Table, a Manual of the International Order of the Knights of King Arthur* (1908), a handbook published for the organization in 1898, five years after Forbush, a Rhode Island Congregational pastor, held the first meeting of the Knights of King Arthur. In *The Boys' Roundtable* Forbush imagines the American boy as "an American prince arming himself for the battle of life from crown to foot" who would mature to become a "knightly-hearted m[a]n in the Great Republic" who was capable of righting wrongs (6). According to Forbush, specifically in turn-of-the-century America, there existed a "perceived boy problem": a growing concern that young men who were no longer subjected to the rigorous life experienced by their fathers and grandfathers in their youth were growing "soft and effeminate" (Mintz 192). Forbush's answer was to initiate youth organizations modeled on King Arthur and the chivalric order that were specifically focused on the "moral renovation" of America's boys and that would "help young men navigate" the especially difficult "teen years" (Mintz 192).

The Middle Ages had effectively been reclaimed and the chivalric code promoted as a specifically *masculine* virtue in the nineteenth and twentieth centuries with King Arthur and Robin Hood serving as role models for contemporary male behavior (MacLeod, "Howard Pyle's Robin

Hood" 45). Forbush instructed girls to be pure, loyal, courteous, and to practice self-control, qualities he attributed to some of the female heroines of Arthurian romance (*The Queens*). The Order of the Knights of King Arthur and the Queens of Avalon were founded on the principles of the medieval knight's chivalric code that was developed into a "program emphasizing character building and 'muscular Christianity'—including competitive sports and physical educations" (Mintz 192). Forbush's youth organizations also provided moral instruction, encouraged boys and girls to perform community service, and trained members to become good citizens. A later club founded on the idea of chivalric knighthood was also promoted as a character-building organization that inspired civic responsibility and prepared its young members to become good Americans. Girls were encouraged to join Forbush's Queens of Avalon, established in 1902 and promoted as an organization that would address the "various needs of modern girl life" (*The Queens*). Girls were encouraged to join "the dainty company of Arthurian heroines" inspired by Arthurian heroines the Lady of the Lake and the Lily Maid of Astolat (*The Queens*). Notably excluded from this list of female worthies were Queen Guinevere because of her unheroic qualities (*The Queens*), possibly a reference to her affair with Lancelot, and Morgan le Fay, for obvious reasons. Through her participation in the Queens of Avalon, a girl would grow up to be "the healer of mankind," like Elaine, and aspire to achieve her true calling—"[p]urity, loyalty, reverence, courtesy, and self-control," similar virtues Banks sought to inspire in men; moreover, a Queen of Avalon would "refine the [coarse] manners of the boys with whom she comes in contact" (Forbush and Forbush, *The Queens* 5–6, 9, 23). Thus, the Queens of Avalon grew into women who were the "ideal" of true "femininity—woman the nurse and healer of mankind, in youth and age, [who] rules by her virtue the kingdom where all men live in peace and purity" (*The Queens* 5–6).

Concurrently, like-minded American conservative thinkers continued to extol the virtues of chivalry. Moreover, chivalry's influence in nineteenth-century America explicitly articulated how "certain chivalric patterns were not only recreated in America but created more fully and purely at times than they had been in Europe" (Banks 49). By the early 1900s, political and civic organizations had joined the Prohibition movement in pushing for the ban of alcohol. To illustrate his argument about the evils of alcohol, Banks described how the British War Department's alcohol ban kept alive a regiment of soldiers who had come under fire during the Battle of Atbara (1898), a conflict during the Second Sudan

War in Egypt. For Banks this incident proved that a "knight" of "twentieth century manhood," whether he was British or American, could not "afford to be indifferent" to the world around him (139). Finally, Banks's commitment to the idea that medieval chivalry was necessary in the modern era was illustrated in his conviction that chivalry never expressed itself so well as when men performed this ideal for the sake of women. Banks believed that chivalry "reached its highest point of nobility in its attitude toward womanhood" (70).

Bankss' book *Twentieth Century Knighthood* also identified the chivalry of the medieval Christian knight with Jesus Christ, a figure Banks considered to be the ultimate knight and "the one standard for noble manhood" (64). Banks's guidebook is divided into the following ten chapters, with each section identifying the virtues of a Christian knight: "The Courage of Christian Knighthood"; "The Simplicity of the True Knight"; "The Beauty of Knightly Generosity"; "The Loyalty of a Noble Soul"; "The White Life of Pure Manhood"; "The Knightly Reverence of Lofty Character"; "Truth and Honor the Spurs of Knighthood"; "Compassion the Glory of the Strong"; "Hardihood the Safeguard of Virtue"; and "Temperance the Flower of Modern Knighthood." "Temperance the Flower of Modern Knighthood" specifically addressed self-control and described alcohol as "the greatest foe to mankind that enters through the door of self-indulgence" (Banks 134).[2] Barbara and Alan Lupack describe such handbooks as the "Americanization of knighthood" that illustrated a "New World–chivalry" that linked the "American flag and knighthood" (*King Arthur* 73–4). For example, they note that in two non-fiction children's books by Annie Fellows Johnston published at about the same time, *Two Little Knights of Kentucky* (1899) and *Keeping Tryst: A Tale of King Arthur's Time* (1906), that the young male protagonists were encouraged to behave as knights and to perform charitable acts no matter the circumstances or the social status of the individual in need (Lupack, *King Arthur* 73). This move to draw parallels between American nationalism and Arthurian legend occurs from the 1920s through the 1940s.

Children's chivalric literature, didactic "handbooks," and youth organizations continued to promote chivalric values infused with American patriotism. Children's radio programs followed these literary examples and character-building projects. King Arthur and Robin Hood would continue to take a "prominent role" in the "construction of a national identity based upon the purported [chivalric qualities of] sincerity, honesty, and courage" (Barczewski 28). Americans idealized the Middle Ages because they saw "the spirit of the pure chivalry of King Arthur and the Knights of the Round Table" as illustrative of the "best ideals for youth to be found in history" (Forbush 22). Youth organizations modeled on King Arthur and the Knights of the Round Table inspired in boys and girls a sense of morality and good citizenship under the rubric of chivalry, while Forbush's handbook *The Boys' Round Table, a Manual of the International Order of the Knights of King Arthur* (1908), first published in 1898, outlined chivalric duties. According to Forbush, an American boy was "an American prince arming himself for the battle of life from crown to foot" who would grow into a "knightly-hearted m[a]n in the Great Republic" (6). This same theme is explored in the juvenile adventure series *Jack Armstrong, the All-American Boy* (1933–1951).

Robert Baden-Powell also encouraged Great Britain's boys and men, the "descendents" of the knight, to "keep up their good name" and to follow in the steps of these chivalric heroes, the original "scouts of Britain" (22). Baden-Powell, a retired lieutenant general with the British Army, and sister Agnes Baden-Powell founded the Boy Scouts and Girl Guides organizations in England in 1908 and 1909 that inspired international scouting movements and the Boys Scouts of America. By 1919 this organization reportedly had 472,538 members consisting of both boys and men (West 30). *The Official Handbook for Boy Scouts*, published by the Boy Scouts of America in 1913, encourages in its members "good character" and "good citizenship" (*Official Handbook*, Preface, v) and encouraged in scouts a duty to self, God, and country. The scout code would later influence the "Cowboy Ten Commandments" created and promoted in the 1940s by Gene Autry, radio and film star and "America's Singing Cowboy." *Publisher's Weekly*, working with the Boy Scouts organization, published a reading list of books titled "Book Needs of Scouts" in January 1922 to reinforce scout training; this reading list encouraged boys to read Pyle's *King Arthur and His Knights* as preparation for "Elementary Scoutcraft" and "The Scout Law" (117).

In an effort to reach children too young to join scout organizations, The Knighthood of Youth was open to boys and girls between the ages of six and twelve. Members chose their favorite heroic knight and adopted that knight's positive attributes as their own (Poe qtd. in "Radio Talk"). In Washington, D.C., the organization, supported by the National Welfare Association and working with parent-teacher organizations, promoted this campaign in the media to encourage enrollment. *The Washington Post* and WOL radio promoted the Knights organization to Washington, D.C., residents in 1920s and 1930s and urged children to "enlist" in its membership. By March 1930, two thousand children had answered the call and were enrolled as "pages" in the Knighthood of Youth ("America of the Future"). A Knight could be promoted in rank for each recorded good deed. In her 1929 radio interview on WOL, Elizabeth Poe, editor of the *Post's Junior Post*, a newspaper for children, explained why the Middle Ages and knights were so popular with children and why the Knights organization would be so appealing to them: "boys and girls approaching the 'teen age' are full of imagination. Ritual and ceremony are highly attractive.... Deeds of chivalry grip them. In the Knighthood they readily picture themselves 'knights' on a journey to their 'castle of knighthood.' They slay dragons—their own bad habits—and supplant them with good deeds" ("Radio Talk"). In language similar to that employed in Gene Autry's "Cowboy Code," a child's good deeds were based on: "obedience, carefulness, promptness, self-reliance, neatness, courtesy, honesty, self-control, cheerfulness, kindness, and service to others" (Poe qtd. in "Radio Talk").

The nineteenth century seemed to reach a pinnacle of adaptations of chivalric literature featuring King Arthur, his Knights of the Round Table, and chivalric themes that remain popular today, but Arthurian romance and the legends of Robin Hood continued to be adapted for literature read by both adults and children. British and American writers continued to borrow from and to expand upon medieval ideas of chivalry while "elements [of chivalry] as a code of behavior" "surviv[ed]" and were unconsciously "absorbed into contemporary manners" (Girouard 17). By the twentieth century, Americans of all ages were familiar with King Arthur, his Knights, and Robin Hood and recognized what the chivalric ethos stood for based on what they already knew about these legends from their reading and membership in one of many Arthurian-themed youth organizations.

In the modern lexicon, chivalry is defined by certain qualities—courtesy, generosity, truthfulness, honor, respect, and chastity—all attributed to the medieval knight and attached to the idea of an individual's conduct, especially exemplary conduct befitting a gentleman. As previously mentioned, according to Burke, the death of chivalry had occurred during the French Revolution. Oddly enough, the demise of chivalry continued to be a hotly debated topic in newspapers and on the radio during the twentieth century. Newspaper columnists and their readers debated the value of chivalry for the modern man and woman but also grumbled about the lapse of chivalric qualities in both sexes. According to a *Los Angeles Times columnist* in 1926, chivalry may have "suffered a setback" in the eighteenth century, but it was not quite dead in the twentieth century. According to one female columnist, if chivalry was dead, women were the culprits. Chivalry had evolved with the times to become a natural virtue reflected in the good manners practiced in daily life (Whitaker). No doubt most people saw chivalry as a code of behavior and important to the social contract. Chivalry was, basically, "human decency" (Noble qtd. in Zylstra). Nevertheless, many people attached chivalry to the behavior of men toward women, but wartime would have much to do with the changing attitudes about gender roles and also chivalry. According to one man, "War has made many changes in everything in the country. Men have been in fox holes, barracks, etc. for so long that they have gotten out of the habits of living. Civilians had their battles, too," but he believed chivalry would "return with everything else" (Carey qtd. in Zylstra).

For some men, the question of how to treat the new "professional woman," who emerged in the 1940s and was hard at work by the 1950s, only added to the confusion. One female columnist offered her male readers sage advice: "treat her with the same courtesies you would extend to a fellow man when you associate with her in business," but still treat her like a woman (Zeliff). For their part, some women were still holding on to the romantic idea of the modern man as a chivalric knight with a "subserviant and romantic ... attitude toward women" (Marianne). This was outdated thinking and only contributed to the problem. According to one female columnist in 1932, it was time for these women, the ones relying too much "on the chivalrous code of the past," to "step down off the pedestal" (Marianne). Writing in 1955, another female columnist points out that because of the gradual change of "attitude[s] toward women since the advent of the franchise and equal rights" and their entrance into the workplace, women were now "ably competing with [men] in most fields" (Dierks). Consequently, women could no longer cry "foul" if things were not going their way. Not only had men's opinions and behavior about women changed by the 1950s, but women's attitudes toward men had shifted as well. Dierks chastises the "modern woman" for lacking the same chivalric qualities traditionally reserved for men. If "the 'old chivalry' is dead, ... women [had] done much to kill it" with their discourteous and rude attitudes toward the opposite sex (Dierks). Radio's bumbling husband and father Chester K. Riley would voice the same male neurosis and insecurity in a hilarious episode of *Life of Riley*.

6. *LIFE OF RILEY*, "CHIVALRY IS DEAD"

In this episode of *Life of Riley*, Riley is a modern husband confused by this very thing when he finds himself in trouble with his wife Peg for failing to act the chivalrous gentleman and show her "how important politeness [is] to a woman" ("Chivalry Is Dead"). In "Chivalry Is Dead aka Politeness," which aired on March 31, 1950, Riley is accused of failing to go out of his way to show his wife "a little common courtesy" ("Chivalry Is Dead"). Riley spends the entire thirty-minute episode trying but failing to change his miserable ways. The focus is on Riley's effort to let his "deeds speak for themselves" ("Chivalry Is Dead"), but in usual fashion, he makes even more of a mess of things.

When Riley is asked by his best friend, Gillis, whether he ever does the "little things that count with women," such as "open[ing] a door for her, help[ing] her on with her coat, or tak[ing] her arm when she" crosses the street, Riley realizes he has no idea how to be chivalrous ("Chivalry Is Dead"). Riley considers this demonstration to be atypical behavior for married people, a comment that causes Gillis to accuse him of not loving Peg and the studio audience to erupt in laughter. For Riley, such little gestures mean nothing to him. Despite his initial uncertainty, Riley asserts to Gillis that Peg is obviously crazy about him. Gillis's warning that Peg may not see things as her husband does and will grow tired of his thoughtlessness and leave him creates for Riley yet another "revoltin' development" ("Chivalry Is Dead"). Things come to a head when Riley and Gillis rush to catch the bus and leave Peg behind at the bus stop.

The characters' conversation about chivalry is prompted by a movie the three have watched that is set in the "olden days"—according to their description probably the Elizabethan era—which they discuss while waiting outside of the movie theater for the bus. Peg comments that she is impressed with the film and especially the politeness the men extended toward the women. Riley, however, sees their gestures as an inaccurate depiction of reality:

> RILEY: I like the movie okay, but one part was not true to life, the big scene at the end. The duke, right in front of dame he loves, takes off his hat with the built in broom and starts sweeping the floor!
> GILLIS: The men spent half of their time bowing.
> PEG: He wasn't sweeping, he was bowing. They were very polite in those days.

3. What Is Radio Medievalism? 79

> RILEY: They would never have gotten me doing that with all them knights standin' around with all them lances.... All that bowin's a lot of bunk. A fellow can be polite without rubbing his chin on the floor ["Chivalry Is Dead"].

Peg's comment is steeped in nostalgia informed by a romantic film. Shortly after this last comment, Riley and Gillis make a run for the bus and unintentionally leave Peg behind. Now on the crowded bus, Gillis assesses the passengers, describes what he sees, and feels satisfied that things are just as he "expected": "All the men are sittin' and all the women are standin'" ("Chivalry Is Dead"), an observation that reflects back to the previous discussion in the newspapers about the death of chivalry.

Once they are home, an exasperated Peg is angry with Riley for neglecting her. What follows is a conversation that has the live studio once again audience rolling with laughter:

> PEG: You ought to be ashamed of yourself. Runnin' off like that for the bus and leavin' me a block behind. Some gentleman!
> RILEY: It was a natural mistake.
> PEG: Natural? Apparently you never heard the expression "Ladies first."
> RILEY: But this was a bus, not a sinking ship ["Chivalry Is Dead"].

Riley promises not to repeat his mistake, but in his usual fashion only manages to make Peg even angrier. The rest of the episode follows Riley's various attempts to mend his ways and to behave with more consideration toward Peg. Toward the end of this episode, one of his attempts to act more chivalrous is to play Sir Walter Raleigh for Peg. His last "extreme gesture of gallantry" is to lay a cloak across a puddle to keep Peg's "tootsies" dry just as Raleigh had done for Queen Elizabeth in the film ("Chivalry Is Dead"). However, Riley fumbles again when he coaxes Peg into the rain and mistakenly covers a puddle of water with her new coat. The story concludes with Peg forgiving Riley as usual but not before he promises to "forget about being a gentleman" and to just be himself ("Chivalry Is Dead").

Radio programs and newspaper columns between the 1920 and 1950s illustrate to some degree how preoccupied men and women were about chivalry. Children were learning how to be chivalric through character-building programs that were supposed to make them exemplary adults and American citizens. They participated in organizations that used chivalric knighthood to influence their behavior, using as examples chivalric knights such as King Arthur, Galahad, and other chivalric heroes like Robin Hood. Even young fans of the Western pledged to follow a "cowboy code" and fight for justice like the masked cowboy-knight Lone Ranger, a derivation of Robin Hood. Chivalric heroes were already entrenched in American popular culture. Despite these misgivings and in spite of these debates, "chivalry [was] not dead" but "[had] only settled down and become a regular citizen" (Whitaker).

The legends of King Arthur and Robin Hood remained popular in American popular culture and were not reserved for the types of books that some literary enthusiasts considered to be representative of "highbrow" culture. Medieval romances, the legends of King Arthur and the Knights of the Round Table and Robin Hood, were featured on the air and in the pages of the comics. Boys and girls continued to be exposed to chivalry in some form or another through their membership in Arthurian-themed youth groups and scouting organizations, reading about medieval heroes in books and comic books, and watching those adventures unfold on screen or come to life on radio.

Chivalry on American Radio

Let's Pretend, Family Theater, and *Jack Armstrong, the All-American Boy* are three highly rated family friendly radio programs that represent how the legends of King Arthur and Robin Hood were brought to an aural medium and, more importantly, how chivalry was conveyed to a radio audience. *Let's Pretend* and *Family Theater* produced a number of adaptations of chivalric tales for radio that will be explored later. The following section provides background on *Let's Pretend* and *Family Theater* and discusses the theme of chivalry specific to an episode of *Jack Armstrong, the All-American Boy*. Specific programs are discussed in detail later.

Let's Pretend

Let's Pretend was a long-running and popular Saturday morning children's program sponsored by Cream of Wheat that was considered to be "an institution in the American home" and an example of a radio series that had done everything right (Weaver 415, 483). The award-winning children's radio program aired on CBS from 1934 to 1954 and featured children's classic tales and original stories with "courtly and respectful" characters (36). Under the direction of writer and producer Nila Mack,[3] cast members known as The Pretenders, a group of voice actors consisting of children and adults, presented adaptations of tales dating from the medieval period (A. Anderson 36). Along with introducing to children to fairyland, Mack and The Pretenders recreated romantic imaginings of the medieval past and chivalric knighthood performed by the Arthurian knight and Robin Hood. Mack's original stories and adaptations have been described as emphasizing the most important "virtues of human nature" (Dunning 392) and were highly regarded for airing folk and fairy tales that conveyed an ideal American morality (Weaver 484). Former cast member Arthur Anderson fondly remembered his time as a young cast member of The Pretenders in his memoir of the show, *Let's Pretend* (1994). According to Anderson, Mack's storylines never intentionally taught children anything, but parents identified a distinct tone in the program and were "pleased that their children enjoyed" the program's "high moral tone" (36). According to Anderson, Mack hoped to teach by example and to show children that good people came from all walks of life, whether they were "royalty or paupers" (36). Mack's scripts also clearly distinguished good from evil for the juvenile audience, as did most radio programs and radio adaptations of the legends of King Arthur and Robin Hood. Villains in *Let's Pretend* storylines were always "punished or ... eliminated" in a nonviolent way by the end of the program (Anderson 36).

Family Theater

Catholic Priest Father Patrick Peyton pioneered *Family Theater*, another award-winning children's radio program. Peyton also intended that his radio program convey a moral lesson, but one relevant to both children and their parents. *Family Theater*, produced by Family Theater Productions, aired from 1947 to 1956 on the Mutual Network and featured stories based on original scripts and adaptations of literary classics and epic poems, such as Geoffrey Chaucer's *Pardoner's Tale* from the *Canterbury Tales*, Walter Scott's *Ivanhoe* (1819), and *The Song of Roland*, an epic poem set during the reign of Charlemagne. Peyton's writers also produced adaptations of Miguel Cervantes's *Don Quixote, Sir Lancelot of the Lake*, the ballads of Robin Hood, and Robert Louis Stevenson's *The Black Arrow* (1883). Peyton's program "mixed religion, politics, and entertainment" that "featured stories about personal growth through suffering by stressing themes of redemption, forgiveness, and self-sacrifice" (Phalen 116, 121). *Family Theater* brought Christian family values and prayer into the American home. Each broadcast opened with the encouraging line, "the family that prays together stays together" (the motto of the Holy Cross Family

Ministries,) and ended with the final words of the dying King Arthur from Tennyson's *Idylls of the King* (1859–1885): "More things are wrought by prayer / Than this world dreams of" (251).

7. JACK ARMSTRONG, THE ALL-AMERICAN BOY

Jack Armstrong, the All-American Boy (1933–1951), aired on all of the major radio networks, was another popular children's radio program that extolled the virtues of chivalric knighthood. Wheaties sponsored the program during its long run from 1933 until 1951 on CBS, NBC, and ABC, where it was re-titled *Armstrong of the SBI*. *Jack Armstrong* was a long-running adventures serial considered to be both educational and entertaining. J. Fred MacDonald describes the program as a "socializing" agent that taught millions of children the American "values and ideals" of "Truth, Justice, Honor, and Decency" (MacDonald 46). Writers for the program were Talbot Munday, the managing editor of *Boys' Life*, Irving Crump, and Colonel Paschal Strong, a West Point graduate and veteran of two wars with ties to the Boy Scout organization. These writers wrote storylines showing Jack as a hero that every boy *and* girl could aspire to become. Crump and Strong, as contributors to *Boys' Life*, a publication of the American Boy Scout organization, featured a number of adventure stories about knights and chivalry that illustrated the importance of the chivalric code as part of the Scouts' code of honor. On radio Jack was the "*perfect* American boy" who embodied "friendship" and practiced the positive character traits of "loyalty, obedience, good sportsmanship, service, perseverance and clean living" (Harmon 79). Along with promoting a young hero of extraordinary character, during the Second World War—the height of radio's popularity—storylines for *Jack Armstrong, the All-American Boy* incorporated the patriotic themes of "fair play and love of country" as a way to inspire patriotism in both boys *and* girls (Boemer 120). The number of Jack Armstrong fans attests to the program's popularity. With the outbreak of the Second World War, fans numbered "more than a million children" who reportedly became "members of Jack Armstrong's Write-a-Fighter Corps" (Boemer 120). As MacDonald points out, radio maintained a neutral policy until the Japanese bombed Pearl Harbor and Germany and Italy declared war on the United States forcing radio to "rall[y] to national needs" (65).

3. What Is Radio Medievalism? 83

Shortly before the outbreak of war, Jack shared with listeners his patriotic enthusiasm and moral ethos. In a 1939 broadcast, Jack travels to Tibet in order to retrieve a stolen scroll (Dunning 353).[4] During this adventure, Jack meets the Great Grand Lama of Tibet. From their conversation, it is obvious that the words of the Grand Lama are not only meant for Jack but all children who are listening. The Grand Lama pointedly suggests in this episode, broadcast on the eve of war, that only American children who practice chivalry in their daily lives will be able to save the world from impending evil. They must be good, brave, honest, and kind. Jack's responsibility is to carry the Grand Laman's message home and to "tell the boys and girls of the United States this world is theirs, and they may use it as they will. As they are, so shall their world become. If they have hearts of gold, a glorious new golden age awaits us all. If they are brave, they shall find a world of chivalry. If they are honest, all riches shall be theirs. If they are kind to one another, they shall save the whole world from the malice and the meanness and the war that is tearing its heart" (qtd. in Harmon 87–88). Jack swears to join the cause and dedicates "the rest of [his] life trying to live that message," illustrating for listeners the important qualities of the "dauntless valor of youth" and the "manly courage" of chivalry that the program's scriptwriter undoubtedly hoped now also resided in the "hearts of American youth" (qtd. in Harmon 87–88).

In addition to the roster of chivalric heroes that include medieval figures such as King Arthur, the various Knights of the Round Table, and even Robin Hood, all-American boys and girls, and cowboys, were added as the chivalric knights of the American West. Gene Autry, Matt Dillon, the Lone Ranger, the Cisco Kid, and many other radio cowboys reflected the morality of the ideal Arthurian knight and practiced the social consciousness of Robin Hood. The radio Western *Gunsmoke* adapted medieval romance and Robin Hood's legend for two 1950s radio episodes, "Lochinvar," based on a ballad in *Marmion*, Walter Scott's nineteenth-century epic poem, and another titled "Robin Hood." In "Lochinvar" a cowboy-knight returns to Dodge to reclaim his lady-love from his rival, and in "Robin Hood" Marshal Matt Dillon and his Deputy Chester Proudfoot trail a thief who is appropriating Robin Hood's persona.

As another example of medievalism on radio, the "Robin Hood" episode of *Gunsmoke* thematically suggests class warfare caused by economic inequality and at the same time stresses the importance of obeying civil authority. However the juvenile radio Western series *The Cisco Kid* took a different approach when the Cisco Kid and his sidekick Pancho encounter medievalism on the 1870s frontier. Though this 1950s radio episode titled "Sir Cisco, Knight of the Round Table" implies that the Cisco Kid played the role of the knight, the "knight" turns out to be an elderly man, an "old geezer," who imagines himself to be one of King Arthur's grail knights. This delusional "knight" in *The Cisco Kid* is based on Miguel de Cervantes' Sancho Panza of his seventeenth-century comic satire *Don Quixote*. The storyline demonstrates through description and sound what happens when an individual loses touch with reality. This episode also seems to parody medievalism.

4

Adapting Malory's *Le Morte Darthur* for Radio

Contemporary social and political circumstances influenced radio adaptations, whether episodes were products of the fifteenth or the twenty-first centuries. Malory, an adapter himself who also engaged with medievalism much like post-medieval writers, had "preserved and reinterpreted the past for, and in light of, the present" to create "his version of Arthur's story" and to "make it his own and reshape it to his own ideals, particularly in his construction of knightly identity" (Davidson 22). *Le Morte Darthur*,[1] written in the 1450s while the author was in and out of prison during the War of the Roses, is Malory's attempt to recreate a utopian ideal of national unification. King Arthur's story is a mirror that reflects the contemporary political turmoil Malory may have been experiencing and the death of chivalry that he was likely mourning. For his adaptation, Malory turned to various thirteenth-century French *Vulgate Cycle* and fourteenth-century Middle English Arthurian texts. As an adaptor, he eliminated episodes of magic and the supernatural and scenes of overt violence and sexual situations, carefully chose episodes and phrasing from a combination of verse and prose source texts, and altered these episodes as he saw fit to better accommodate his aristocratic English audience.

Bravery, loyalty, honesty, courtesy, generosity, and mercy were the qualities of chivalry attributed to both King Arthur and Robin Hood in pre- and post-modern adaptations. As mentioned earlier, a reader or auditor's exposure to these positive qualities was a good thing. For many people King Arthur especially represents the "moral and ethical ideals" which would help "define the larger culture" (Karl 387). For example, Debra Mancoff's discussion of the elasticity of the Arthurian legend attributes the nineteenth-century chivalric revival to a number of factors: "a convergence of nostalgia, cultural pride, a desire for national identity, and the romantic imagination fueled" by "scholarly investigations and the escapist inventions that characterize the early Gothic revival" (xii). Inga Bryden locates this "cultural fascination with Arthur" as "mythmaking" and as the outcome of the publication of Arthurian literature that was "reinvented as part of a new historicism" and the "Medieval Revival, which embodied both an historical and a mythical Middle Ages" (18). This cultural mythmaking continued well into the twentieth century, sometimes with disturbing results. Robert Maxwell's appropriation of Arthurian and medieval tropes deliberately identifies the Ku Klux Klan with the dark side of self-serving chivalry in a storyline titled "Knights of the White Carnation" written for the radio program *The Adventures of Superman.*

The Historical Arthur

The historical Arthur was a warrior, a *dux bellorum*, who appeared in historical documents and chronicles as early as the fifth or sixth century, after the Romans withdrew from Britain around 410 A.D., and also in Welsh legends and oral tradition. A popular figure by the 1100s, the chivalric King Arthur, the one recognized by modern audiences today, originated with the twelfth-century historian Geoffrey of Monmouth in his book *Historia Regum Britanniae* (*History of the British Kings*), a pseudo-history. Twelfth- and thirteenth-century narratives by French writer Chrétien de Troyes, influenced by Geoffrey and William of Malmesbury, made the Arthurian legend the subject of courtly romance, focused on individual tales of Arthur's knights, and introduced the French knight Lancelot (the personification of the chivalric ideal), the Grail, and Camelot. The *Brut*, a French adaptation of Geoffrey's work by Wace, first mentioned the Round Table in 1155. By the thirteenth century, the familiar motifs of the Grail Quest, the love affair of Lancelot and Guinevere, plus other episodes, were incorporated into the vast Arthurian cycle of romances. Eighteenth-century antiquarians and Romantics such as Thomas Warton and Thomas Percy and the Gothic Revival encouraged the Arthurian revival. Warton's *Observations on the Faerie Queene of Spenser* (1754), which was reprinted in 1816, renewed interest in Malory's *Le Morte Darthur* as did other publications. By the nineteenth century, Arthurian legends were adapted for children and adults from a cultural desire to reinvent King Arthur in nationalistic terms.

King Arthur in the Twentieth Century

Clearly for twentieth-century American writers and radio scriptwriters, King Arthur and his knights were conservative champions of morality. According to Alan Lupack and Barbara Tepa Lupack, the popularity of American Arthuriana made the legend "accessible and attainable" and "cultivated" a value system that culminated in the "democratization of Arthurian tradition" (*Arthur in America* 326). Twentieth-century audiences consumed Arthurian legend in print, in film, and on radio. The early 1950s was an especially prolific period for Arthurian adaptations. The earlier release of Eugène Vinaver's *The Works of Sir Thomas Malory* (1947), T. H. White's four novels, *The Once and Future King* (1958), *The Sword in the Stone* (1939), *The Queen of Air and Darkness* (1940), and *The Ill-Made Knight* (1941), and general Arthuriana kept King Arthur alive in popular culture (Lynch 28). Moviegoers were treated to Arthurian films produced in the 1940s and 1950s: *The Adventures of Sir Galahad* (1950); *Knights of the Round Table* (1953)[2]; and *Prince Valiant* (1954), a film adaptation of Hal Foster's comic strip, which also was heard on radio and will be discussed later; and *The Black Knight* (1954).

Radio scriptwriters borrowed but bowdlerized the legends of King Arthur and Robin Hood for juvenile and adult programs in all genres, whether for the children's storytelling programs, the dramatic anthology, the crime drama, or the Western. Malory's rambling tales had to be compressed to fit fifteen- or thirty-minute time slots, focusing on such iconic scenes as King Arthur drawing out the sword from the stone, his receiving the sword Excalibur from the Lady of the Lake, Sir Lancelot's quest for the grail, or Morgan le Fay's treachery to usurp the throne. Following the dictates of the radio broadcasting code meant cleaning up questionable content such as explicit violence and sex. Some programs adapted the theme of wholeness in relation to the fellowship of the Knights of the Round Table and only tentatively explored the illicit affair of Queen Guinevere and Sir Lancelot. One notable difference is the 1940s adult anthology series *Crime Classics*, a dramatization of historical criminal cases, refused to shy away from the illicit love affair of Lancelot and Guinevere, King Arthur's jealousy, Mordred's obsession with the queen, or details of the events that led to the death of King Arthur.

Keep the Lady in Her Place: Gender Roles in Radio Adaptations

Radio broadcasters generally favored airing moral tales of good overcoming evil and restricted men and women to prescribed gender roles. Female characters on radio, like their counterparts in medieval film, were often "relegated to the margins" (Rose 9). On radio adaptations the focus is typically the knight and his quest, though in some of these adaptations Arthurian ladies—Guinevere, Morgan, Elaine, and the Lady of the Lake—are given some airtime and feature as secondary or tertiary characters. Queen Guinevere and Morgan le Fay are shown as disruptive forces that undermine the chivalric ideal, in contrast to Elaine, the chivalric counterpart to the knight, and the benevolently powerful Lady of the Lake, advisor to King Arthur and Lancelot. King Arthur and his knights, especially Lancelot, and Robin Hood are associated with masculine traits emphasizing the chivalric ideal, such as service, duty, loyalty, honor, wisdom, courage, and generosity. However, if a knight transgresses in the episode, the woman is usually to blame. Although Margaret of Hereford is the reason her husband is accused of treason against William the Conqueror in "The Valiant Lady," a *Family Theater* production, she proves to be a chivalric female knight. Not only can Margaret shoot an arrow as straight as Robin Hood, but she shows unusual courage in the face of adversity, winning the respect of a hardened, battle-scarred king. Margaret is an extreme example of the lady-knight, who bears some similarity to Elaine in the *Family Theater* episode "Sir Lancelot of the Lake" as a heroine with the qualities worthy of emulation.

"The Triangle on the Round Table," broadcast on *Crime Classics*, was based on Lancelot's failure to fulfill the grail quest and demonstrates little compassion for the suffering of either Queen Guinevere or Lancelot, exploring instead King Arthur's bitterness upon discovering their relationship. Worth noting are radio adaptations produced in the 1940s and 1950s for a mixed audience that presented Morgan le Fay, the Lady of the Lake, Queen Guinevere, and Elaine the Lily Maid of Astolat as women who resist male authority and who refuse to remain marginal figures. In contrast, *Family Theater* firmly kept the lady in her place with its productions featuring knights and ladies. In the episode "In Shining Armor," a wife and mother must reconsider her convictions about marriage. By playing the role of Lancelot's healer and protector in *Family Theater's* "Sir Lancelot of the Lake," Elaine is equally as chivalric as Arthur's favorite knight. In the same episode, Morgan and Guinevere, in contrast to the gentle Elaine, are driven by destructive desires that destroy both Arthur and Lancelot. In the children's program *Let's Pretend*, the episode "King Arthur and How He Won His Sword, shows how Morgan's jealousy of Arthur drives her to treachery and murder. As a product of the mid–1940s, "Knives of the Square Table," reinforces traditional thinking about femininity.

8. *The Land of the Lost*, "Knives of the Square Table"

Consumers of mass media are more familiar with the role television, film, magazines, and advertising played in portraying stereotypes, but radio was equally responsible in shaping gender, as previously mentioned. A postwar episode of *The Land of the Lost* titled "Knives of the Square Table" is a light-hearted and entertaining adaptation that incorporates Arthurian themes. Aired on October 28, 1945, a month following the end of the Second World War, the episode makes a passing reference to tyranny. This thirty-minute episode is a playful adaptation of Arthurian tropes that conveys to boys and girls the importance of behaving according to traditional gender roles. Male and female characters exhibit behavior that results in praise and success for the male but risk and failure on the female's part. *The Land of the Lost*, sponsored by Bosco Chocolate Syrup, aired from 1943 to 1948, first on Mutual and later on ABC, and was narrated by Isabel Manning Hewson. The series followed the undersea adventures of Isabel, played by Betty Jane Tyler, and her brother Billy, played by Ray Ives, as they travel in an underwater kingdom of lost things guided by the wise fish Red Lantern.

The title "Knives of the Square Table" is an obvious reference to the Knights of the Round Table and bears a similar title to the much earlier Edison film *The Knights of the Square Table* (1913), a family friendly Arthurian film endorsed by the Boy Scouts of America (Harty 320).[3] However, there is no evidence to suggest that this early film is the source for this tongue-in-cheek radio adaptation. The pun-riddled story features "The Great Horn Spoon" ruler of the "Knives of Redstone Castle" and the "gleaming" Knights of the Table Square: Sir Keen Carver, Sir Crusty Breadknife, Sir Penknife, Sir Slice Well, and Sir Pie Man ("Knives of"). As knights they pledge to live "life without reproach", "fight tyranny," and accomplish "deeds of high renown and achievement," such as saving a helpless animal by "cutting through a wire" and aiding a modern bride, a damsel in distress, valiantly struggling to learn to cook ("Knives of").

Male characters are chivalric knights of action and female characters are secondary, needy women. In contrast to the women who need succor, the women in the episode who bend the rules are suitably punished. For instance, Lavinia, the damsel in distress, disregards the king's ban on elopement, elopes with a highwayman, and, as a result, is victimized and risks losing her reputation. Additionally, Billy voices contemporary anxieties brought on by women stepping outside of their traditional gender roles into a designated male sphere when he is unable to hide his surprise on meeting a female boat captain named Lazy Susan. Lazy Susan has identifiable male characteristics—a deep voice and "tough" mannerisms. She is also stereotyped as a woman driver.

Jack Knife, a squire, wishes to join the ranks of the Knights of the Table Square but must "stay back in rank and file" where he belongs until he proves himself up to the task ("Knives of"). The plot is driven by the rescue of Lavinia, the young "ladle" in distress who discovers she loves Sir Salahad, a play on the name Galahad, the chivalric Arthurian Christian knight who achieved the grail quest. The "young, gay" highwayman named Tuning Fork, with whom Lavinia eloped ("Knives of"), is blamed for leading her astray. Jack's perseverance pays off where the other knives failed. After Jack rescues Lavinia, the listener expects a fairytale ending; however, the conclusion is unusual for a children's program. Lavinia shares with Red Lantern and listeners her fear that because of her elopement, she now has a bad reputation that will cost her Salahad. Red Lantern quickly puts to rest her worries with the reassurance that Salahad will be "glad" she is "still untarnished" ("Knives of"), a reference to her virginity and an interesting choice of words for a children's program. It is difficult not to read into this a direct message for females in the radio audience to practice chastity.

Despite the bad puns and overall silliness of the tale—representing common table flatware as medieval Arthurian knights and ladies—"Knives of the Square Table" has some interesting moments, such as the reference to chastity. On the surface, this children's program is an innocent thirty-minute fantasy obviously modeled on Arthurian romance, but a close "reading" of this episode suggests something more serious at work: conflicting images of women's roles. Shortly before the airing of this broadcast, the Second World War had ended and the expectation was that working women would give up the jobs reserved for men that they had temporarily shouldered and resume their earlier roles as homemakers.

9. *Family Theater*, "In Shining Armor"

Another storyline inspired by chivalrous knighthood that features a woman in a gendered role aired on *Family Theater* in the 1950s. Although King Arthur, Sir Lancelot, Queen Guinevere, and Elaine are absent from this adaptation, "In Shining Armor" does make use of medieval tropes. Writer Jack Van Nostrand's modern love story is a lesson on "humility" and "understanding" meant to inspire positive chivalric traits in the audience. "In Shining Armor" aired on September 5, 1951, and featured Lee Bowman as Bill Monkton, Ruth Hussey as Linda Monkton, Anne Whitfield as Judy, and Roddy McDowall as the host. Bill Monkton is a modern-day Lochinvar who "came from out of the west" (from California) to sweep Linda off her feet. As a young attorney, Bill aspires to become a prosecutor and run for governor; however, his career goals cause him to lose sight of the importance of family life and lead to the couple's separation.

The story picks up after the couple's separation and is told as a story within a story, conveyed by the couple's young daughter following her weekly visits with her father. During their time together, Bill tells his daughter a fairy tale about an unhappy princess and a knight in shining armor who lost his way, a tale intended to act as an apology and convey to his soon-to-be ex-wife his desire to rekindle their relationship. Judy shares the fairy tale with her mother after her visits with her father. The tale is divided into three chapters summarizing the couple's initial meeting, their courtship, and marriage. The narrative events acted out by Bill and Linda foreshadow their separation: Linda's hesitation about marrying Bill because of his career aspirations to become a prosecutor and run for governor or the "high up castle," and Bill's resulting neglect of his marriage and family.

In the fairy tale, Bill, an attorney, a "knight in shining armor," explains how he saw the princess Linda among the knights and ladies "gathered around the Round Table" and asked her to dance (Nostrand). Their relationship evolved from there, they fell in love, and he proposed. At first Linda refused him, pointing out that he did not need her and her love would not make him any stronger as a man: "A girl wants weakness in a man, ... a chink in her knight's armor, ... some quality lacking in him she has" (Nostrand). According to Linda, a woman must "feel that she contributes something to the marriage," but Bill is a "world unto himself" (Nostrand). This conversation is one-sided and focuses only on what Linda brings to the marriage.

While she respects the importance of his work, Linda reminds Bill that he must also enjoy his life. Nothing changes, and despite their birth of the "little princess" Judy, Bill is absent from home eagerly pursuing the job of prosecutor. The couple's separation is imminent when Linda and her brother Tony are involved in an auto accident that almost kills the driver of the other car. The crash is her fault, not his. Nevertheless, and without hesitating, Bill threatens to prosecute Tony for manslaughter if the driver of the other car dies. Bill disregards Linda's explanation that she was at fault and caused the accident by grabbing the wheel to avoid Tony hitting a dog in the road. Bill thinks Linda is a liar, and she accuses him of only seeing himself as the "champion of truth and justice" (Nostrand). Bill has turned into a man without compassion.

In the episode, Julie travels between parents, updating her mother on the latest installment of her father's fairy tale, then sharing with him her mother's reaction to the story. Following the last chapter of the tale, Linda tells her daughter to convey her wish to the knight that he achieve his quest for the "high up castle" (Nostrand). Bill's plan to win back his wife pays off. He relays back that the knight has changed his mind, "found a hole in his shining armor right where his heart is supposed to be," and is "unable to go on without Princess Linda beside him" (Nostrand). Once they are together again, Linda reconsiders and urges Bill to run for governor. At first he refuses, explaining that she spoke the truth, and that he has failed as a human being because he lacked "humility" and "understanding" (Nostrand). By the predictably happy conclusion, it is obvious to listeners that Linda also sees in herself a lack of humility and understanding when she stubbornly refused to support Bill's decision to run for governor. At the end of the program, Linda has submitted to Bill's wishes, has returned to her husband, and firmly "stands by her man."

10. *Let's Pretend,* "King Arthur and How He Won His Sword"

"King Arthur and How He Won His Sword" aired on October 2, 1954, on CBS. This adaptation of Arthurian romance was written by Johanna Johnston for the popular and highly acclaimed children's radio program *Let's Pretend.* The series first aired on CBS as *The Adventures of Helen and Mary* (1929–1934). Nila Mack would produce and write for the program until her death in 1953, after which Johnston took over. Johnston remained faithful to Mack's vision for *Let's Pretend,* ensuring that characters should always emphasize "the virtues of human nature[:] ... honor, service in a good cause, courtesy, and kindness'" (Dunning 392).

As listeners tuned in to "King Arthur and How He Won His Sword," the young audience was encouraged to imagine that they had time traveled back to the Middle Ages, "one thousand years or more," to the reign of King Arthur on a very modern convenience: an imaginary jet plane (Johnston, "King Arthur"). This entertaining and fast-paced thirty-minute episode loosely adapts and compresses three early tales in Malory's *Works*: "The Knight with the Two Swords," "The War with Five Kings," and "Arthur and Accolon" from *The Tale of King Arthur*. Merlin's conversations with King Uther Pendragon and King Arthur frame the episode. Johnston adapted and conflated the familiar episodes of King Arthur's legend that were favored by adapters for radio: Arthur's birth, his accession to the throne, his receiving of Excalibur from the Lady of the Lake, the machinations of Morgan to become queen instead of her brother, Arthur's trial by battle with Sir Accolon, and the establishment of the Round Table. The by-now familiar sound effects used to recreate the Middle Ages included galloping horses' hooves, the clash of metal on metal to recreate the illusion of armored knights in combat, and the magical appearance and disappearance of Morgan le Fay and Merlin.

Characters featured in "King Arthur and How He Won His Sword" are Uther Pendragon, King Arthur, Merlin, Morgan le Fay, the Lady of the Lake, and Sir Accolon. Absent from this child-friendly adaptation is any mention of the eventual destruction of the Round Table fellowship, a gathering of "all the bravest boldest knights of the world" (Johnston, "King Arthur"). Also excised are the extramarital affair of Morgan le Fay and Accolon, although "King Arthur and How He Won His Sword" alluded to a relationship between the two; King Arthur and Morgan's incestuous relationship that produced his illegitimate offspring, Mordred; Mordred's treachery and murder of Arthur; the extramarital affair of Lancelot and Guinevere; and Arthur's death.

Although Johnston focuses on the early days of King Arthur's reign, she omitted scenes rightly judged as inappropriate for a children's program, such as Arthur's conception through Uther's magical deception and rape of Igrayne and Arthur's incestuous relationship with Morgan. In this production, Uther is a lonely widower; he is not Malory's lecherous king who "out of mesure [out of control]," so driven with desire for Igrayne, a married woman, that he asks Merlin to use magic to transform him into the image of Igrayne's husband, the Duke of Tintagel, later killed by Uther (Malory, *Works* 3). In Johnston's version, Arthur is described as a "strong, brave and handsome" sixteen-year-old boy who wishes to grow up to become a knight "riding out on adventure," not a king by "God's will" (Johnston, "King Arthur"), a very democratic sentiment. Once he becomes king, Arthur promises to seat one hundred and fifty of the best knights around the Round Table and take Guinevere as his bride.

Morgan, half-sister to King Arthur and an enchantress schooled by Merlin, is determined to rule England. Johnston's Morgan, like Malory's Nynyve and Morgan le Fay, is a "marginalized" woman who attempts but fails to break "down the barriers of artificial gender constructions" (Kaufman, "The Law" 56). With the help of her enchanted lover Accolon, she plans to murder King Arthur, who is at first blind to her ambition and is later very forgiving of her flaws. Johnston keeps Morgan as "essentially ancillary," an Arthurian woman who like her Malorian counterpart is a "sorceress [who] never casts her magic in the open" (Kaufman, "The Law" 65). However, because Morgan is driven to be queen, her "female magic and female desire" eventually surface (Kaufman, "The Law" 65). In addition to the danger she poses to Arthur as a sorceress, she is also dangerous because she is a combination of beauty, intelligence, and deceit. Merlin warns Uther after the birth of Arthur that Morgan will use her "dangerous enchantment[s]," her beauty, intelligence, and deceit, against her stepbrother (Johnston, "King Arthur").

Merlin cautions Uther "not to let her beauty or [his] father's heart blind" him to the scheming Morgan who wants to rule England (Johnston, "King Arthur"). However, both Uther and Arthur ignore their wizened advisor and protector and wrongly assume that because Morgan is "beautiful and clever," she is not evil (Johnston, "King Arthur"). Apparently,

Uther had a history of judging events incorrectly, as suggested earlier in the episode when Merlin reminds the still-living king that without his magic, the Celts would not have been defeated. Morgan asks Accolon to help her take the throne from its rightful heir with the promise that he will be the "most powerful knight in the realm" (Johnson, "King Arthur"). Arthur may doubt the validity of divine right, but Merlin predicts that a sign from Heaven will eventually prove Arthur's kingship. A "great stone" and an anvil appear in the churchyard etched in gold with the familiar words: "Who so pulleth out this sword from this anvil is right wise king born of England," a line that angers Morgan because the word "queen" is absent (Johnston, "King Arthur").

Morgan orders Accolon to attempt to draw the sword from the stone, which he fails to do. What follows is, of course, the now familiar scene of Arthur's successful drawing of the sword. Later in the episode, Arthur receives an equally important sword—Excalibur from the Lady of the Lake. With his kingship secured, Morgan begrudgingly shares her thought that "fair words would better serve [her] purpose for awhile than hard ones" (Johnston, "King Arthur"). In the next scene, a loose adaption of the marriage of Arthur and Guinevere in Malory, Morgan organizes a hunt for a white hart giving Accolon the chance to engage Arthur in a swordfight. He lures King Arthur into the forest where they discover a white canvas pavilion with food and drink. They dismount, feast on the enchanted food and wine, and fall into a drugged sleep. Morgan steals Excalibur from Arthur, replaces it with a false sword, and places the magic sword on Accolon. Magic and the trope of disguise make it possible for Accolon to follow through with Morgan's orders. King Arthur awakens and is immediately suspicious of the Lady of the Lake (Morgan in disguise) and her claim that the pavilion belongs to an evil knight. Now a damsel in distress, the Lady requests that Arthur champion her in a trail by battle with an unnamed knight (the now disguised Accolon). Following his short disappearance from the scene, Accolon reappears with his sword held high, charges King Arthur, and forces him to prove his bravery in hand-to-hand combat, but within minutes of their struggle, Accolon surrenders, revealing his identity.

In a voice filled with remorse, he pleads for death, but King Arthur shows true compassion by refusing to kill his enemy. Instead of blaming Accolon, Arthur blames Morgan, and Accolon likewise voices his anger at being "bewitched" (Johnston, "King Arthur"). In Malory's version, Accolon dies within four days of being wounded. King Arthur then sends the corpse to Morgan as "a present" along with the message that he retrieved his "swerde Excalyber and the scawberde [sword Excalibur and the scabbard]" (*Works* 90). By the conclusion of this episode, Merlin is satisfied that Arthur recognizes Morgan's treachery, though for the king this "knowledge is more bitter than the [physical] wound" (Johnston, "King Arthur"). Arthur forgives her nonetheless. In contrast to Johnston's forgiving version of Arthur, Malory's Arthur recognized Morgan as a traitor: "God knowyth I have honoured hir and worshipped hir more than all my kyn, and more have I trusted hir than my wyff and all my kyn aftir [God knows I have honored her and worshipped her more than all my kin, and more have I trusted her than my wife and all my kin after]" (*Works* 88). According to Merlin, Arthur has shown great compassion. Both the king and the listener are reminded that evil and good exist in the world, so the battle must continue to "right wrong everywhere" (Johnston, "King Arthur"). Merlin directs King Arthur, "the Once and Future King," to look to the future, to turn his face to the sun and to Camelot, and to think of the Round Table and the knights who will serve him. In his closing remarks, Merlin promises King Arthur, and the program's listeners, that his "most splendid days are ... ahead" (Johnston, "King Arthur").

11. *Family Theater,* "Sir Lancelot of the Lake"

Another adaptation that illustrated a conflict between love and loyalty was "Sir Lancelot of the Lake," a *Family Theater* episode broadcast June 28, 1950. Dagonet, King Arthur's fool, narrates this entertaining episode about Sir Lancelot's quest for the grail. Featured characters are Sir Lancelot, Queen Guinevere, Elaine the Fair Maid of Astolat, Sir Ector as Sir Lancelot's brother, and King Arthur, who makes a brief appearance. Similar to the *Let's Pretend* episode, this thirty-minute adaptation packs a lot of action into a short program by compressing familiar but complex scenes in Malory, such as "The Fair Maid of Astolat" in the book of *Launcelot and Guinevere*. Malory's Elaine was so "'oute of mesure [out of control]'" and "keste such a love unto sir Launcelot that she cowde never withdraw hir love, wherefore she dyed [cast such a love unto Sir Lancelot that she could never withdraw her love, wherefore she died]" (Malory *Works* 623, 641). Malory writes that before her death, Elaine requested that her body be put in a richly outfitted barge and set afloat on the Thames. Her dead hands clasp a letter attesting to her purity later read by King Arthur, Queen Guinevere, and Sir Lancelot. Elaine claims to have died a "clene maydyn, ... God to wytnesse [clean maiden.... God as witness]" (Malory, *Works* 641). In the *Family Theater* production, however, Elaine is a chivalric female who gives succor to Sir Lancelot.

Lancelot's relationships with Queen Guinevere and Elaine are the focus of this adaptation. Following his introduction establishing the setting, Dagonet describes the figures of Sir Lancelot and Queen Guinevere approaching on horseback, a scene reminiscent of the spring reverie of medieval romance. Guinevere is described as dressed in green and gold and looks as if she embodies "joyous spring" ("Sir Lancelot"). Ava Gardner's Guinevere would be similarly dressed in an early scene from the 1953 film *Knights of the Round Table*. Guinevere's vocals indicate that she is a young, carefree woman, but her actions suggest otherwise. In their first verbal exchange, the queen tests Lancelot's loyalty by referring to him as her "knight, right or wrong" and, in a breathless, *sotto voce* to better illustrate for listeners her nearness to Lancelot, requests that he define chivalry ("Sir Lancelot"). Guinevere's voice noticeably deepens and softens as she moves physically closer to Lancelot, but his voice grows louder as the conversation intensifies, indicating that he has now moved away from Guinevere to avoid physical contact. As Lancelot explains, he took a vow before Arthur as a knight of the Round Table to spend his life searching for the Holy Grail, an experience he describes as "heaven on this fair earth," and for him "knightly chivalry" is the "truest emotion" ("Sir Lancelot").

As the queen leans in to kiss him, suggested by the volume of her voice and the actresses' position near the microphone, Lancelot suggests that they return to Camelot, "a safer" place for "thee and me" ("Sir Lancelot"). This last line is confusing since so far Lancelot's conduct during this exchange had never suggested that the more sexually aggressive Guinevere has tempted him. Readers of Malory would be familiar with Lancelot's feelings for the queen and would recognize his failings, though Guinevere is blamed for the events that follow. As the Lady of the Lake reminds Lancelot in this radio adaptation, as the son of a king, he must perform his duty "with great heart," and because he walks in the "human world," he must remain "separate from the world of reality" ("Sir Lancelot"). He embodies the virtues of a grail knight who is faithful to God above all others. Lancelot arrives home and is confronted by his brother Sir Ector. Ector shares with him the gossip in Camelot that

Lancelot and Guinevere are "lovers" ("Sir Lancelot"), a surprising word choice for a conservative, faith-based family program.

Lancelot is angry that such "fetid whispers besmirch the Holy Grail," which is a confusing choice of words since he could be referring to the grail, himself as the knight of the grail, or even Guinevere ("Sir Lancelot"). Now filled with rage, Lancelot turns his anger on Ector. Sound effects suggest a brief physical confrontation between the brothers before Lancelot promptly departs for a "cleaner climate" ("Sir Lancelot"), a pointed remark directed at the gossip and possibly the queen. Lancelot next visits a hermit as he does in Malory where he, and the *Family Theater* audience, learns the importance of the "sublimation of the soul" through "service to others" ("Sir Lancelot"). Disguised as Chevalier Monfe, Lancelot performs his service well. He slays the dragon of Corbin, meets Elaine, and suffers injuries in a tournament with the Knights of the Round Table. Lancelot and Elaine fall in love, he sees the Holy Grail, and dies from his wounds.

Queen Guinevere's uninvited and persistent desire for Lancelot forces him to leave Camelot but also allows him to fulfill his destiny, with the help of a wise hermit and Elaine. Lancelot's quest ends with his spiritual transformation and death. "Sir Lancelot of the Lake" features strong female characters that encourage Lancelot to prove his worth "through deeds not words ("Sir Lancelot"). Elaine is a female knight, a "queen of Avalon," and a positive role model for girls listening to the program. She is neither deluded nor naïve, giddy nor girlish, unlike Guinevere in this adaptation. Elaine is not the mirror of Elaine of Malory or of Tennyson's *Idylls of the King* (1859–1885), who remained "outside the Arthurian cycle" and had a "bittersweet, graceful death," as suggested by Mark Lambert (qtd. in Scala 397). Sir Lancelot reinforces this image of Elaine's innocence by referring to her as a "child" and calling her "Lily Maid" (Sir Lancelot). Despite Sir Lancelot's inability to see Elaine's true qualities, they are obvious to the listener. Elaine's voice indicates youthfulness, but her steely character and level-headedness suggest much more.

Queen Guinevere bears some similarity to the character of Morgan le Fay in the previously discussed 1954 radio episode "King Arthur and How He Won His Sword," broadcast on *Let's Pretend*, given that both women are divisive forces. In failing to mediate her desire, Queen Guinevere tests Sir Lancelot's loyalty to King Arthur, who has a minor role in this episode and is somewhat pitiful and ineffective both as a king and as a husband. The listener may not have been surprised that Guinevere so easily transfers her feelings to Sir Lancelot. Shortly after Sir Lancelot leaves court, King Arthur asks Guinevere to confirm her love for him. Though as a king, he cannot command her to love him, King Arthur states that at least she be considerate of him as a man ("Sir Lancelot"). In a voice heavy with regret, the queen, with emphasis, remarks that she is *his* queen and ends the conversation. King Arthur's last attempt to win back Guinevere is to remind her that she was the reason the Knights of the Round Table were assembled.

Most surprising about this episode is the allusion to the adulterous love affair of Queen Guinevere and Sir Lancelot. Even though Guinevere expresses her depth of feelings for Sir Lancelot, he never reciprocates but continues to behave as a chivalric knight. It is the rumor of an illicit affair that forces him to leave court and allows him to fulfill his destiny and spiritual quest, with the help of the love of the good woman Elaine. What the audience may have taken from this particular adaptation of the tale "Lancelot of the Lake" was the importance of honor, loyalty, faith, and personal sacrifice.

12. *Family Theater,* "The Valiant Lady"

In this next *Family Theater* production, another woman proves herself to be as worthy as any knight when she faces down William the Conqueror. In order to save her husband, the valiant Margaret disguises herself as a yeoman and as a knight to better navigate a violent, male-dominated world at war. According to Rod O'Connor, the announcer for that evening, the program's listeners were asked to submit their favorite stories for adaptation on the show. The result was a series of stories that reflected the audience's preferences. It is impossible to determine when this request for stories first went out, but prior to this episode, Twain's *The Prince and the Pauper* and Broun's "Fifty-first Dragon" aired. In the coming months, fans of *Family Theater* were also treated to adaptations of Bret Hartes's "The Outcast of Poker Flats," Stevenson's *Treasure Island*, Lancelot's legend, William Shakespeare's *Julius Caesar*, and other "classics."

"The Valiant Lady" was broadcast on *Family Theater* on April 26, 1950, and tells the story of Margaret of Hereford who risks everything to save her husband, Ralph de Guader, from execution. Following their marriage, which William the Conqueror defines as an act of treason, the

Hereford-Norfolk families go to war with their king. During the battle with William's army, Ralph is injured and captured. As he awaits execution, Norfolk explains to William why he defied the king and married the woman he loved. William's narrative, inserted at the beginning of the tale and into his interior monologue at the end, provides an unusual rendering of an historically formidable king. Sidney Marshall adapted this story for radio based on the works of G. P. R. James, a nineteenth-century British author who also penned *The History of Chivalry*. Gale Storm is Margaret Hereford, the Valiant Lady, Daniel O'Herlihy is Ralph de Guader, and William Conrad is William the Conqueror, the first Norman king of England. Also included in the cast are Hy Averback and James Eagles.

"The Valiant Lady" is loosely based on an incident in history that occurred after the Norman Conquest when the Earl of Norfolk Ralph de Guader, a Norman, defied William the Conqueror (1066–1087) and married Emma FitzOsbern, the daughter of William FitzOsbern, the first earl of Hereford. William the Conqueror refused to sanction his marriage and de Guader and Hereford revolted. Ralph did leave Emma behind to defend Norwich Castle when he sailed to Denmark for reinforcements. Meanwhile, Emma, playing a real life valiant lady, agreed with William's terms and the family forfeited lands. The de Guaders died on the First Crusade sometime in 1101. Margaret of Hereford, a twelfth-century English noblewoman also known as Margaret de Boun and Margaret of Gloucester, also lived a colorful and eventful life.

In his introduction to this episode, host Rob O'Connor describes the period following the Norman Conquest with a tinge of nineteenth-century nostalgia that celebrates the Middle Ages as an idyllic time in "Merry England" of "fair days when knighthood was in flower," and suggests that his American radio audience is "thrilled by the tales of romance and chivalry" (Marshall). Music transitions between scenes establishes the temporality of the scenes and mood. The first scene is marked with dissonant music overlaid with the sound of a fierce sword battle and knights shouting, while a voice narrates a brief account of the cause of the battle. Just as quickly as the audience is brought into the story with the battlefield scene, the setting transitions to William the Conqueror's tent and introduces Norfolk's story, narrated through flashbacks.

According to the episode, Norfolk was once the king's right hand and had been entrusted with the kingdom. William fails to understand why Norfolk, now his prisoner, risks dying for a woman. Norfolk, in turn, accuses William of having a hardened heart with "only fire and sword" as his "marrow of life" (Marshall). Believing his wife is dead, Norfolk accuses William of causing him to lose "that which is dearer than life" and declares his "heart owes no allegiance to thee" (Marshall). This scene flashes back to the past and the romance of Margaret and Ralph. In a scene familiar to readers of Robin Hood tales, and incorporating the trope of disguise, Margaret appears in the woods dressed as a "lad" and, like Robin Hood, is a true archer who manages to take down a stag before Ralph's arrow hits its mark. An enraged Norfolk accuses the "lad" of poaching, but the interloper reminds Norfolk that he has permission to hunt the woods. The "lad," who is without a doubt a woman based on the soft, modulated tone of her voice, gifts Norfolk with the stag but with the caveat that he dine at Hereford Castle and give the "first and choicest cut to the Lady Margaret" (Marshall). The "lad" exits, wishing Norfolk the "happiest of hunting" (Marshall).

The game of courtly love is underway and Margaret is clearly the prize. Ralph's flowery descriptions of his "gallant" lady contrast with her strength of character. Norfolk is besotted with Margaret's beauty and describes her in hyperbolic romantic language, calling her an "angel" and "the most beautiful woman in the world" who means more to him "than life itself" (Marshall). Margaret, in contrast, is guided by reason. She hesitates to marry Norfolk because, she argues, William arranges marriages to benefit himself and points out that Norman nobles treat their women as "play things" to be tossed aside like dolls. The most dangerous reason of all for not marrying him is that uniting the Norfolk and Hereford families is an act of treason against William. Despite her misgivings, Norfolk convinces Margaret that their marriage is based on love and not revenge against William. He assures her that as his wife she will be his "friend" and "companion" (Marshall). To Norfolk, the possibility of death is of no consequence. Norfolk sends a messenger to William informing him of the pending marriage. Sir Otto, described as a "richly dressed knight," delivers a message to Norfolk on behalf of his brother, William (Marshall). The couple has two choices: fight and die or surrender and die under the executioner's axe. Together the couple choose war. William is confused as to why a nobleman would risk losing his lands and his life for love. Norfolk's response is that the king is unable to understand because he is a warrior who cares more for "conquest" and "self-advancement" than for the "meaning of life" (Marshall).

Margaret, dressed in armor and carrying her bow and arrow, stands next to her husband on the castle wall, determined to fight by his side.

But months of fighting and heavy casualties force the couple to accept the king's offer to accept their surrender. Margaret suggests a plan that will save both her brother and her husband: escape. A secret tunnel will help Roger, her brother, escape to France to find reinforcements. In the confusion of battle, Margaret disappears. Transitioning to the present, the scene returns to the imprisoned Norfolk and William the Conqueror. Margaret now appears dressed in armor and makes a timely arrival to save her husband. She had used the tunnel to escape the castle, carefully making her way through the soldiers, and killing the king's guard by shooting him with an arrow, finally reaching the king's tent. Margaret of Hereford's actions proved she was as brave and determined as even the most courageous knight and, by the end of the story, even wins the admiration of William the Conqueror. William the Conqueror attempts to explain to his brother, Sir Otto, who is shocked by the turn of events and why he let the couple go free. According to William he would trade everything, even his power and kingdom, if he "could ever be worthy enough" to "be beloved by such a valiant lady" (Marshall).

13. *Sealtest Variety Theater*, "Sir Lancelot of the Lake"

Sealtest Variety Theater aired its adaptation of the encounter between Sir Lancelot and Elaine in a skit titled "Sir Lancelot of the Lake" airing on September 16, 1948, hosted by Dorothy Lamour.[4] In the episode, actor Ray Milland[5] steps in as co-host and plays Lancelot to Lamour's Elaine. This original radio sketch was written by Milton Geiger and is a loose adaptation of Tennyson's "Lancelot and Elaine," a section of the *Idylls*. *Sealtest Variety Theater* was a variety show broadcast on NBC from 1947 to 1949. Among the guest stars of radio and screen who appeared on the program were James Stewart, Ronald Colman, Bob Hope, Gregory Peck, and Eddie Bracken, the episode's evening guest. *Sealtest Variety Theater* was directed by Glenhall Taylor and sponsored by Sealtest Milk.

Larry Gardner, played by Milland, and Elaine Booth, played by Lamour, are high-school classmates who meet in the hospital. Larry, hospitalized for an unknown illness or injury, is being tended to by Elaine, his night nurse, an obvious pun on the word "knight." As the plot unfolds, the audience discovers that in high school, Elaine, a romantic and fan of

4. Adapting Malory's Le Morte Darthur for Radio

Tennyson's *Idylls*, had a crush on Larry, who was nicknamed "Sir Lunch of the Lake" because of his voracious appetite. Now his nurse, Elaine, has the opportunity to clue him in on who she is and to make a confession. However, all he can remember about Elaine is that she was the "awkward, freckle-faced girl who recited Tennyson" in his English class:

> ELAINE the fair, Elaine the lovable,
> Elaine, the lily maid of Astolat,
> High in her chamber up a tower to the east Guarded the sacred shield of Lancelot [Tennyson 138–139].

At the time, Larry was in love with a beautiful girl named Eunice, and he was prepared to propose to her when his fraternity pin, a gold and enamel fraternity shield, went missing. After high school, he apparently went to war as his recent encounter with Elaine takes place eight years later and this program aired in 1948. All this time Elaine's conscience had troubled her. In fact, the pin was not lost. Elaine had stolen the fraternity shield and kept it as a token all these years.

In the next scene, a dream sequence, Elaine relives the fictional Elaine's encounter with Lancelot when she falls asleep at Larry's bedside. As she sleeps, she unwittingly reveals her secret to Larry. In this "lovely dream" she is "Elaine the fair" visited by a "knight in gleaming armor" bearing the shield of "great lions of Lancelot of the Lake" ("Sir Lancelot"). Lancelot (Larry), travelling to Camelot for a tournament, stops to request "a boon"—something of Elaine's to wear into battle ("Sir Lancelot"). Elaine presents a shield and proclaims she is his "squire," as the fictional Elaine does in Tennyson. Lancelot rides into the tournament but is injured by Gawain. This radio play relies on hoof beats and clashing steel to help the audience imagine armored knights in combat. Other than these minimal sound effects and music to set the mood and announce scene changes, listeners have little other than the actors' line delivery to imagine King Arthur's Briton. In an attempt at humor, the fallen Sir Lancelot calls himself a "gone goose," but Elaine reassures him that she can "take care of knights" because she is a "night nurse" ("Sir Lancelot"). She awakens to Larry calling her name.

Elaine realizes she exposed her secret and swears to return the pin, "the sacred shield of Lancelot" ("Sir Lancelot"). Larry reassures her that all is forgiven and explains how insignificant her crime was compared to his experiences in war, experiences that turned him into a man: "I spent two of those eight years [away] growing up in a foxhole. Old values change. A man [sees] things more maturely, clearly, more deeply. He begins to listen to fundamental things deep inside him, like 'The Lord is my shepherd,' like 'Entreat me not to leave me,' or like "Elaine the fair. Elaine the lovable. Elaine, the Lily Maid of Lake High School" ("Sir Lancelot"). Larry explains that Elaine is the right girl to own his pin and then, quoting Tennyson, asks her: "Do me this grace, and keep this pin. From Lancelot with all my love" ("Sir Lancelot"). Instead of the title "Sir Lancelot of the Lake," this episode should be titled "Elaine the Fair." The plot is driven by Elaine's choices and her acts of female chivalry. In the end, the lady is rewarded with marriage for taking care of Larry/Lancelot.

14. *Smilin' Ed's Buster Brown Gang*, "Knights and Tournaments"

Smilin' Ed's Buster Brown Gang gave equal airtime to Arthurian tales and Robin Hood's legend. Tristan, or Tristram, was featured in the "Knights and Tournaments" broadcast on July 26, 1946. *Buster Brown Gang* originated as a comic strip in the 1930s with host Ed McConnell of Buster Brown shoes fame. McConnell hosted the Saturday morning program on NBC from 1944 through 1953. The children's program aired on television in 1950. McConnell and the characters, Froggie the Gremlin, Squeaky the Mouse, Midnight the Cat, and Grandie the Piano, voiced by McConnell and a cast of radio actors, entertained a live studio audience of children with tales set in the Old West, the jungle, and Robin Hood's "merry England" (Dunning 620–621). Buster Brown originated as a comic strip character created by R. F. Outcault and was adapted for radio in 1929. Originally, the program followed the adventures of a little boy named Buster Brown and his dog, Tige.

McConnell opens the "Knights and Tournaments" episode by inviting listeners to travel back in time with him to the "days of chivalry" and "good King Arthur and his Knights of the Round Table," when "many of them met adventures and many of them met death" (McConnell, "Knights"). Presuming his listeners are familiar with King Arthur, McConnell makes no other reference to the legend and provides no additional details. "Knights and Tournaments" is a didactic tale that addresses the importance of honor and courage. In addition to entertaining young fans with a chivalric tale, McConnell has an agenda. This storyline also draws a parallel between the deaths of medieval knights and modern soldiers on the battlefield.

McConnell took advantage of the medium's ability to reach and to influence listeners, but in this instance he used King Arthur as a vehicle to encourage children toward a social conscience with the pointed reminder that, as Americans, they were lucky compared to other children starving around the world. Joining the Clean Plate Club, a nationwide campaign to prevent waste promoted by President Harry Truman, becomes an act of good global citizenship and patriotism. The Clean Plate Club campaign was initiated by Herbert Hoover and supported by President Woodrow Wilson following World War I and the passing of the Lever Act. The campaign was revived during the Depression and the Second World War[6] to encourage children to make the same sacrifices as adults: to not be wasteful, to ration, and to volunteer, all in support of the troops fighting overseas. McConnell's call went out in 1946 at about the same time as the creation of the United Nations International Children's Emergency Fund (UNICEF), an organization aiding children in war-torn Europe and China.

Children listening to "Knights and Tournaments" would have associated their own actions with those of the episode's hero, Tristan, a young man training to become a knight after the death of his father in the Crusades. Tristan risks his own life to help someone in need. In Arthurian tradition, the story of Tristan or Tristram was linked to the fated love story of Tristan and Isolde, while in Malory, Tristan is a young knight undergoing a series of trials to become a Knight of the Round Table. Tristan's actions in this radio adaptation illustrate the "noble soul" of chivalry that was written about and encouraged in children's chivalric literature and Arthurian organizations (Banks 50). Tristan's charity toward someone in distress, along with his honor and bravery in conduct and in battle, are qualities to which McConnell's fans could and should aspire. Smilin' Ed's explanation of chivalry draws upon the Old French *chevalerie*, the equivalent of the English word for knighthood.

"Knights and Tournaments" opens with a scene between Tristan and his mother, Lady Eleanor, who are discussing the death of Tristan's father, a "brave," "chivalrous and gentle" knight who "fell before [the] swords of the infidels" (McConnell, "Knights"). Now that Tristan's time has come to train as a knight, Eleanor delivers a short lecture on the nature of diplomacy, war, and bravery in combat. Eleanor assures Tristan that, while death in war is "never good," "no good comes from an unsheathed sword" either since "no man must be cowardly" (McConnell, "Knights"). Even though she stresses courage as an important trait on and off the battlefield, Tristan should attempt diplomacy to "conquer with a soft word when [he] may" before turning to the sword—although, as she reminds him, "the bare sword is a mighty persuasion" (McConnell, "Knights"). Perhaps the audience was supposed to understand that while diplomacy worked, sometimes situations could call for brutal measures. Tristan takes his mother's words to heart as he trains for knighthood. A year passes and Tristan is ready to "go into the world and earn his spurs" causing Lady Eleanor to express a mother's regret at "losing her little son" to maturity, or more likely to war; nevertheless, she supports Tristan in the best way she can by providing him with a suit of armor (McConnell, "Knights"). As Tristan begins his journey, the setting switches to the interior of a cottage and to John, another young man ready to begin his own quest.

Tristan and John have much in common: they are near the same age, boys on the cusp of adulthood; they are both of the noble class; and they both have lost a father in battle. After the death of his father, John was fostered by the former gatekeeper of Asbury Castle and his wife, who John believes is his dying grandmother. To protect John's identity and to keep him safe, John has been hidden from his uncle, who would kill him for his inheritance, another popular theme in many of these radio programs. After John's grandmother dies (on the air), he journeys to Asbury Castle to claim his inheritance. Before he arrives, however, John is accosted by four horsemen. McConnell keys listeners into the fact that the horsemen were sent by John's uncle, who intended that John die in the skirmish. Tristan immediately appears on the scene, kills one attacker and scares the others away. John and Tristan become fast friends, and Tristan takes John home to train him as a knight and prepare him for an upcoming tournament so he can win back the Asbury property. McConnell uses a similar storyline for his 1949 "Robin Hood" adaptation in which Robin Hood and Little John "best" the Sheriff of Nottingham.

"Knights and Tournaments" concludes with Tristan disguising himself as John, taking to the field wearing the Asbury crest, killing John's uncle, Gregory, and winning back the Asbury lands. As the disguised Tristan and Gregory take their places, the duke threatens his opponent with the warning that "his crest will lie in the bloody mud" (McConnell, "Knights"). Within seconds of taking the field, Tristan kills Gregory. Tristan's bravery emphasizes the episode's point that chivalry, especially courage, honor, and prowess, win in the end. As with all of the radio adaptations of the legends of King Arthur and Robin Hood, this episode also ends happily: John regains his inheritance and his dukedom.

Many radio programs addressed contemporary social issues, such as gender roles and post-war anxieties, or encouraged in listeners a sense of right and wrong. American children familiar with King Arthur and the Knights of the Round Table would recognize chivalry when they heard it on radio. This selection of radio programs conveyed ethical ideas already associated with chivalric culture and identified with American mores and expectations of ethical personal conduct. *Let's Pretend* and *Family Theater* thus simultaneously fulfilled their network's policies and their listener's expectations.

15. *Gunsmoke*, "Lochinvar"

Les Crutchfield adapts the plot of Walter Scott's chivalric tale "Lochinvar" for an October 17, 1952, episode of *Gunsmoke*, titled "Lochinvar" after Sir Walter Scott's Lochinvar, the knight protagonist who Lady Heron sung about in a ballad in the story-within-a-story *Marmion: A Tale of Flodden Field* (1808), a popular epic poem. Only listeners familiar with Scott's "Lochinvar" would readily identify how the early nineteenth-century ballad informed Crutchfield's story. Crutchfield borrows Scott's Canto First, the story of Lochinvar and his lady Ellen, who elope on the day of her wedding. Elements of time and place undergo a significant shift in this radio Western. The setting moves from Galloway, Scotland, to Dodge City, Kansas, and focuses on two cowboys and their mutual love interest. Doc, the town's soft-spoken physician with a soft spot for romance, aptly sums up the excitement in Dodge when this erstwhile cowboy returns to Dodge for his lady-love: "a man comes back from the West, sees girl, finds out that she's on the point of marrying someone else" (Crutchfield).

In Scott's tale, "Lady Heron's Song" is the story of

> young Lochinvar ... come out of the west,
> Through all the wide Border his steed was the best;
> And save his good broadsword he weapons had none,
> He rode all unarmed and he rode all alone.
> So faithful in love and so dauntless in war,
> There never was knight like the young Lochinvar.
> He stayed not for brake and he stopped not for stone,
> He swam the Eske river where ford there was none;
> But ere he alighted at Netherby gate
> The bride had consented, the gallant came late:

> For a laggard in love and a dastard in war
> Was to wed the fair Ellen of brave Lochinvar [Canto V, li. 313–XII, 136–324].

Frank Craig, the cowboy-knight, a "fancy dresser who wears silver spurs, a red silk handkerchief, and yellow boots," replaces Scott's Lochinvar as the knight of "Shield, lance, and brand, and plume, and scarf" on a quest to win his lady love, Artis Nash (Introduction to Canto First, li. 226). Ben Martin, Frank's rival and Artis's intended, is a mean "bull neck plow boy" (Crutchfield) and the "laggard in love and a dastard in war" of Scott's work (XII, "Lady Heron's Song," li. 323). Kitty, the owner of Long Branch Saloon and Marshal Matt Dillon's long-time friend, speaks for the women of Dodge City when she associates Frank with the romantic figure and knight of medieval romance. Kitty, too, seems drawn to Arthurian tales of "warriors wrought in steely weeds" (Scott, Introduction to Canto First, li. 256).

Artis, absent from all but the final scene, is the lady of medieval romance, an object of exchange between the male rivals. For most of the play, she keeps silent as her fiancé and former lover come close to solving their differences through a gunfight. Oddly, Chester Proudfoot, Matt's deputy, voices his frustration that all the trouble in Dodge would have been avoided had Artis only spoken her mind early on and identified what she really wanted (Crutchfield). Not until later in the episode do listeners discover that she and Frank had all along been working behind the scenes to plan their elopement.

Act One introduces the characters and the back story, followed by Act Two, which fleshes out the conflict. Frank Martin arrives in Dodge City to retrieve Artis Nash, the woman he still loves and a woman "every man in Dodge was crazy about" (Crutchfield). Matt considers this romantic drama ridiculous, and he voices his inability to understand why women "go after men like that" (Crutchfield). Kitty agrees with Matt, in part, but as a woman, which is emphasized in this episode of *Gunsmoke*, she cannot help but identify Frank as a romantic figure and see the love triangle as a romance. Matt, always the rational lawman, incorrectly identifies Frank as drifter and troublemaker but has a change of heart when Frank shows his true character. As the storyline unfolds, Frank evolves from a suspected murderer into the romantic Lochinvar figure of Kitty's imaginings, the faithful knight "dauntless in war" (Scott, Canto V, li. 317).

Frank's back story includes a rapid departure from Dodge City a year earlier under mysterious circumstances and a likely frame up by rival Ben. Frank's return happens to coincide with his former girlfriend's impending

4. *Adapting Malory's* Le Morte Darthur *for Radio* 109

wedding to Ben. Describing himself as a changed man who has "gotten over [his] wildness," Frank claims he is ready to settle down (Crutchfield). Matt senses trouble when Ben states that a "man's got a right to protect what's his" and stations armed men around Artis's house making her a prisoner in her own home (Crutchfield). Angered by his actions, Frank needles Ben at every opportunity and snidely remarks that, unlike Artis's betrothed, he needs no weapon to keep her (Crutchfield). Ben's last desperate act is to frame Frank for murder. Ben shoots and kills an office clerk, stages a robbery, and plants at the scene a red handkerchief later identified as Frank's. Matt and Chester stake out Frank's room in the boarding house, hoping to arrest him. As they wait, the lawmen wonder why Frank would rob and kill a clerk when he obviously had no need for money. Frank enters the room but escapes through a window before he is arrested.

Artis had claimed that she was finished with Frank, but listeners are alerted that the two lovers had planned to elope all along. Just as Lochinvar entered Netherby Hall to claim his bride as the bridal party looks on, Frank, like Lochinvar, "...stopp'd not for stone, / ... / But ere he alighted at Netherby gate / The bride had consented, the gallant came late; / For a laggard in love, and a dastard in war, / was to wed the fair Ellen of brave Lochinvar. (Canto XII, "Lady Heron's Song," li. 319, 321–326). Frank hides in the church as the ceremony begins, and then causes a commotion. Artis faints and is carried to the minister's study. Ben, brandishing a gun, follows her, but he is too slow. The couple escapes in a scene right out of Scott's "Lochinvar", when Lochinvar and Ellen "reached the hall-door, and the charger stood near; / So light to the croupe the fair lady he swung, / So light to the saddle before her he sprung! / 'She is won! we are gone, over bank, bush, and scaur: They'll have fleet steeds that follow,' quoth young / Lochinvar" (Scott, "Marmion," 184–185). As Matt and Chester head out in search of the couple, the news arrives that the clerk is dead. Frank is accused of murder.

In the last scene, Matt and Chester return to the jail, intending to issue a an arrest warrant for Frank. As Matt lights the lamp, his eyes fall on Frank and Artis. Listeners are finally treated to Artis's story. Scott's Ellen, unlike Crutchfield's Artis, never explained why she chose to elope with her knight. According to Artis, she is to blame for the events of the last two days and describes herself as a "victim of her own foolishness" since she loved Frank from the moment he returned to Dodge (Crutchfield). In fact, she says she loved him enough to provide him an alibi for the night the clerk was shot. For his part, Frank says he preferred being hung for murder rather than risk damaging his lady's honor and admitting they were alone together. Artis also pushes Matt to confront Ben about what happened to her red silk scarf. She knows Ben killed the clerk to ruin Frank. Matt believes their tale.

Suspense builds as hoof beats fill the air, announcing Ben's arrival at the jail, but the couple has enough time to escape. In a gesture that suggests the Marshal is a romantic at heart, Matt gives the couple his extra horse, and they ride to Wyoming. Ben enters the jail ready for a fight. Matt confronts Ben, trying to get him to give himself up, but Ben prefers death over a trial. Ben draws his gun and Matt shoots, killing him. Matt describes for listeners the sad scene meant to invoke compassion for Ben—a marriage license falls out of the dead man's pocket.

16. *Crime Classics*, "The Triangle on the Round Table"

"The Triangle on the Round Table," broadcast on November 18, 1954, on *Crime Classics*, compressed Malory's "The Book of Sir Lancelot and Queen Guinevere" and "the Poisoned Apple." *Crime Classics* was an entertaining thirty-minute dramatic CBS series that aired on radio from June 15, 1953, to June 30, 1954; the series incorporated dark humor for presentations of pre-twentieth-century true crime stories adapted by Morton Fine and David Friedkin. Fine and Friedkin claimed "The Triangle on the Round Table" was based on the "accounts and legends of King Arthur." Elliott Lewis, a well-known and highly respected radio actor, director, and producer, produced and directed *Crime Classics*. Lou Merrill voiced the program's fictional narrator, Thomas Hyland, aptly transmitting his character's sardonic wit. William Conrad, who played Matt Dillon on *Gunsmoke* and voiced a number of characters on radio, including Robin Hood in "Robert of Huntingdon" on *Escape*, voices King Arthur.

"The Triangle on the Round Table" focuses on the love affair of Sir Lancelot and Queen Guinevere; the episode explores Mordred's lust for the queen and the death of King Arthur, both of which caused the rift in Camelot and illustrates the paradoxical nature of chivalry, the failure of the chivalric code, and the futility of war. Because of audience sensitivity,

Let's Pretend, Family Theater, and the *Buster Brown* show downplayed violence and emphasized good overcoming evil, choosing to present King Arthur as a mature and controlled individual. Fine and Friedkin do not idealize King Arthur or hold him above reproach. Listeners are treated to a version of King Arthur other radio adaptors ignored, a version which shows his very human qualities. In Fine and Friedkin's take on the legend, King Arthur is emotionally devastated by Sir Lancelot and Guinevere's affair, and he wants revenge. Their Arthur is sharp-tongued and violent. The storyline is driven by the affair and by Mordred's treason. Chivalry associated with courtly love proved problematic because the ideal was predominately restricted to and was practiced by the ruling class as a code of manners relevant in war and in love (Tuchman 62). Fine and Friedkin explore the "fiction of chivalry" as a standard of behavior which, according to Barbara Tuchman, "molded outward behavior to some extent" but "did not, any more than other models that man has made for himself, transform human nature" (69). Events in this radio adaptation are evidence of what happens when a governing system such as chivalry breaks down.

The likely source for Fine and Friedkin's adaptation was Malory's *Le Morte Darthur* and specifically "The Most Piteous Tale of the Morte Arthur Saunz Guerdon [The Death of Arthur Without Reward]" covering the incidents that culminated in the dissolution of the Round Table, along with the deaths of King Arthur, Sir Lancelot, and Guinevere. "The Most Piteous Tale of the Morte Arthur Saunz Guerdon" is about the destruction of the Round Table fellowship and ends the days known as the flower of chivalry (Malory, *Le Morte* 673). Based on its violence and mild sexuality, this adaptation was probably intended for an adult audience. Listeners already familiar with Arthurian legend knew of Sir Lancelot and Guinevere's "ado" with one another when "Launcelot began to resorte unto queen Gwenivere agayne and forgate the promise and the perfeccion that he made in the queste (of the Grail) [Lancelot began to resort unto queen Guinevere again and forgot the promise and the perfection that he made in the quest]" (Malory, *Le Morte* 611). Likely, they also knew that Mordred's passion for the queen drove him to treason and to patricide.

War seems to have held the attention of Fine and Friedkin just as it did McConnell. "The Triangle on the Round Table" covers the events leading up to King Arthur's death for a supposedly "true story of crime" (Fine and Friedkin), managed in only two acts framed by a musical bridge. Hyland, the name of the fictional narrator, imposes himself on listeners throughout the program, but one comment in particular attests to the underlying theme of the episode: Hyland stresses that four thousand men were killed, further saying that this act occurred in the name of chivalry. The former comment is a criticism of the chivalric code, a theme repeated throughout the episode, while the latter comment may have reflected the very real and growing number of casualties caused by the conflict in Korea. When this episode aired, war was in the headlines and the number of military casualties continued to grow. Even with President Dwight D. Eisenhower's order to begin withdrawing American troops from Korea in January 1954, some people still feared a possible third war with Russia.

Fine and Friedkin set their adaptation in sixth-century Britain, located in the court of King Arthur in Camelot, a romantic "time of myths and legend, of hunting horns and streaming banners, and maidens and thistle, of sunlight slanting like a tapestry into cold castles, and pagan rites and magic and stone" (Fine and Friedkin), yet they present a different, non-romantic reality. Listeners are treated to a tale of a barbaric age alive with "shaggy" heroes, who allow their "outlaw feelings" to prevail (Eco 69). Like the narrators who introduce Arthurian adaptations on *Family Theater* and *Let's Pretend*, Hyland urges imaginative play as the audience hears King Arthur putting on his armor, picking up his sword, and walking out of his tent into the sunlight to the sound of a cheering crowd (Fine and Friedkin). Hyland's vivid description of the scene draws the audience into the radio play. Hyland next explains that King Arthur dresses for war "against a friend of his" in which "four thousand men will be killed over a woman, which is known as chivalry," and he explains that Mordred's behavior toward Queen Guinevere was the result of his *mis*understanding of the rules of courtly love.

Act One is set in Camelot, in a hall housing the Round Table at which Arthur's knights are seated, discussing Sir Lancelot's reason for "fail[ing] on the quest for the Holy Grail" (Fine and Friedkin). Sir Lancelot is described as a failure of a knight because he spent his free time with Guinevere instead of honing his skills as a warrior. Sir Galahad's report on his killing of a "scurvy knave" for looking "askance at the Lady Vivienne" and Percival's suggestion that a party of knights should "be sent to slay the seven wicked knights at the Castle of Maidens" are based on incidents in Malory (Fine and Friedkin). Fine and Friedkin also borrow from Malory's "Slander and Strife, Book XX, the scene in which Sir Aggravane and his fellow knights reveal their suspicions about Lancelot and Guinevere, the same suspicions shared by King Arthur. King Arthur is reminded that "three times before" he wished his wife "burned at the stake" but failed to

4. Adapting Malory's *Le Morte Darthur* for Radio

carry through with his plan to "feed [Guinevere and Lancelot] to the flames" (Fine and Friedkin). The king does wonder, for a brief moment, why the queen is poisoned against him, but this passes and he declares that Guinevere will "roast" for her behavior (Fine and Friedkin). Only the queen is to be subjected to this punishment, a slightly different version of the events in Malory.

Fine and Friedkin's Aggravayne and Mordred are also more concerned about the possible reward of a province if they kill Lancelot in the queen's chamber before King Arthur gets him (Fine and Friedkin). This version of Lancelot would be unfamiliar to listeners, who likely expected the chivalric Lancelot portrayed in other radio adaptations, or even Howard Pyle's Arthuriana. Malory's favorite knight is here a vengeful warrior who, when confronted, attacks and kills Aggravayne before turning on Mordred and harshly accuses him of being a "sniveler" who "sneaks like a crawling thing and [a] spy" (Fine and Friedkin). The king sends Mordred away with a warning not to say Guinevere's name or else his "tongue will be fed" to her goldfish (Fine and Friedkin), a line delivered most likely in an attempt to inject a bit of dark humor. Lancelot leaves Camelot to rescue the queen; however, his "spectacular" plan, as Hyland drily remarks, results in the death of "some fifty people" (Fine and Friedkin). Lancelot and Guinevere escape to Joyous Bastion, a castle named "after the good times had there" where, as Hyland explains, they "set up house in Lancelot's castle" (Fine and Friedkin), another allusion to an incident in the Arthurian cycle. Months of "war" and "siege" passed with "many knights" dead and wounded before a "papal bull arrive[d]" ordering an end to the conflict (Fine and Friedkin). With the exception of the explanation that Lancelot returns to France and Guinevere to Camelot, no other information about the couple is provided. Arthur orders Gawain to France to kill Sir Lancelot, shouting "let there be war, let the killing start" on "this day of blood," but soon follows Gawain himself (Fine and Friedkin). The audience does not know of King Arthur's fate until Gawain's ghostly visit.

Hyland explains away Mordred's wickedness as the result of his "blood thirsty" character. Before he follows Lancelot to France, Hyland offers an explanation: "somehow ... [Mordred] made King Arthur let him stay home to watch Camelot, to watch Britain, to watch Queen Guinevere" (Fine and Friedkin). In Malory's words, King Arthur left Mordred "chyeff ruler of all Ingelonde" and "puts the queen undir hys governaunce [chief ruler of all England, and also ... puts the queen under his governance]" (Malory, *Le Morte* 700). Mordred declares himself regent, and predicts on this "dolorous day" that King Arthur will die (Fine and Friedkin), a reference to the events in the "The Dolorous Death and Departing Out of this World of Sir Launcelot and Queen Guinevere" of Malory's final tale, "The Moste Piteous Tele of the Morte Arthur Saunz Guerdon." As Hyland snidely explains, Mordred's pursuit of Guinevere to the Tower of London is evidence of his chivalric code or "personal code of how to behave in love" (Fine and Friedkin). According to Malory, Mordred fails to retrieve Guinevere despite his "mighty syge aboute the Towre and ... many assautis, [and the] threw[ing] of engynnes unto them, and grete gunnes [mighty siege about the Tower and ... many assaults ... throwing of engines unto them and great guns]" (Malory, *Le Morte* 707).

Before returning to the story and to set the upcoming battle scene, Hyland provides an accurate description of medieval knighthood—training at age seven, lessons in manners, morals, battle techniques, arms care, jousting, and horsemanship—though knights tended to be killers (Fine and Friedkin). Hyland also interjects that Mordred was "one graduate of the curriculum [who] skipped the course on advanced morals" (Fine and Friedkin). King Arthur and Mordred both experience spectral visits. Gawain's ghost appears to warn Arthur to disband his army and come to a truce with Mordred or he will die. Mordred's father appears to him with the prediction that he will be king. As these events unfold, King Arthur returns to Dover by ship to fight for Camelot, a choice that, as Hyland explains, only results in "more battle" and "more blood" (Fine and Friedkin). Mordred accuses Arthur of deserting him when he left for France, and predicts that the result will be "war and killing, killing and war, no peace until Arthur is dead," and the additional death of four thousand "good men" (Fine and Friedkin). In the final scene, and the only instance when the radio audience is given a sense of King Arthur's inner turmoil, the king shares his feelings of betrayal. Disturbed by Gawain's eerie warning, King Arthur seeks a truce with Mordred. However, when they next met, Mordred arrogantly declares he has beaten the king who wanted "no more dying" (Fine and Friedkin). As in the *Le Morte Darthur*, King Arthur spots an adder at Mordred's feet, but in this adaptation, King Arthur, not the knight, is "stonge [stung]" (Malory 713). When King Arthur, now illustrating chivalry, draws his sword to slay the adder, Mordred seizes this opportunity and accuses the king of drawing his sword for battle.

"A great battle" follows in which "every man who died, died a hero" (Fine and Friedkin). On the fourth day of the battle, only "two horsemen," Arthur and Mordred, remain alive. The sound of clashing steel indicates

4. Adapting Malory's Le Morte Darthur for Radio

this is the last bloody fight between these opponents. King Arthur's final sword thrust mortally wounds Mordred, though he still has the ability to deliver the fatal deathblow to Arthur. Arthur's dying words, adapted from the death scene in Malory, suggest that the blood spilled over Guinevere was in vain: "I could have found a woman as good as Guinevere, but such a fellowship of knights as was mine can never be brought together again" (Fine and Friedkin). Hyland dryly remarks that this is the "end of King Arthur," while Guinevere and Lancelot will share a long life (Fine and Friedkin).

Adaptations of the medieval romance have a long history in popular culture, including the serial comics and the comic book, once the genre emerged in the 1920s. Radio scriptwriters continued to find inspiration in Arthurian legend, adapting and compressing Malory's voluminous work into short, entertaining radio programs. During the 1950s especially, a number of popular radio programs—*The Land of the Lost, Let's Pretend, Family Theater*, and *Smilin' Ed's Buster Brown Gang*—adapted Arthurian romance for children and adults:. Not only do these programs prove the flexibility of Arthurian romance, but they illustrate the various approaches scriptwriters took with the legend. Family-friendly programs preferred to recreate a fairytale world of romance and chivalry, in which the Arthurian knight operated as a chivalric hero worthy of emulation. These programs stand in sharp contrast to the more violent and adult-themed rendering produced for *Crime Classics* that defined chivalry predominately in terms of war. The next two radio adaptations feature comic book heroes who, through words and deeds, demonstrate chivalric qualities.

5

The Chivalric Ethos of the Comic Hero
Superman and Prince Valiant

Robert Maxwell and Hal Foster, the writers of the comics *The Adventures of Superman* and *Prince Valiant*, were well-versed in Arthurian romance and created fast-paced, entertaining programs of high adventure. Maxwell, responsible for the "Operation Tolerance" project, aired his anti–KKK storylines a couple of years following World War II, but then moved beyond an adaptation of Arthurian legend to code a series of *Superman* adventures on radio that engaged with medievalism. Maxwell linked the destructive forces of the medieval warrior's code to prejudice in post-war America. Prince Valiant evoked the chivalry of knighthood, though unlike Superman, his adventures on radio were more typical of Arthurian romance.

Cartoonist Hal Foster created *Prince Valiant* in 1937 and, three years later, produced a series of comic strips in which Prince Valiant fought fascism. In Andrew E. Mathis's estimation, the wartime *Prince Valiant* comic strips were a "morale-building series, showing as they do that even when outnumbered the righteous may conquer evil" (62). When *Prince Valiant* was brought to radio, Foster's long-running comic strip was transformed into a *Bildungsroman* meant for boys using a narrative that takes liberties with King Arthur's legend. For instance, through his deeds and his chivalric language, Prince Valiant taught young male listeners the importance of bravery, honor, and fair play.

Even though as radio adaptations "Knights of the White Carnation" and *Prince Valiant* differed in their adaptation of the legend, specifically in time and setting, they represented the liberties writers for radio took with adaptation, and even in the case of *Superman*, these adaptations were examples of medievalism on radio.

Superman versus the Klan

The steady increase in the activities of the Ku Klux Klan drew federal attention and legislative action following the organization's first meeting in Pulaski, Tennessee, in May 1866. Under pressure, the group had disbanded by the 1870s but some branches remained active until the 1880s, taking racially coded names such as "The White League," "White Brotherhood," "Constitutional Union Guards," and "Knights of the White Camelia" (Jones 46, 47, 51; Bowers, 60). Although the Klan's national organization officially disbanded in the 1880s, unofficial branches remained underground. Colonel William Joseph Simmons, Georgia native, veteran of the Spanish-American War, former Methodist minister, and founder of the modern Klan, was named Imperial Wizard of the "Invisible Empire" and revived the Klan in 1915 (Jones 57).

With the help of a savvy public relations team, the Klan's tarnished image was recouped for a short time, though scandal continued to plague the group's "wealthy organizers" and undermined Simmons's efforts (Bowers 73–74). Among the organization's members were prosperous businessmen and lawyers, the same individuals who re-emerge in Maxwell's radio play. As Imperial Wizard, Simmons had earlier "planned to perpetuate [the Klan's] spiritual purpose, and to make it a national, standard, fraternal order composed of *American manhood*, who believed in the preservation of pure Anglo-Saxon institutions, ideals, and principles" (Jones 57, 62, emphasis added). The organization shared with Hitler a desire for racial purity, swore by similar ideals that had been promoted in western chivalric literature, and worried that Anglo-Saxon racial superiority was under threat. Simmons revived and preserved the Klan's original precepts.

In the 1930s Depression-era problems emerged. Some saw the crisis as an opportunity to affect social and political change, while others feared that the United States was headed toward an apocalyptic future that might include dictatorship (Cooney 9; Barnouw, *The Golden* 43). In wartime, radio was vital to maintaining a sense of national unity after the bombing of Pearl Harbor and the official declaration of war in December 1941. As Barbara Savage writes in her book *Broadcasting Freedom: Radio, War, and the Politics of Race, 1938–1948*, "Hitler's rhetoric" resonated "so closely with the predominant racial thinking in the United States that it created a demand for a new, differentiating language of tolerance" (59). As she explains, "the threat of another world war capped off a decade of depression, unemployment, insecurity, and social upheaval. Some of the anxiety of that period was turned against America's 'others,' whether judged to be different because of race, national origin, or religion" (59).

Economic and social tensions following the Depression and the war had compounded anxieties in the United States and "turned" American against American (Savage 59). Fascists and radical thinkers in Europe and America in the 1930s used radio as a vehicle to promote hate-filled messages that were intended to "construct" a "radical ideology" (Cooney 19). Radical radio personalities such as Father Charles E. Coughlin, the "radio priest," and Louisiana senator Huey Long made the most of the situation, using radio as a platform to influence public opinion and to tap into their listeners' fears and prejudices, prompting their critics to warn that these two would "Hitlerize America" (Savage 49–50). Coughlin's rants against President Herbert Hoover, communism, international banking, and the wealthy played into the "hopes and fears gripping the nation" (Barnouw, *Golden Web* 45).[1] Americans radio audiences were already familiar with the hate speech of Hitler and his obsession with creating a "race of supermen," a pure German race, through the obliteration of "foreign blood" ("Nazi's"). "Hitler's rhetoric" resonated "so closely with the predominant racial thinking in the United States that it created a demand for a new ... language of tolerance" (Savage 59).

By the Second World War, the Ku Klux Klan and similar groups had re-emerged; Americans were becoming increasingly sensitive to their anti–Semitism and could no longer ignore the problem. Similarly-oriented groups organized, taking such names as the American Nazi League, the German American Bund (an American Nazi organization), the Black Legion, The Anglo-Saxon Federation, and the Commoner Party. Even women, historically barred from membership in the Klan, were recruited to organize their own branches. Americans grew increasingly sensitive to anti–Semitism. Newspapers warned of the Klan's revival and called on Americans "to stem the tide of hate before the most susceptible among us are swept into the stream" ("Hate"). In response to this correctly perceived threat, secular and civic leaders mounted a defense against the Klan, gathering their forces from the American Jewish Committee, the Council for Democracy, and the American Council Against Nazi Propaganda (Hilmes 238).

5. The Chivalric Ethos of the Comic Hero

Americans felt they had been "battling a foreign enemy who was steeped in racist ideology, [so] it was difficult for many ... to decry fascism abroad and tolerate bigotry at home" (MacDonald 75). In the past, radio had been used as a propaganda machine and had proved effective in the war on prejudice, at least once networks got involved. However, radio had been slow to join this home-waged war on intolerance because of the United States' isolationist position and the radio networks' fear of losing advertising dollars. Howard Blue writes that "when radio dramas" finally "dealt with the rise of fascism in Europe and the consequent outbreak of hostilities [in the 1940s], it did so indirectly" (Blue 79). Public service announcements and other radio programs addressed prejudice and encouraged tolerance, including the Mutual Network's *Mr. District Attorney* (1939–1953), *Big Town* (1937–1952), and *Jack Armstrong, the All-American Boy* (1933–1951).

With Kellogg's acquisition of Superman, the time had come for the program to delve into "the realm of the previously untouched" for juveniles— "everyday life, with the problems and solutions spelled out in strong language that no child could misunderstand" (Lewis 75). *The Adventures of Superman* was the first children's radio program to join the nationwide "campaign for tolerance" ("Radio: Plan"). As one of the producers and writers for Mutual's radio series *The Adventures of Superman* (1940–1950), Robert Maxwell considered his radio series to be a public service and Superman, America's favorite superhero at the time, to be America's moral compass ("Superman Combats"). To Maxwell, the United States needed Superman. Troubled by what he undoubtedly observed as a growing problem with prejudice and the rise of fascist organizations, Maxwell used radio to combat prejudice, taking aim at the Ku Klux Klan and launching "Operation Tolerance" in 1947 with a series of three storylines: "The Clan of the Fiery Cross," "The Hate Mongers Organization," and "Knights of the White Carnation." Each installment of "Knights of the White Carnation" is framed with an anti-bigotry message and begins and ends with the reminder that Superman "defends the truly American principle of fair play and equality against a group of men preaching the doctrine of hate" ("Knights of").

Recovering the Middle Ages in popular culture has always been at least one way to come to terms with the present by concurrently analyzing existing social and political issues or anxieties camouflaged as medieval plots and characters. In brief, this is medievalism, an engagement with the Middle Ages and/or the adaptation of some aspect of the medieval, such as coding a medieval storyline with contemporary anxieties. However "conjoining [of] past and present" can also prove problematic when the process of medievalism results in "communal misremembrance" (Giles 954).[2] According to Laurie Finke and Martin Shichtman's examination of the Nazis' appropriation of Arthurian history, the Nazi Party engaged with medievalism when it "located the origins of the SS in the chivalric Middle Ages" and "promoted" a racial theory that identified "knighthood ... [as] a genealogy of the blood and demanded the ruthless destruction of all those who posed the threat of contamination," though "medieval knights could not possibly have conceived of themselves as fascists" (189, 191, 193).

17. *The Adventures of Superman*, "Knights of the White Carnation"

According to Joseph Goebbels, Hitler's Nazi propagandist, radio was the "eighth great power" of the twentieth century, a power that equaled that of the nineteenth-century press ("Radio"). Goebbels correctly identified radio as the "most influential and important intermediary between a spiritual movement and the nation, between the idea and the people" and recognized the significant impact that the medium had on society ("Radio"). Cantril and Allport worried in 1935 that radio's ability to move the "will of the ... masses" might be able to ease a listener's sense of "dread and apprehension" or even shut down the rumor mill; however, the medium could just as easily create mob mentality and incite "racial hatred" (21). Radio's reach was never more obvious than the hysterical reaction caused by Orson Welles's 1938 radio broadcast of a fictional Martian invasion that frightened the nation.

Radio was to become a powerful ally in the war on fascism. In response to this perceived American crisis, radio networks produced programs that encouraged, among other things, a "unifying national commitment" (Cooney 98). Comic book heroes even joined the effort. Superman made his first appearance in 1938 in the first edition of *Action Comics* and became America's moral compass, an orphan and immigrant from the planet Kryptonite, a superhero "Faster than a speeding bullet!' 'More powerful than a locomotive!' [, and] 'Able to leap tall buildings at a single bound!'" (Dunning 14). Jerry Siegel and Joe Shuster, the children of Jewish immigrants, created Superman partly in response to the prejudice they experienced as children. Superman represented the "best parts of the

5. The Chivalric Ethos of the Comic Hero 121

American way of life" and was intended to "raise awareness of 'un–American' attitudes" rampant in the country (Bowers 97). William Lewis, president and radio director of the Kenyon & Eckhardt advertising agency sponsoring *The Adventures of Superman*, expected Mutual's *Superman* to be a "socially conscious" program that would pave the way for other radio networks to raise awareness of prejudice (Lewis).

Superman could easily spread his message. Between 1941 and 1944 approximately "thirty million Americans," including soldiers stationed overseas, read Superman comics (Tye 63). Fans of the *Superman* radio series also numbered in the millions. *The Adventures of Superman* was originally transcribed (pre-recorded and broadcast later) and syndicated (licensed to be aired on simultaneous radio networks) on WOR, New York, beginning in February 1940; the series was picked up by Mutual in 1942 and sponsored by Kellogg's Pep cereal in 1943. Six years later, the series was extended to a thirty-minute format, picked up by ABC, and aired until 1951. In wartime, Superman was described in terms that demonstrate medievalism. The Man of Steel was a modern-day crusader, "a hell-raiser and insurrectionist[,] ... half Huckleberry Finn, half Robin Hood," the "knight of Metropolis[,]" and a "flying Uncle Sam" (Tye 31, 60–61). Superman straddled the past and the present as a permutation of British and American legend, at once an American patriot and a medieval knight. Superman, played on radio by Clayton "Bud" Collyer, took on "real-world hatemongers" in chivalric style, battling "neo–Nazi thugs and hooded Klansmen [without] pulling any punches" (Bowers 118).

Maxwell had two reasons for putting Superman on the radio. First, this radio offered an opportunity to further the success of the Superman enterprise. Second, Maxwell, like Superman's creators, was motivated by a personal moral agenda. Superman promoted American values and represented true patriotism, a concept carefully illustrated in the radio episode "Knights of the White Carnation." In spite of Superman's social consciousness (Tye 84), his power of influence made some people uncomfortable. Early in Superman's radio career, NBC's management had also been concerned that the Man of Steel's "powerful personality could potentially" harm children; however, Maxwell assured the network that his program "was aligned with the prevailing cultural values of the day" (Santo 16). According to Tye, "radio Superman carefully picked his enemies: Nazi saboteurs, jewel thieves, witch doctors, and others unlikely to generate sympathy or controversy" (83).

"Operation Tolerance" was Maxwell's attempt to stop the advance of prejudice and particularly anti–Semitism in the United States (Tye 82). Even before embarking upon his project, Maxwell had carefully researched the Klan and sought the input of educators and religious and community leaders to produce a program appropriate for younger listeners. Unlike radicals and anti–Semites Coughlin and Long, Maxwell used radio to encourage brotherhood and tolerance, not divisiveness and hate. In an article penned by Maxwell in 1946 titled "Superman Combats Race Intolerance," published in the *Atlanta Daily World*, Maxwell suggests that *The Adventures of Superman* was more than an entertaining children's show; rather, Maxwell asserts that the program performed a public service, and Superman was America's moral compass ("Superman"). In this same article, the reporter praises Maxwell for taking "up the cudgels for tolerance, in support of a movement which has the blessing of every church and the endorsement of President Truman and various organizations" ("Superman"). The reporter's medievalism is evident in his rhetoric and word choice: "cudgel" is a medieval term for club (*MED*). This reporter's word choice is also interesting because it evokes the image of a medieval weapon also favored by Robin Hood, yet associates it with Superman, a modern hero described as the "knight of Metropolis." Despite the admiration many had for Maxwell's humanitarian project, critics doubted it would achieve its desired effect. First, debates were on going over the quality of children's radio programming. *Superman* was considered by some to be just another "blood and thunder" adventure program for children who were too unsophisticated to understand the program's deep message. Critics argued that Maxwell's project would be more valuable for children if it dealt with topics that were important to them.

Medievalist and literary theorist Umberto Eco identifies some teachable moments in the *Superman* comics (960), but he ignores Superman's history on the radio. Nevertheless, Eco's essay "The Myth of Superman" is applicable to a "reading" of the radio series. At their foundation, the Superman storylines, and typically most children's radio programs, had a civic and political consciousness that operated in a world in which good always overcame evil. According to Eco:

> The pedagogic message of these stories would be, at least on the plane of children's literature, highly acceptable, and the same episodes of violence with which the various stories are interspersed would appear directed toward this final indictment of evil; Superman *must* make virtue consist of many little activities on a small scale, never achieving a total awareness. Conversely, virtue must be characterized in the accomplishment of only partial acts, so that the plot can remain static [960–961].

5. The Chivalric Ethos of the Comic Hero

For Eco, Superman's world is too narrow as it limits him to fighting evil within his own communities of Smallville and Metropolis. Eco also compares Superman to a medieval pilgrim with a limited worldview who "practically ignores, not exactly the dimension of the 'world,' but that of the 'United States'" (961). Although Eco is correct that much of Superman's time is spent fighting the criminal underworld in Metropolis, Eco overlooks an important point. Between 1941 and 1945 in the comic strip, and eventually on the air, Superman supported the war effort and even headed to the front line to fight Hitler, Mussolini, and Tojo.

As Rick Bowers points out in his book *Superman Versus the Ku Klux Klan*, during wartime the "radio version of Superman, like his counterpart in print, did his part to turn back the Axis powers" (104). Furthermore, Superman's battles were not only limited to petty thieves and "attempts on private property" (Eco 961). In fact, Superman's exploits had far-reaching consequences. According to Tye,

> on the airwaves [Superman] was commissioned as an undercover Secret Service operative.... Superman ... had always fought for patriotic principles, but it was only with the nation at war—and Americans thinking more than ever about why their country was worth fighting and dying for—that the idea of a distinctly American way of believing and acting took hold in the public mind and the Superman mythos. Yet again, Superman was reflecting and refracting his era in a way that helped define it [89–90].

When the Man of Steel took on intolerance in the city of Metropolis, by extension he took on fascism in America. Metropolis is a microcosm of the United States, and the United States is a microcosm of the world. Presumably, Superman's fans recognized this for themselves. "Knights of the White Carnation" addressed prejudice as a serious threat to American democracy while at the same time teaching radio fans about good citizenship. Maxwell's moral message was then articulated through medievalism.

Employing medievalism for negative goals, Klansmen imagined themselves as crusading knights performing chivalry, though for the Klan chivalry was a pretext for maintaining the white race via their protection of white women. In contrast to Superman and the other male characters who exhibit a true chivalric ethos in this radio adaptation, the villain Vincent Kirby, an American version of the German fascist Adolf Hitler, and his Knights of the White Carnation, the leading figures in the City of Metropolis, represent the danger of collectivism. Collectivism had helped breed radical ideas such as fascism, which many people feared as the 1940s came to a close. Through his radio program, Maxwell condemned prejudice bred by fascist organizations like the Klan by comparing it to the original medieval fraternal organization of knighthood, but a knighthood gone terribly wrong.

Medieval chivalry is best described as "proud" and "egocentric" knight-errantry that proved problematic as the profession promoted "self-fulfillment" and "personal values" (Saul 369). In post-war America, the knight errant morphed into a superhero like Superman, an American soldier, or even the ordinary man who preferred individualism to collectivism, and who, when he was called upon to do so, made the moral choice. In fact, Maxwell used the contradictory nature of knighthood to full advantage in a series of segments for "Knights of the White Carnation." This skewed value system plays out in the "Knights of the White Carnation." Maxwell, a writer and producer of the radio series *The Adventures of Superman*, linked the chivalric code to the modern Ku Klux Klan. His fictional knights promote a unique version of chivalry informed by the actions of the real Klan, a fraternal organization that claimed to be "pledged to wholesome service" (Jones, W., *Story* 8), though history proved otherwise. In his study of chivalry and the English gentleman, Mark Girouard identifies "one of the great dangers of chivalry" as the ability to "make people totally out of touch with reality" and to turn "chivalrous Galahads and Lancelots" into "White Knights" "gallantly charging in the wrong direction" (Girouard 270)—an example of this can be found in the misguided knights that Maxwell exposes in his *Superman* storyline.

Debra A. Mancoff explains the American "cultural fascination with Arthur" as the result of "nostalgia, cultural pride, a desire for national identity, and the romantic imagination" (xii). Arthurian legend has continued to be a favorite source for adapters across all media—literature, art, film, and radio, an all-but-forgotten medium. Arthurian legend is easy to appropriate across media, especially for radio. King Arthur, Sir Lancelot, Merlin, and Queen Guinevere appeared in every radio genre: the drama, the Western, the adventure series, variety shows, and juvenile programming. We cannot be certain why Maxwell chose Arthurian tropes for "Knights of the White Carnation." Perhaps it was because of the malleability of Arthurian legend or the obvious connection between medieval knights, King Arthur and his Knights of the Round Table, and the Ku Klux Klan, an organization that had appropriated but subverted the chivalric code.

Maxwell's "Operation Tolerance" project was a direct attack on

5. The Chivalric Ethos of the Comic Hero

prejudice meant to send a "thoroughly American message of brotherhood" to inspire in children a desire "to be friendly with all other children regardless of ... race, creed or color" ("Superman Combats"). He alludes to the Klan's subversion of the chivalric code and points to the similarities between the Klan and the Knights of the White Carnation. Maxwell chooses for his "Klan" the name "Knights of the White Carnation"—an obvious parallel to the names of KKK branches "Knights of the White Camelia," "The White League," and the "White Brotherhood"—and identifies the groups' members as Metropolis's business and civic leaders. According to Winfield Jones's early biography of the Klan, published in the 1920s, the Klan's membership included prosperous businessmen and lawyers, similar to Maxwell's envisioning of Metropolis's leading citizens as members of the "Knights of the White Carnation." Additionally, Maxwell's fictional knights, like the Klan, promoted a dangerous racial ideology. Klansman were "a fraternal order composed of American manhood [swore to] perpetuate its spiritual purpose, [to preserve] pure Anglo-Saxon institutions, ideals, and principles, [to protect] womanhood; to maintain forever white supremacy in all things; commemorate the holy and chivalric achievements of [their] fathers ... to safeguard the sacred rights, exalted privileges and distinctive institution of our civil government; to bless mankind ... and to keep America pure" (Jones, W., *Story* 57, 62, 64). Although radio is an aural medium, the format's limitations did not interfere with Maxwell's ability to use verbal and aural cues to draw a comparison between a fictional Round Table of racist knights and the real Klan. Though Maxwell did not set "Knights of the White Carnation" in the Middle Ages, the script has a medieval context.

The opening line of "Knights of the White Carnation" immediately catches the listener's attention and imagination: "while Metropolis sleeps an ugly menace to America is being prepared to strike against the freedom and well-being of all Americans" ("Knights"). As innocent as this line may sound, more is at work here. A younger listener may have anticipated yet another exciting *Superman* adventure, but a mature listener would have read between the lines. Metropolis is the United States, while the "ugly menace" that threatens this fictional city actually threatens every city: racism. Vincent Kirby, the antagonist of the story, adopts a racist rhetoric and directs his Knights—Metropolis's leading male citizens—to protect the city and the United States from foreigners. Kirby's first move is to rid the high school varsity basketball team of foreigners, a status based on their surnames: Casimere "Cass" Pulaski (Polish), Michael [Kelley] (Irish),

Tony R[ozutti][3] (Italian), and Bill Kaplan (Jewish). Kirby's verbal attack on children, his violent, racist language, might recall for listeners their own experiences with prejudice or parallel the hardships of the Jews during the Second World War.

In the first installment of the "Knights of the White Carnation," Kirby provides a detailed description of his Knights. Each "knight" is dressed in a "conservative dark business suit" and has in his lapel a white carnation ("Knights"). This is an innocuous description, except for the fact that their attire is similar to the black uniform adopted by the German Schutzstaffel (SS) as a means of group identification. Maxwell makes other clever but subtle allusions to the Klan and Arthurian legend. The white carnation is a symbol of racial purity and a heraldic symbol, or other means of group identification, similar to the Klan's white ceremonial robe and hood. White also appears consistently throughout the *Le Morte Darthur* in descriptions of clothing, flowers, and animals. Kirby and his Knights sit around a table, an arrangement that re-enacts King Arthur's Round Table. "Ku Klux" is supposedly a corruption of the Greek word *kuklos*, meaning circle or ring (Jones, W., *Story* 22), and another allusion to the Round Table. The surname "Pulaski" is ironically the surname of Casimir Pulaski, a cavalry officer of Polish descent and a real patriot of the American Revolution; it is also a reference to the name of the town in Tennessee where the Klan held its initial meeting.

Kirby implicates the four foreign high school boys in racketeering, accuses them of "un–American" behavior, and of being "dirty little foreigners" with "different ideals" from real Americans because they will "do anything for money" ("Knights"). Narrator Jackson Beck describes the newspaper clipping and photograph of the Metropolis High School team featured in *The Daily Planet* that fuels Kirby's racism and pushes him to murder. Despite the positive news that the team won the "crown," Kirby's voice drips with venom as he points out that, according to the list of names mentioned earlier, only Jack Wilson is an American ("Knights")—perhaps as American as radio's popular teen patriot Jack Armstrong. Kirby's disgust and rage are obvious in the tone of his voice. Charles Canfield, a solid citizen and "a wealthy industrialist," is the only member of Kirby's Knights who defends the boys, arguing that perhaps the basketball players are good players, even better players than their own sons ("Knights").

Kirby disregards Canfield's defense of the boys despite the other man's point that a number of American patriots were immigrants, including Pulaski's Polish ancestor, a general remembered as the Father of the

American Cavalry. Shortly before withdrawing his membership from the Knights, Canfield asserts to Kirby that the organization's original premise has been lost. Originally, the group had organized in an effort to preserve the American Constitution and the Bill of Rights, to "combat ... communism, fascism, and all other 'isms" that threatened to undermine the First Amendment ("Knights"). Kirby's Knights perform contrary to his expectations of true patriotism. In this storyline, the true knights who illustrate chivalry—good citizenship, bravery, and honor—are Superman and his alter-ego Clark Kent, as well as characters Jimmy Olson, Jack Wilson, and Canfield. Canfield warns Kirby that he is dangerously close to becoming another "Hitler or Mussolini" leading a meeting "in pre-war Germany" ("Knights").

Behind the scenes, Kirby orders Canfield's murder and orchestrates further brutality against Ro[zutti] and Pulaski. Because of their injuries, the boys are unable to play well in the tournament and are accused of throwing the game. They are accused of racketeering, kicked off the team, and arrested. Clark Kent and Jimmy Olson, newsboy and aid to Clark Kent/Superman, eventually clear the boys of all charges. In a later installment, Kirby's agitators, armed with inflammatory pamphlets, try to instigate unrest among the students at Benjamin Franklin High School, but Superman and Clark Kent arrive in time to prevent mob violence. Each takes a turn lecturing the students, and presumably the audience, against hate speech. In each of the installments, violence progressively escalates in dialogue and action. Kirby predicts that within the next twenty-four hours "hate" will "sweep through the city ... directed against all people of foreign ancestry" ("Knights").

"Knights of the White Carnation" concludes with installment fifteen, when Clark Kent solves Canfield's murder and Superman captures Kirby and his Knights. In the final scene set in a courtroom, Kirby and his cronies are sentenced for perpetuating violence and spreading hate. The judge's pronouncement, directed at the defendant and *Superman* fans, warns that "only the bigot and the demagogue," whose "minds and hearts are twisted and poisoned," attempt to "corrupt [their] countrymen" ("Knights"). Whatever their reasons, in addition to their skewed senses of patriotism, Kirby and his Knights have failed to uphold their civic responsibilities, first as members of their socio-economic class, and second as American citizens. They saw themselves as knights and the champions of American democracy. Kirby and his Knights took seriously their charge to "protect" their "sacred heritage," "this great country, with its millions of human souls, resources, and material possessions," a heavy responsibility that is instead given to the "citizens of tomorrow," the radio generation of children in the 1920s and 1930s, by the character-building organization the Knighthood of Youth ("America of the Future").

Additionally, the wealthy and influential men of Kirby's Knights demonstrate no sense of *noblesse oblige*. Kirby gave into "blind unreasonable hatred," fed his own "desire for power by discriminating against minorities," and used his wealth and "influence to corrupt, to murder, [and] to become a traitor to [his] country" ("Knights"). Kirby, of course, swears he and his Knights acted in America's best interest, arguing that their targets were not real true Americans, only individuals he identified as foreign. Kirby's argument fails to move the judge, and he is sentenced to the electric chair. His Knights are each given a twenty-year sentence in the Metropolis city jail. By the last installment, Superman's radio audience would easily relate the operation of fascist organizations such as the Ku Klux Klan to un–American and unpatriotic ideologies, they would recognize fascism and bigotry when they saw it, and they would now be able to identify true chivalric qualities by what they were not.

Maxwell created a timely storyline that resonated with a radio audience aware of the continuing problem of intolerance in the country, and he used the medium of radio to join the fight against homegrown bigotry. Maxwell uses the broadcast as an opportunity to educate young listeners about the dangers of prejudice perpetuated by groups like the Klan. "Knights of the White Carnation" employed Arthurian and medieval tropes to call attention to a contemporary crisis, the rise of the Ku Klux Klan, a group of individuals with a "collective consciousness of the [medieval] knightly class" who were committed to fighting for a just and noble cause based on a racist ideology and a misguided "sense of social obligation" (Saul 127).

The knight-errant of radio was a superhero named Superman, a Prince Valiant from a fabled land, a detective called the Saint, a cowboy named Paladin, or an American boy named Jack Armstrong. The Arthurian knight demonstrated chivalry through bravery, loyalty, courtesy, truthfulness, and his defense of the oppressed. Superman, the modern caped crusader of the comics, crossed paths with the criminal underworld and "foreign dictators [who] followed a philosophy of racial and religious superiority and [whose] quest for world domination included plans to conquer America" (Bowers 99). *Prince Valiant* perhaps appears quite different from *The Adventures of Superman*, but like Maxwell's adaptation,

Hal Foster's adaptation is another example of the liberties that could be taken with Arthurian legend.

18. *Prince Valiant*

Hal Foster created *Prince Valiant* in 1937; three years later he produced a series of comic strips in which Prince Valiant fought fascism in what is now regarded "as a morale-building series, showing as they do that even when outnumbered the righteous may conquer evil" (Mathis 62). Through his deeds and his chivalric language, Prince Valiant taught boys the importance of bravery, honor, and fair play in comics, on radio, and in film. This radio adaptation of Foster's *Prince Valiant*, which is not affiliated with a network and does not state a broadcast date, is based on the early episodes of the long-running *Prince Valiant* comic strip and follows the conventions of the genre of medieval romance. Had it aired in the 1950s, the radio adaptation would have joined the film adaptation *Prince Valiant* (1954) written by Foster and Dudley Nichols. Henry Hathaway directed James Mason, Janet Leigh, and Robert Wagner in the starring roles. In the radio production, titled both "Val Becomes a Knight" or "Valiant Becomes a Knight," the prince and his father are displaced noblemen accompanied by twenty of their retainers who fled a Viking invasion of their homeland on the Norwegian west coast and landed in the fens of Britain ("Valiant Becomes"). The plot follows Valiant's efforts to become one of King Arthur's Round Table Knights. Despite his arrogance and "impetuous" nature, Valiant is "destined by deeds of his valor to win his spurs at the court of King Arthur" ("Valiant Becomes"). Before Valiant can achieve his goal, however, he must learn how to be courageous ("Valiant Becomes"), an important male characteristic.

The *Prince Valiant* radio adaptation provides an overview of the first two years of Valiant's adventures in the comic strip *Prince Valiant in the Days of King Arthur*, originally titled *Derek, Prince of Thane*. The comic strip debuted February 13, 1937, and was bought and distributed by King Features in the late 1930s. For fans, Tondro considers *Prince Valiant* the "quintessential example of the traditional Arthurian comic" (171). For his part, Foster, who was influenced by Howard Pyle's illustrations, was one of the first creators of a comic book character credited with adapting Arthurian legend for the medium (Tondro 170, 178). Foster's foray into the world of comic books occurred in 1929 when he adapted Edgar Rice

Burroughs's novel *Tarzan*. *Tarzan* first ran as a comic strip on March 15, 1931, and was first illustrated by Rex Maxon.

Foster's choice to let words and not pictures tell the story in the comics "places Valiant at odds with the American comic-book tradition, but ... contributes to the strip's appeal among scholars of Arthurian literature" (Tondro 171). Despite Foster's methodical research and his accurate portrayal of medieval England, both the *Prince Valiant* comic strip and the radio program are described by DeForest as a "combination of accuracy and anachronism, seasoned with an occasional element of pure fantasy" from which Foster "create[d] a believable alternate history—a world in which the nobility of the Round Table co-existed with the ugliness of the real world" (*Storytelling* 139). On radio, King Arthur existed alongside Vikings, Saxons, and dragons, while the Viking chief leading the attack on Britain was a British sea captain rather than the Norse chieftain he most likely would have been. Foster primarily engages Arthurian legend in this radio episode, but also present are nuances of the Robin Hood legend as well.

Prince Valiant is narrated by an unnamed male voice and the aged, cackling female voice of Horrit the witch, who sounds like the witch Old Nancy, narrator of the popular radio horror program *The Witch's Tale* (1931–1935). Horrit predicts the outcome of Valiant's adventures over her bubbling cauldron and warns that his "bravado and confidence" will cause him nothing but "pain and sorrow" ("Valiant Becomes"). Prince Valiant stepped "out of the legends" and typical of the Malorian knight "yearns for adventure" ("Valiant Becomes") and spends the entirety of the program proving his manhood and performing chivalry. Valiant's fair looks—Horrit calls him "my pretty one"—have nothing to do with his ability to become a knight ("Valiant Becomes"). He is described for the listener as a young, good-looking, brave, honorable young man (a nobleman at that), and a skilled swordsman, the sort of man boys should aspire to become and girls should aspire to marry. Also making an appearance on radio are Arthurian knights King Arthur and a much older and wiser Sir Gawain; Prince Arn, described as equally handsome as Prince Valiant; Lady Ilene, the fiancée of Prince Arn and the object of exchange between the two princes; and Prince Arn's magical Singing Sword, described as Excalibur's sister sword. The setting moves from swampland, to sea, to the beautiful and magical city of Camelot, a celestial city, that looks like a "hundred cathedrals all joined together" ("Valiant Becomes").

The Middle Ages is recreated primarily through what Robert L. Mott

5. The Chivalric Ethos of the Comic Hero   131

describes as natural and characteristic sound (85). Most of the action occurs outdoors while the sound effects are fairly standard—galloping horses' hooves and the clash of steel to illustrate armored knights in battle. In addition to the usual fare of armored knights and battle scenes, a fire-breathing dragon makes an appearance. Instrumental music, a mix of brass and percussion instruments, combined with realistic sound effects, create an air of aural discord and produce an atmosphere of suspense. Nature's wrath is conjured through the sound of violent winds and equally violent seas. In one particularly exciting scene, a Viking vessel that is tossed about on a stormy sea and pummeled by gale-force winds, creaks with the effort to stay afloat.

King Arthur has a minor role in this adaptation, but more surprising is Gawain's role as a patient father figure to Valiant: this is in contrast to the arrogant, womanizing knight eager for adventure in Malory; the Gawain of the fourteenth-century alliterative romance *Sir Gawain and the Green Knight*, written by the *Pearl* poet and influenced by Geoffrey of Monmouth's heroic depiction of the knight; or even Pyle's Gawaine in the "Story of Gawaine," a section in *The Story of King Arthur and His Knights* (1903). Gawain is often depicted as a Christian knight who understands the meaning of *gentilesse* (nobility). In this radio adaptation, however, Prince Valiant and Gawain trade places. Gawain is an experienced semi-retired older knight full of advice for the young prince, in contrast to the blindly ambitious and arrogant young man who requests King Arthur make him a knight, even before has earned his spurs. King Arthur is impressed by Valiant's prowess but not enough to bestow knighthood upon someone so young.

This rise from insignificant squire to knight was another favorite trope borrowed by radio scriptwriters adapting King Arthur's legend, wherein they depicted a squire hungry for recognition and eager to take his place among the ranks of King Arthur's knights. This same desire to be knighted is expressed by the squire Gryfflet la Fyse de Deu in the *Le Morte Darthur*, described to be as fierce a warrior as even Arthur's most experienced knights. Gryfflet, a young squire, is among the knights praised for his chivalry; Merlin predicts Gryfflet will be a "passynge good man whan he ys of ayge [passing good man when he is of age]" and will prove himself to be "one of the beste knyghtes of the worlde and the strengyst man of armys [one of the best knights of the world and the strongest man of arms]" (Malory, *Works* 31).

Gawain identifies Valiant as a younger version of himself and attempts to stop Valiant from challenging Prince Arn for the Lady Ilene, an act he describes as the impetuousness of youth ("Valiant Becomes"). Perhaps Gawain is addressing both the squire and young listener with the remark that "we can't all have our heart's desire" ("Valiant Becomes"). Valiant repeatedly proves be a stronger, more agile knight than Gawain. Twice Valiant defends the older knight. First, he saves Gawain from the clutches of a dragon, and then he champions the injured Gawain when the Red Knight demands their horses and Lady Ilene. Valiant kills the Red Knight and, in a scene fashioned upon "The Fair Maid of Astolat" in Malory, when Lady Elaine travels with the injured Lancelot to a hermit and reprised in "Sir Lancelot of the Lake," carries the injured Gawain to a hermit for a cure.

Other tropes of medieval romance in the program include the love triangle, the damsel as an object of exchange, the besting match between two equally skilled combatants, and the trope of disguise. Prince Valiant, Prince Arn of Ord, and Lady Ilene form a love triangle similar to that of King Arthur, Queen Guinevere, and Sir Lancelot, a situation adapted or alluded to in a number of radio adaptations. However, here the two princes fulfill their bond of fellowship and embody chivalry when they join forces to save Lady Ilene, after she is captured by Vikings, a "common foe" ("Valiant Becomes"). When it becomes clear that the search for Lady Ilene is fruitless, Arn declares that she is better off dead than alive. Their bond stays firm because, unlike the rift Guinevere caused between King Arthur and Lancelot, his favorite knight, had Ilene "lived, there would have been grief for her" since only one of them would have survived to win her ("Valiant Becomes").

In a scene directly from the Robin Hood ballads, the equally stubborn Valiant and Arn meet on a bridge, refuse to surrender the way, and exchange blows. While in the Robin Hood tradition Robin Hood and Little John try to outdo one another, exchange cudgel blows, end up in stream, and become allies in the process, in *Prince Valiant* the combined weight of the heavily armored princes and their equally armored warhorses collapses the bridge and sends men and horse into the water. Neglecting his own safety, Valiant gallantly puts aside their differences and risks his own life to save Arn. Prince Valiant has eight separate adventures during which he seeks to prove himself or die trying ("Valiant Becomes"). During his most trying adventures, Valiant is required to kill his foes, thus proving himself an expert swordsman. On his way to Camelot, Valiant encounters a fire-breathing dragon, described as "an oversized lizard the size of a

5. The Chivalric Ethos of the Comic Hero 133

house, breathing flame," and an ogre with the face of a resurrected demon; Valiant also battles Viking marauders and beats back Saxon invaders ("Valiant Becomes").

Although *Prince Valiant* illustrates the chivalric code as an ideal behavior, this radio play also sends a mixed message. Valiant blatantly ignores the sage advice of Gawain and King Arthur that he is too young to become a knight. Before King Arthur knights him, Valiant arrogantly presents himself as a fully equipped *chevalier* of Arthur's court. Valiant assumes that because he is a nobleman and a prince, knighthood will automatically be conferred. Instead of the much desired knighthood that Valiant hopes for, Gawain makes him a squire, much to the younger man's chagrin. Gawain warns Valiant that Camelot "has not place ... for anyone who won't play by the rules" ("Valiant Becomes"). However, Gawain's claim proves false. In the final scene, Valiant finally proves his prowess as a knight. Despite breaking tournament rules and "unseating Sir Tristram," a skilled knight, Valiant impresses King Arthur who refuses to "punish such a brave lad" and instead gives him an army to lead against the Saxons ("Valiant Becomes"). At the conclusion of the radio play, Valiant is knighted for fighting "valiantly" for his country and for protecting Britain from an onslaught of invaders ("Valiant Becomes"). In the last lines, the narrator predicts that the search for Lady Ilene will be the catalyst for Valiant's next quest.

Despite this somewhat inconsistent message, the radio adaptation of *Prince Valiant* offers an entertaining half hour for radio fans, whatever their gender or age. Prince Valiant therefore joins the list of medieval and modern chivalric heroes that also include the Boy Scout, the cowboy, the detective, the superhero, and even the outlaw.

6

White Knight of the Range
The Arthurian Knight in the Radio Western

Re-Imagining the Old West

Western dime novels, Wild West shows, rodeos, western art, and western fashions ensured the Old West a place in American popular culture. Early cowboy literature—a genre widely popular in the nineteenth century because of the writings of James Fenimore Cooper, Bret Harte, Max Brand, Owen Wister, and Zane Grey—mythologized the cowboy as a knight with Robin Hood's sense of social justice. Wister even produced a comic medieval romance set in the fourteenth-century, titled *The Dragon of Wantley: His Tale* (1892), an adaptation of a comic ballad and parody of the medieval romance collected in Thomas Percy's *Reliques of Ancient Poetry* (1767). Stories of the Old West emerged in the 1830s at approximately the same time that American interest in the legends of King Arthur and Robin Hood was surging. Frederick Jackson Turner and Theodore Roosevelt further added to these romanticized depictions of the Old West. Turner's thesis "The Significance of the Frontier in American History" (1893) and Roosevelt's reminiscence of his time with the Rough Riders and his embellished descriptions of the cowboy lifestyle both stirred more interest in the frontier and helped promote frontier masculinity in American culture. Cooper, also influenced by Walter Scott, "made Medievalism an integral if unobtrusive aspect of a myth that has powerfully influenced [American] popular culture" and transferred the "virtues of Sir Gawain to Natty Bumppo," the hero of his *Leatherstocking Tales* (Rosenthal and Szarmach 8).

Wister presented a romanticized rendering of the cow-puncher as a mythic cowboy-knight errant and Robin Hood figure in his essay, "The Evolution of the Cow-Puncher," published in *Harper's Magazine* in 1895. In this lengthy, romanticized rendering of the American West, Wister fully engages with medievalism in the following passage, wherein he waxes nostalgic for a by-gone era of the imaginary days of King Arthur by offering a portrait of the cow-puncher as a descendent of the medieval knight:

> The blood and the sweat of his jousting, and all the dirt and stains, have faded in the long sunlight of tradition, and in the chronicles of romance we hear none of his curses or obscenity; the clash of his armor rings mellow and heroic down the ages into our modern ears.... No doubt Sir Lancelot bore himself with a grace and breeding of which our unpolished fellow of the cattle trail has only the latent possibility; but in personal daring and in skill as to the horse, the knight and the cowboy are nothing but the same Saxon of different environments, the nobleman in London and nobleman in Texas; and no hoof in Sir Thomas Mallory shakes the crumbling plains with quadruped sound more valiant than the galloping that has been echoed from the Rio Grande to the Big Horn Mountains.... There you have him ... the American variety of the Saxon [Wister 604, 606].

Wister then laments that, alas, the American West has "no Sir Thomas Mallory!" (606). Wister is navigating between fiction and reality, drawing comparisons between the fictional grail knight Sir Lancelot; the very real Sir Thomas Malory, a knight and the author of Arthurian legend; and the cow-puncher. Wister's cow-puncher is "the American descendent of Saxon ancestry," a courageous and self-sufficient men with the "spirit of adventure" who enjoys the companionship of his horse, "his foster-brother, his ally, [and] his playfellow from the tournament at Camelot to the round-up at Abilene" (604, 617). Moreover, Wister's "roving Saxon" ruffian, a "'rude and rough'" fellow, nevertheless, has admirable chivalric qualities as well, providing succor when the poor and defenseless cross his path (Wister 606).

A cowboy-knight was honest, fair, loyal, and kind, like radio and television's Hopalong "Hoppy" Cassidy and the Lone Ranger, both of whom played fair and fought for justice. At the turn of the century, Clarence Edward Mulford created Hopalong Cassidy for a series of short stories. Unlike the Hopalong Cassidy adapted for radio and the movies between the 1930s and 1950s, Mulford's original character more realistically depicted cowboy life as a hard-working cowboy who drank, smoked, cussed, and cheated at cards (W. Savage 143–44). On radio and on screen, however, Hopalong Cassidy was transformed into a cowboy every child could imitate. William Boyd played the title role, with Andy Clyde as his sidekick California Carson. Hopalong was a knight of the range who brought justice to the Old West.

Other radio cowboys who practiced chivalry on radio and screen were Paladin of *Have Gun—Will Travel*, Gene Autry the "Singing Cowboy" in *Melody Ranch*, Marshal Matt Dillon in *Gunsmoke*, Britt Ponset in *The Six Shooter*, "Wild" Bill Hickok, and the Cisco Kid, also known as the "Robin Hood of the West." In his other role as a cowboy-knight, Autry was one of radio's "good guys," a Paladin who, armed or unarmed, fought Indians, defended women and brought justice to the frontier (Bloomfield 20). Paladin was also the title character and hero of *Have Gun—Will Travel*, a Western that originated on television before coming to radio in 1958. John Dehner played the title role of Paladin, a knight errant–gunfighter whose symbol was the white chess knight. "Paladin" was a derivation of the medieval term *paladine*, which originated in Old French. In the thirteenth century, "palatine" referred to "noble," and by the fourteenth century the word identified a "defender" or a "supporter" (*OED*). In the sixteenth century, *paladine* meant a "very brave and chivalrous man" (*OED*). *Paladin* also referred to the twelve peers of Charlemagne's court or, more generally, a knight renowned for heroism and chivalry.

Lejeune compares the Western in American popular culture to Arthurian legend in British culture suggesting, "just as the legends of King Arthur were 'the Matter of Britain,' so Westerns have been the Matter of America" (23). For Anne Scott MacLeod, the popularity of King Arthur and Robin Hood, and "other equally romanticized legends suggests the disquiet" that began in turn-of-the-century America in reaction to economic disparity, class division, immigration, and industrial growth ("Howard" 44–45). Unsettled times threatened the national spirit, civic virtue, and the developing sense of masculinity. Conservative thinkers recognized a need to promote a new masculinity of virility and chivalry that began with America's youth. As William Savage explains in his book, *The Cowboy Hero: His Image in American History and Culture* (1979), the cowboy's image functioned as an example of the American way of life and as a "system of beliefs" that included "truth, honor, justice, preparedness, righteousness, free enterprise, and a great many more noble nouns" (151).

The Old West, imagined as a land of "openness, drive, manliness, [and] movement," and the cowboy, imagined as the champion of justice, was "partly a continuation of the real Middle Ages and partly a new Medievalism with the cowboys taking the role of the good knights and the crooks and hangers-on assuming the role of the bad knights" (Bloomfield 19).

Both the knight and the cowboy were larger-than-life lone heroes who navigated a barbaric society (Fulton, Intro. 9). They equally protected the romanticized pastoral west and its folk from greedy landowners, corrupt lawmen, and other villains. At least in children's radio programs, the "good" guy was a cowboy who rode the range, or a lawman of a dusty frontier town who acted as a peacekeeper, fighting corruption and greed and handing out justice without resorting to heavy-handed violence.

Scriptwriters adapting medieval romance for the radio Western reconciled the violence inherent in Malory's *Le Morte Darthur*. Adapters glossed over or simply ignored a cowboy's penchant for violence, just as adapters had glossed over the Malorian knight's violent encounters. Though Wild Bill Hickok and the Cisco Kid were chivalric cowboys on radio and in other media, their originating counterparts had engaged in less than commendable behavior. The historical Hickok had been a Federal Marshal in Abilene, Kansas, who killed two men in cold blood; yet he became the hero of the children's radio and television program *Wild Bill Hickok* and was featured in a number of films produced from the 1920s onward. The fictional Cisco Kid, a Mexican adventurer and outlaw made popular on radio, on television, and in movies, was originally portrayed as a Robin Hood figure who "victimized the rich and the greedy" (Dunning 155), though for the purpose of this study an episode of *The Cisco Kid* falls in the Arthurian category. The popular Mexican caballero and the Lone Ranger operated as a combination knight errant and Robin Hood. The cowboy heroes of radio and the movies were honorable and just. As long as their values were obtainable, they too contributed to what Lupack and Lupack regard as the "democratization of the Arthurian tradition" (*Arthur* 326).

The Chivalric Code of the American Cowboy

The cowboy "never became personified and idealized in any one character but has remained a composite telescoped into a single folk type ... alongside ... traditional heroes in accomplishment" (Frantz and Choate 71). The cowboy-knight is so much a part of the American psyche that the announcer for Gene Autry's *Melody Ranch* commented that boys and girls had at one time probably imagined themselves as knights dressed "in shining armor, astride a powerful charger, thundering through adventure and hardships, to a romantic rescue" ("Gene Gets"). *Melody Ranch* was praised for storylines that promoted "old-fashioned American values and the code of the old west" (Boemer 101). Autry debuted on radio in 1929, began broadcasting Melody Ranch on CBS in January 1940, and remained a fixture on radio for sixteen years. Doublemint sponsored the Sunday evening program, a mix of music and adventures. Autry's legacy to young cowboy "wannabes" was a cowboy code that encouraged them to work hard, to live clean, and to be patriotic.

Autry had much to do with this image of the chivalric cowboy since he originated the idea of the "cowboy code" as a model of proper behavior for his American fans. Autry was the "hero of Melody Ranch ... [,] America's favorite singing cowboy [, and] ... a symbol of the clean-thinking, honesty, and integrity of the American people" (Boemer 101). Specifically, the "Cowboy Ten Commandments" encouraged the same behavior expected of America's Boy Scouts. Actually, Autry's cowboy code, the Boy Scout code, and the medieval chivalric code had many basic principles in common. According to Autry's "Cowboy Code":

> (1) The cowboy must never shoot first, hit a smaller man, or take unfair advantage; (2) He must never go back on his word, or a trust confided in him; (3) He must always tell the truth; (4) He must be gentle with children, the elderly, and animals; (5) He must not advocate or possess racially or religiously intolerant ideas; (6) He must help people in distress; (7) He must be a good worker; (8) He must keep himself clean in thought, speech, action, and personal habits; (9) He must respect women, parents, and his nation's laws; (10) The cowboy is a patriot [qtd. in McGillis 38].

These rules encouraged "a sense of stewardship that has national and racial and gender implications" (McGillis 39). This code served as a slightly modified and modernized version of medieval chivalry that taught boys how to grow up as "good" men but better Americans.

Especially in America during the nineteenth and twentieth centuries, the medieval chivalric code was reflected in the chivalric language in children's books, in the chivalric codes that guided members of the Boy Scouts and Arthurian youth organizations, and, eventually, in the behavior of anyone who wanted to be a cowboy. According to the fourth edition of *The Official Handbook for Boys* produced by the Boy Scouts of America, distributed in 1913, scouts were to "cultivate courage, loyalty, patriotism, brotherliness, self-control, courtesy, kindness to animals, usefulness, cheerfulness, cleanliness, thrift, purity, and honor" (Preface vi). The following sections consider radio adaptations of Arthurian romance and Robin Hood that aired on three mid-century radio Western series, *The Cisco Kid*, *Wild*

Bill Hickok, and *Gunsmoke* and how they present medieval tropes and chivalry to listeners.

19. *The Cisco Kid*, "Sir Cisco, Knight of the Round Table"

The Cisco Kid was the Robin Hood of the West, a Mexican outlaw and an important popular culture figure, who, along with his sidekick Pancho, righted wrongs and, just like Robin Hood, "victimized the rich and greedy" but stayed on the wrong side of the law (Dunning 155). In addition to a radio presence on the Mutual Network from 1942 to 1946, the Cisco Kid appeared in comics, on television between 1950 and 1956, and in a number of films produced between 1929 and 1955, beginning with *Old Arizona*, produced by Fox Movie Corporation. Cisco first appeared in comics in 1944, but Dell Comics was behind *The Cisco Kid* comic book series published in the 1950s. A syndicated *Cisco Kid* comic strip published by King Features and drawn by Jose Luis Salinas and Rod Reed ran from 1951 to 1967.

The Cisco Kid radio program aired on the Mutual network in the 1940s and in the 1950s was adapted for television. If fans did not automatically identify the Cisco Kid with Robin Hood, the broadcast opened with the well-known lines: "Here's adventure, here's romance, here's the famous Robin Hood of the Old West," followed by Pancho's warning, "Cisco, the Sheriff, he's getting closer!," and Cisco's reply, "This way Pancho!" From 1942 to 1945 Jackson Beck played Cisco on radio, with Louis Sorin in the role of Pancho. In 1946 Jack Mather took over the role of Cisco and Harry Lang played Pancho. The Cisco Kid was the creation of O. Henry, William Sydney Porter's pen name, and was made famous by the short story "The Caballero's Way," published in 1907 in *Heart of the West*, a collection of Western stories. Caballero, a reference to a Mexican cowboy, was actually the medieval Spanish term for knight. O. Henry's literary creation was originally a non–Hispanic character and an outlaw of Billy the Kid's caliber, a far cry from the heroic Cisco Kid adapted for radio, film, television, and comic books. The Cisco Kid of radio was O. Henry's Robin Hood of the West, who caught criminals but left their punishment to the law.

The storyline for "Sir Cisco, Knight of the Round Table," written by Larry Hays and aired June 5, 1958, is informed by Arthurian legend; it is also informed by Miguel de Cervantes's *Don Quixote*, a seventeenth-century picaresque novel and parody of chivalric romance about the adventures of Alonso Quixano and his squire Sancho Panza. "Sir Cisco, Knight of the Round Table" focuses on Cisco's protection of Hubert, an elderly man who imagines himself an Arthurian knight with all of the trappings of medieval knighthood and Englishness: Hubert lives in a castle with a moat; wears armor, and wields a lance named "Excalibur; rides on horseback; adopts the honorific "Sir" before his name to distinguish himself as an English nobleman; and affects medieval British speak and an antiquated vocabulary using such words as "varlet,"[1] "forsooth," and "knave" ("Sir Cisco").

Specific references are made to Arthurian characters and the Holy Grail, though no further details are given about the quest or the part the Grail plays in Arthurian romance. Rather the Grail symbolizes an eternal quest for an unattainable spiritual ideal. Elaboration on the scriptwriter/adapter's part for the benefit of the listener may have been unnecessary given that this reference to "the quest for the Holy Grail" was already part of the American lexicon as a metaphor for the pursuit of a significant but nearly unattainable goal. This quest is illustrated repeatedly in radio adaptations: examples in *The Cisco Kid* include Hubert's desire to live in the Middle Ages or a desperado's desire for treasure; the grail legend also features in *Wild Bill Hickok*, where a young cowboy knight named Tommy adopts a quest to dispense with Greed. Undoubtedly, the radio audience would also recognize the passing reference to the legend of Saint George, a well-known figure and patron saint of England and of the Boy Scouts. The legend of the dragon-slaying Christian knight actually originated in the East and was brought to the West during the Crusades. In the thirteenth century, the Dominican Jacobus de Voragine, later the Archbishop of Genoa, recorded the legend in his collection of saint's lives *Historia Longobardica seu Lengda Sanctorum* [*The Golden Legend*], another text edited and printed by Caxton. Voragine's history was among the most popular books of the Middle Ages.

"Sir Cisco, Knight of the Round Table" opens with the announcer's description of the Old West of the 1870s in terms usually used in reference to the United States. The Old West was a "brawling, sprawling Western frontier," a "melting pot for many nations and many customs," and a place where "people from every strait of society journeyed to this new land,

6. *White Knight of the Range*   141

most of them in search of a common goal, a home of their own" ("Sir Cisco"). Hubert and his daughter Julie are among these men and women trying to achieve the American dream, though Hubert has trouble leaving the past behind. Greedy and desperate men like Dell and Spike, men with a "lust [that] was not satisfied with this measure of security" ("Sir Cisco"), wait for the opportunity to take advantage of these hardworking men and women. Dell and Spike mistakenly believe that because Hubert "transported every stone, rock, and stick of that castle ... from England," he must be wealthy enough to have "brought over a trunk full of money and jewels" ("Sir Cisco"). Their plan is to lure Hubert into the woods, kill him, and use his armor as a disguise to gain entrance into the castle, murder Julie, and steal the alleged treasure. Julie must die because, according to the criminal code, "never leave a witness to a job" and the "law can never touch you" ("Sir Cisco").

As the episode opens, Cisco and Pancho are riding out to see the peculiar sight of a medieval castle on the frontier and share with listeners what little they know about the Middle Ages, as acquired through books and artwork on the medieval period ("Sir Cisco"). Hubert, a Don Quixote tilting at windmills and an "hombre dressed like a knight in armor," charges them and threatens to kill the "varlets," Cisco and Pancho ("Sir Cisco"), a scene similar to the meeting between Hank and the armored Sir Kay in *CBS Mystery Theater*'s 1976 adaptation of Twain's *A Connecticut Yankee in King Arthur's Court*. In this adaptation as well, the knight with lance in hand gallops toward his surprised opponent, shouting the challenge, "varlet, stand and fight" (Dann). Similar to Hank, Pancho and Cisco feel as if they, too, have been transported back to the Middle Ages. Pancho, unlike Hank and Cisco, does not know what to make of this knight riding toward him at full tilt, challenging him to a trial by battle. From the following exchange, it appears that Pancho is without a point of reference with regard to the Middle Ages or the knight errant. Speaking in an "Americanized Mexican dialect" (Dunning 155), Pancho asks Cisco why he "chase after Pancho with that big pointy stick?" ("Sir Cisco"). Hubert mistakenly believes that the caballeros are a threat and accuses them of attempting to murder him. Seeing himself as a "noble knight," Hubert warns them "not [to] attempt to beguile [him] with words of peace" ("Sir Cisco"). Pancho responds by asking Cisco why Hubert "talk of 'de nighttime when 'dis 'de daytime" ("Sir Cisco"). Insulted by Pancho's wordplay, Hubert calls Pancho a "country bumpkin" and threatens to slay him as Saint George slew the dragon ("Sir Cisco"). This last remark assumes a familiarity on the audience's part with Arthurian romance; however, according to Hubert, a lack of such knowledge is indicative of a lack of culture.

Hubert takes his imagined role to heart, warning Cisco and Pancho that "no mortal man shall stay the fulfillment of my quest for the Holy Gail" and vows to refrain from eating "earthly food until success crowns [his] knightly wish" ("Sir Cisco"). When Hubert accuses Cisco and Pancho of colluding with the treacherous Morgan le Fay, Cisco finally realizes Hubert is mentally unstable. As Cisco explains for the benefit of Pancho and the listener, Hubert relives the tales of King Arthur and the Round Table in his imagination. Pancho comically interjects his literal interpretation of the Round Table as a large table that allowed the knights to "eat more," a facetious comment that angers Hubert, who takes the legend seriously ("Sir Cisco"). Cisco and Pancho leave the old man to his daughter's care, not realizing that Dale and Spike are waiting them out. Cisco later anticipates trouble and heads back to the castle.

Disguised as a doctor (another example of the trope of disguise), Dale enters the castle and threatens Julie. Hubert attacks and is knocked unconscious in a scuffle with the desperadoes, who force Julie to lead them to the treasure. Fortunately, Cisco has anticipated trouble all along: he swims across the moat and enters the castle in time to save Julie, the damsel in distress. A gunshot and a struggle follow. Sound effects suggest Cisco lands a timely punch, knocking out Spike, and another blow "send[ing] Dale over the ledge, into the courtyard" ("Sir Cisco"). This episode concludes with the jailing of the desperadoes and placing Hubert under a doctor's care. "Sir Cisco, Knight of the Round Table" parodies medievalism with Sir Hubert in the role of Don Quixote in the Old West. In this radio adaptation of Arthurian legend, the tables have turned. This episode cleverly pokes fun at medievalism, and intentionally or not, at the nineteenth-century chivalric revival that saw an enthusiasm for all things medieval and even encouraged the revival of jousting tournaments, but this time on American soil.[2] Unexpectedly, it is Cisco, the Mexican caballero, who demonstrates chivalric knighthood, not "Sir" Hubert, the self-proclaimed Grail knight.

20. *Wild Bill Hickok*, "Sir Tommy, the Silver Knight"

Wild Bill Hickok offers another adaptation of Arthurian romance that teaches listeners the virtues of generosity and gratitude through the actions of a young boy who dreams he is a knight. "Sir Tommy, the Silver Knight" differs from the usual *Wild Bill* storyline that has Wild Bill and Jingles bringing criminals to justice. This 1951 Christmas Eve storyline is instead a fantasy framed by a dream vision, in which Wild Bill Hickok and Jingles dream they are knights who help ten-year-old Tommy Duncan on his quest to rid men's hearts of Greed, one of the Seven Deadly Sins. As Wild Bill Hickok explained to Tommy and to the program's fans, "bandits of the West took no time off for the holidays, so a lawman's work went right on as usual" ("Sir Tommy"). *Wild Bill Hickok* was a thirty-minute western series for children sponsored by Kellogg Cereals that aired on radio's Mutual Network and on television from 1951 to 1956. Guy Madison starred in the title role with Andy Devine as his sidekick, Jingles. Together they solved crimes and brought justice to the Old West, even on Christmas.

"Sir Tommy, the Silver Knight" was written specifically to impart to the program's juvenile audience the maxim "*Radix malorum est cupiditas* [Greed is the root of evil]," a maxim that was also the moral of Chaucer's "Pardoner's Tale" in *The Canterbury Tales*. A few of the characters in this episode are named for *New Testament* figures: John and Thomas (Tommy is a derivative of Thomas) were two of Christ's twelve Apostles; Mary is a reference to the Virgin Mary, Christ's mother. This morally tinged episode with Christian nuances also incorporates the allegorical dream vision, a strange choice for a radio program enjoyed by children. The dream vision is typically found in some of the greatest works of the thirteenth and fourteenth centuries, including Guillaume de Lorris and Jean de Meun's *The Romance of the Rose*, William Langland's *Piers Plowman*, and Chaucer's *The Book of the Duchess*, among others.

The Romance of the Rose is a thirteenth-century French dream vision and satire of courtly love and court life in which Amant, the lovesick dreamer, falls asleep and dreams that he is pursuing a rose, the symbol of a young woman. Amant awakens in an enclosed garden, its walls decorated with images of allegorical figures that represent human characteristics and courtly vices, such as Covetousness, Hatred, Envy, and Avarice. *Piers Plowman* is an alliterative dream vision in which the dreamer Will, a simple plowman and an allegorical figure representing "every man," embarks on a pilgrimage or quest to investigate the human soul. Will also encounters allegorical figures represented as vices, including Covetousness, Sloth, and Gluttony. *The Book of the Duchess* is a consolation poem written early in Chaucer's career as a poet and is likely linked to the death of John of

Gaunt's wife, Blanche of Lancaster, a victim of the 1368 plague, who is referred to in the text. After falling asleep while reading Ovid's *Metamorphoses*, the unnamed narrator encounters a bereaved Black knight grieving the loss of his lady, represented as a white chess piece. Chaucer's allegorical dream vision struggles with the knight's natural state of grief and the need to move beyond it.

Features of the medieval dream vision may include the following elements: a prologue that illustrates the conditions leading up to the dream; a dreamer who narrates an account of his dream, after falling asleep in a "pleasant place" (*locus amoenus*) or being lulled into sleep while reading a book, which may have informed the dream; and the arrival of an authority figure who teaches the dreamer a lesson about himself or his life. The dream vision in these texts reveals much about the human psyche. As Amant, the narrator of *The Romance of the Rose*, the most famous dream vision, explains, "a dream signifies the good and evil that come to men, for most men at night dream many things in a hidden way which may afterward be seen openly" (de Lorris 32). Although this adaptation was in no way comparable to the above-mentioned medieval works, it was sophisticated for a children's program and imparted an important lesson.

Wild Bill and Jingles accompany Tommy on a quest to the allegorical Shadow Land to fight the Giant of Greed, a monster that resides in the human heart. As Tommy explains, for the past five years on Christmas Eve, he has dreamed that he was Sir Tommy, the Silver Knight, who fights the Giant. His earlier failures to conquer his foe are never explained. Before they can set off on their allegorical quest, Wild Bill, Jingles, and Tommy say a prayer in which they swear to always be "good" ("Sir Tommy"), an explicit directive to young radio listeners. The three "knights" awaken in the dream sequence to find themselves in the Shadow Land. Standing in front of a gate "guarded against bad temper and bad manners" is John, Tommy's father, though he fails to recognize his son ("Sir Tommy").

Before setting off to find Greed in the Valley of Hate, described for listeners as "an awful place, worse than Death Valley and an African valley" ("Sir Tommy"), the three knights receive horses and buckshot instead of the usual bullets, which somewhat tones down the suggestion of violence. Again, the scriptwriters leave out particular details about these "valleys," though the assumption must have been that schoolchildren listening to the program would be familiar with the extreme temperatures of these locations, possibly connecting the dream landscape to what they imagined

Hell was like. In fact, images of Hell come alive through sound and vivid description when the knights must wade through a crowd of cackling demons, allegorical figures for temptation. However, Jingles struggles with self-control and gives into temptation when he gorges on candy. As punishment for his greediness, Jingles spends the next few minutes of the program in the castle's dungeon awaiting rescue. Meanwhile Wild Bill looks for the Giant of Greed, "a mean lookin' critter" ("Sir Tommy").

Once they all confront Greed, the monster warns the three cowboy knights that no one will ever find happiness because "nobody can kill the greed in people's hearts," meaning people will remain "too greedy to have a Christmas at all" ("Sir Tommy"). The scene transitions quickly from a verbal encounter into a physical encounter between the knights and the monster. Possibly because of their earlier Christmastime encounters, Greed is frightened of Tommy. After a brief struggle with the boy, Greed tumbles over the edge of the balcony (presumably) to his death, leaving Tommy free to rescue the Christmas Lady, who happens to look like his mother, Mary. With their quest completed, the knights awaken on Christmas morning to his mother's voice calling them to breakfast. She directs their attention to an envelope containing a letter that is hanging from the Christmas tree. According to a letter written by the neighbor Mr. Grudge, who reads the letter using the voice of the Giant of Greed, ownership of the Duncans' ranch has transferred to the family. This is, of course, the explanation for Tommy's nightmare.

Young listeners would understand the obvious final message of the program that they should always "be good" and never "yield to temptation" ("Sir Tommy"). Any adult concerned with radio's potentially negative influence on children would likely have been reassured that youngsters were enjoying wholesome entertainment when they tuned their radio dials to *Wild Bill Hickok*.

7

Radio Adaptations of Robin Hood

As "socializing agents," children's radio programs were educating, entertaining, and "bringing to youngsters ... the values and ideals of America society," preferably through the example of heroes (MacDonald 42, 45), either traditional figures like King Arthur or non-traditional figures such as the anti-authoritarianist Robin Hood. Adapters of Robin Hood's legend took liberties with their sources, as had adapters of Malory and Arthurian legend. Modern readers are familiar with the benevolent yeoman and host of Sherwood Forest, who distributed the crown's wealth and aided the weak, not the violent bandit of the original myth. However, the "real" Robin Hood was neither benevolent nor chivalric.[1] Radio adaptations of Robin Hood's legend privileged adventure as a masculine experience that included rescuing maidens, or even squires in distress, and overcoming equally capable opponents in battle. Characteristically, radio plays written for a broad audience of children and adults toned down the violent incidents of the ballads, choosing not to feature scenes such as, Robin Hood's beheading and defacing of Guy of Gisborne, or Robin Hood's death by the hand of the Kirklees prioress.

Medieval audiences heard oral performances of the "rimes of Robyn Hode" referred to by William Langland in his fourteenth-century dream vision *Piers Plowman.* Fifteenth-century British audiences enjoyed Robin Hood ballads: *Robin Hood and the Monk, Robin Hood and the Potter, Robin Hood and Guy of Gisborne,* and *A Little Geste of Robyn Hode,* all sources for later adapters. In the sixteenth century, British playwrite Anthony Munday wrote and staged *The Downfall of Robert Earl of Huntington* and *The Death of Robert Earl of Huntington.* Following Munday's lead, Martin Parker's seventeenth-century *A True Tale of Robin Hood* (1632) continued the gentrification tradition and influenced Ben Jonson's and Shakespeare's forest outlaw story, the pastoral comedy. Robin Hood's existence under the reign of King Richard was an attempt by adapters of the legend to invent an official "biography" for the mythic figure. Munday also medievalized his plot inserting into the play fifteenth-century poet laureate John Skelton, who also plays Friar Tuck. Skelton performed a "Robin Hood" play-within-a-play being staged for King Henry VIII. The play's "character" John Skelton worries that his loose adaptation of the yeoman outlaw tale based on the Robin Hood ballads will offend Henry VIII. (As a side note, the king enjoyed disguising himself as Robin Hood for court festivities.) Munday was also responsible for the gentrification of Robin Hood, renaming the character Earl Robert of Huntington, giving him Maid Marian as his love interest, and renegotiating Robin Hood's Catholicism and his participation in the Third Crusade. These elements would become standard features of later adaptations of Robin Hood's legend. Though Munday was the first to refashion Robin Hood's earlier outlaw image into that of a "socially respected" nobleman, he was not as successful as he hoped (Dobson and Taylor 44–5). Munday's adaptations and later Parker's influenced the "forest outlaw stories" staged by British author Ben Jonson in *The Sad Shepherd* (1637) and Shakespeare's *As You Like It* (c. 1599) (Knight and Ohlgren 10). Robin Hood in the eighteenth century was the subject of ballad operas, bourgeois comedy, and antiquarian collections, such as those produced by Bishop Thomas Percy, *Reliques of Ancient Poetry* (1767), a collection of medieval romances and Robin Hood ballads.

Benjamin Franklin's observations and opinions of Robin Hood's popularity in the American colonies attests to how firmly entrenched the British outlaw was in early American culture. Franklin observed that like the British, colonists preferred reading Robin Hood ballads to reading their scripture. In his editorial "An Apology for Printers," published in *The Pennsylvania Gazette* in the summer of 1731, Franklin defends such "lowbrow" literature which forced him and his fellow printers to print "vicious or silly things" ("An Apology" 7). "An Apology to Printers" was the printer-politician's satiric response to readers who claimed outrage over a controversial statement he had made earlier in print. Franklin's alleged "apology" was actually his defense of the print trade in the American colonies. Writing under the pseudonym of John Paul Jones in a letter to the *Supplement to the Boston Independent Chronicle* dated March 1781, Franklin defends America's declaration of war on England, citing it as a defense of liberty and of property from England's spirit of conquest; Franklin further suggests that the literary tastes of the British were limited to reading about pirates, the deer-stealing highwayman Robin Hood, and ancient conquests ("Supplement" 341). By the twentieth century, Robin Hood had featured in all mediums of popular culture, even radio. Especially in children's radio programs, Robin Hood illustrated for young listeners chivalric qualities usually identified with King Arthur.

American scriptwriters for radio wove together legends of Robin Hood made popular by two British authors. The eighteenth-century publication of Joseph Ritson's collection of ballads *Robin Hood: A Collection of all the Ancient Poems, Songs, and Ballads, Now Extant, Relative to that Celebrated English Outlaw: To which are Prefixed Historical Anecdotes of His Life in Two Volumes* (1795) and many later adaptations, including Sir Walter Scott's *Ivanhoe* (1819) and Pyle's tales, as well as numerous fictional modernizations of the outlaw legends published by British and American authors. All but one of these radio adaptations of Robin Hood's legend aired on a family-friendly radio program, so it is surprising that the majority of the adaptations feature suggestively violent or overtly violent scenes, such as bullying, sword fights, death threats, or even death as when the Sheriff of Nottingham threatens to hang Robin Hood, Little John, or Maid Marian, and the death of Guy of Gisbornne. A storyline featuring mild violence was, of course, entertaining, and made good radio. More importantly, Robin Hood's chivalric conduct in such situations illustrated for listeners, young and old alike, ideal masculine behavior in the face of a personal challenge. For instance, in these adaptations, Robin Hood never loses control of his emotions but rather conducts himself with honor and bravery in every situation.

21. *Popeye the Sailor*, "Popeye Meets Robin Hood"

The Middle Ages, imagined as time of pageantry and chivalry, was a period when Robin Hood, a "merry-hearted, idealistic, impulsive" "chivalric hero" (MacLeod, *"Howard"* 46) roamed the greenwood, defied authority, and championed the weak. Rather than the violent character portrayed in medieval ballads about the outlaw, this tamer version was the Robin Hood favored by radio scriptwriters writing for *Popeye the Sailor, Buster Brown,* and *Family Theater. Popeye the Sailor,* a King Feature's comic strip character brought to radio in 1935, aired first on NBC and then on CBS in 1936, and was sponsored by Wheatena Cereal. Despite his short tenure on radio, Popeye and his gang—his girlfriend Olive Lamoy (Olive Oyl), J. Wellington Wimpy, Matey (Popeye's adopted son and the newsboy), Swee'Pea, and the bully Bluto—remained popular in comics, on television, and in the movies.

"Popeye Meets Robin Hood" is the earliest radio adaptation of Robin Hood covered in this study of radio adaptations. Lasting only fifteen minutes, this radio fairytale nonetheless manages to pack a lot of action into a short period. "Popeye Meets Robin Hood" focuses on a series of competitions between Popeye and Robin Hood, borrowing from medieval ballads that tell of Robin Hood meeting his match by either besting or being bested by Little John, Friar Tuck, the Sheriff of Nottingham, or Guy of Gisborne. During a series of games in which Popeye and Robin Hood try to outdo one another, Popeye, not Robin Hood, exhibits good sportsmanship and athletic ability. Thematically this episode is about proving one's masculinity through athletic prowess. This time-travel narrative opens with Olive Oyl, Popeye, Swee'Pea, and Wimpy transported to Sherwood Forest during a discussion about their favorite book *Robin Hood*, perhaps a reference to Pyle's *Merry Adventures of Robin Hood* (1883). Note that this episode also borrows from the medieval dream vision trope in its reference to a book: in many medieval dream visions, a book lulls the narrator to sleep. Popeye attempts "medieval speak," communicating in an Americanized British accent. Robin Hood appears and volunteers to carry Popeye across the river, but he is accused of turning the spinach-munching tattooed sailor with bulging forearms into a "sissy" (*Popeye*).

This particular scene is an adaptation of the seventeenth-century comic ballad "Robin Hood and the Curtal Friar" in which Robin Hood and the Friar attempt to outdo one another in a game in which each man tries to carry the other across a river multiple times.[2] In the ballad, Robin Hood hears of a friar who can match his skill with a bow and arrow. Once he locates the friar, Robin Hood feigns to be a "wet weary man" and asks to be carried across a river "For sweete Saint Charity" (Knight and Ohlgren 52, 461). The friar, recalling Robin Hood's "good deed; / He had done none of long before," takes Robin Hood upon his back (Knight and Ohlgren 53–4, 461). Now on the other side of the river, the friar draws his sword and demands that he be carried back across the river. This scenario is repeated twice more until he friar tosses Robin Hood into the stream and declares that he must choose to "sink or swim" (Knight and Ohlgren 76, 462). Robin

Hood and the friar continue their fight onshore but this time using arrows and swords. As the challenge reaches a fevered pitch, Robin Hood blows his horn three times calling, "Half a hundred yeoman, with bows bent" (Knight and Ohlgren 106–08, 463). Likewise the friar blasts a "lowd … blow" calling "halfe a hundred good bandoggs" (Knight and Ohlgren 122–23, 464). At a stalemate, they call a truce. Robin Hood asks the friar for his friendship and pledges to clothe him in a new suit every year if he joins Robin Hood's band of Merry Men (Knight and Ohlgren 464).

In this radio adaptation, Popeye plays the friar's role and clears the stream in one jump. Popeye encounters Robin Hood and calls him a "fair and noble sportsman" (*Popeye*). Popeye agrees to an archery tournament in which Robin Hood is the winner, as in the ballads. The audience quickly discovers that archery is not the sailor's game, but Popeye is reminded that he is good at other things when Swee'Pea suggests that Popeye's chivalric deeds made him "a sort of Robin Hood" (*Popeye*). Possibly these comments were meant to also boost the self-esteem of a young listener who, like Popeye, had tried but failed to achieve a goal. Product placement puts two bowls of Wheatena cereal in Popeye's hands, giving him enough strength to break the longbow, though not enough accuracy to hit the bull's eye. As in many "Robin meets his match" ballads, the segment concludes with a celebratory feast. In a show of good sportsmanship, Robin Hood and Popeye part as friends.

22. *Smilin' Ed's Buster Brown Gang*, "Robin Hood"

"Robin Hood" aired on the half hour Saturday morning children's program *Smilin' Ed's Buster Brown Gang* in 1949. Smilin' Ed's adaptation of the Robin Hood legend is an exciting tale, casting Robin Hood as the same charitable fellow that appears in *Family Theater's* adaptation "An Adventure with Robin Hood," discussed next. McConnell introduces Robin Hood as Sir Locksley, a man who "took back the gold stolen from the poor people in the first place" and who, only out of necessity, kept some of the wealth for himself and his Merry Men (McConnell, "Robin"). Through Robin Hood's words and deeds, listeners learned the importance of personal morality. Robin Hood is the heroic outlaw of Ritson's pseudo-biographical *Robin Hood collection*, he is "active, brave, prudent, patient; possessed of uncommon bodily strength, and considerable skill; just, generous, benevolent, faithful, and beloved ... by his followers" (xii).

McConnell introduces the Robin Hood of history, a man who was both a "robber" and a "benevolent bandit," who once lived in "Merry old England" (McConnell, "Robin"). Radio listeners imagined they too could "see" the village through the eyes of Robin Hood and Little John as they strolled alongside the medieval heroes, taking in the "dusty streets of Nottingham" or heading to a tavern for a tankard of ale and plate of mutton, "as was the fashion of the day" (McConnell, "Robin"). McConnell's vivid descriptions bring to life the tournament setting and typical medieval characters speaking with an Americanized British accent. McConnell also does a fair job describing down to the last detail the rules of a medieval tournament, including the protocols of engagement, such as when the sound of metal on metal illustrates for listeners Sir Gilbert's lance striking Gregory Clive dale's shield hanging in front of the young nobleman's tent, announcing the knight's challenge. Next the "air rings with clash of steel on steel" as heralds proclaim that the joust has begun (McConnell, "Robin"). Complex sound effects lend a medieval air and create atmosphere: the sound of horses' hooves, the notes of a trumpet, and the clash of steel bring a jousting tournament to life.

The episode's story opens with Robin Hood and Little John discussing their chances of meeting the Sheriff, here replaced by a similarly greedy nobleman of the ballad tradition, who uses tricks to gain property. Listeners are introduced to the Robin Hood and Little John of the ballads: Robin Hood is the skilled archer who wins the golden arrow in the Sheriff's contest, and Little John demonstrates his skill with the quarterstaff. Little John expresses his hope that he once again has the "opportunity to tweak the Sheriff's nose" (McConnell, "Robin"), an allusion to the many times Robin Hood and Little John bested the Sheriff in *A Gest of Robyn Hode*, a collection of Robin Hood ballads dated to around the mid-fifteenth century (Knight and Ohlgren 81).[3] In Fitt Three of the *Gest*, an episode also retold by Pyle in *The Merry Adventures of Robin Hood* (1883), Little John, a skilled archer calling himself Reynolde Grenelef (Knight and Ohlgren 595, 109) pretends to be a faithful steward to the Sheriff while planning to steal from his employer. In Fitte Five, a disguised Robin Hood wins the Sheriff's archery contest and angers the Sheriff. Later titled "Robin Hood and the Butcher," which was adapted by Pyle, Robin Hood, disguised as a butcher named Robert of Locksley, barters with the Sheriff for five hundred head of "horned beasts" during a feast at the Guild Hall. The "beasts" turned out to be Robin Hood's "good stout yeomen" who merrily sent the Sheriff on his way (Pyle 53). By Fitte Six of the *Gest*, Robin Hood beheads the Sheriff, an incident never included in literary adaptations or in radio adaptations of Robin Hood.

The plot of the radio adaptation centers upon Miriam and Gregory, the Clivesdale heirs who wish to reclaim their inheritance. The lands will increase Gilbert's holdings and will encourage other knights to support him. For Robin Hood the tournament is not only an opportunity to help the Clivesdale heirs but also a chance to repay an old debt to the elder Clivesdale, who once gave him refuge (McConnell, "Robin"). For the benefit of younger listeners, McConnell stresses the importance of the chivalric code, especially the chivalric qualities of honor and loyalty. Young Gregory illustrates exceptional bravery when he enters the joust against Sir Gilbert, but Gregory is injured, which requires Robin Hood to assume his place. In the ballads and on radio, Robin Hood usually adopts the disguise of a tradesman—a butcher or potter—to trick the Sheriff of Nottingham. However, a variation of this disguise motif is introduced when Robin Hood dresses himself in the Clivesdale family armor to regain the Clivesdale inheritance stolen by Gilbert of Middlebury, the Black Knight (McConnell, "Robin"). Championing the Clivesdale children is for Robin Hood an opportunity to repay his old debt to the family and unseat a tyrant. Robin Hood defeats Sir Gilbert and returns the property to its rightful owners.

23. *Family Theater,* "An Adventure with Robin Hood"

Especially in wartime, radio programs taught listeners, young and old, how to be good citizens and better Americans. Father Patrick Peyton's dramatic anthology *Family Theater* was one of those didactic programs. In addition to the Arthurian tale "Sir Lancelot of the Lake," the program also brought Robin Hood to the air. "An Adventure with Robin Hood," broadcast on July 27, 1949, is likely influenced by Errol Flynn's high-flying Technicolor swashbuckler film *The Adventures of Robin Hood* (1938) and closely models the adaptation titled "Robin Hood" that aired that same year on *Your Playhouse of Favorites*, discussed next. In addition to an action-packed storyline, complex sound effects and a cast of familiar and personable characters engaged the listener's imagination.

7. Radio Adaptations of Robin Hood   153

Narrator Edmond O'Brien introduces "An Adventure with Robin Hood" as a story of romance and adventure taken from the "immortal" classics of yesterday, a story that still "captures the fancy and transports the spirit" ("An Adventure"). Listeners undoubtedly recalled what they already knew about Robin Hood, the benevolent hero, and recognized a shared love of liberty when they heard O'Brien's description of Robin Hood, also called Robin of Locksley, and his Merry Men: "the bold, green-clad men of Sherwood Forest lived ... carefree lives ... untroubled by want or restraint ... [and] were all men to whom liberty was a personal thing, a privilege that was to be abused neither by them nor by those whom they met on their adventures" ("An Adventure"). O'Brien next invites listeners to imagine they have returned to "Sherwood Forest and [have] become young again" ("An Adventure"). In an effort to authenticate the period, the actors affect the usual Americanized British accents.

The audience is encouraged to imagine that they have traveled back to the Middle Ages and now stand among Robin Hood's men, "watching" the famed archer and Little John engage in a friendly cudgel match, a scene often repeated in adaptations of Robin Hood ("An Adventure"). This announcer again instructs the audience with the "look-see" radio device—"*Look* you at the scene before them"—wherein the listener in his imagination becomes part of excitement unfolding ("An Adventure" emphasis added). This engagement with the action and characters is further enhanced when, in the next scene, listeners are told to "*Picture* them, sweet folk, Robin Hood's Merry Men" resting in Sherwood Forest ("An Adventure" emphasis added). Robin of Locksley is a wronged nobleman who seeks social justice, and the spunky Maid Marian is his love interest and a damsel in distress. In addition to the usual cast of characters populating a Robin Hood radio adaptation, Robin Hood, Little John, the Sheriff of Nottingham, and Maid Marian, secondary characters appear, including Little John, who towers "above the band"; Will Scarlet; and Allen a Dale, the troubadour of Sherwood. This adaptation also incorporates some of the most familiar scenes in ballads and modern adaptations: the cudgel match, Robin Hood's robbing of the Sheriff in Sherwood Forest, a benevolent Robin Hood distributing the stolen taxes among the general populace and back to the king, and the Sheriff's capture of Maid Marian. The trope of disguise, characteristic of many of these radio adaptations, is used again when Robin Hood and his men disguise themselves as servants and sneak into the Sheriff's banquet hall to rescue Maid Marian.

The story opens in Sherwood Forest with the reenactment of the cudgel match between Robin Hood and Little John, a key scene in Flynn's 1938 film. One of Robin's men signals the arrival of the Sheriff of Nottingham, who is carrying a bag of coins, the taxes collected from the citizens of Nottingham. Robin Hood's usual disdain for the Sheriff is obvious in the tone of his voice when he orders the Sheriff to pay a toll for "traveling the lanes of Sherwood" before being permitted to leave the forest ("An Adventure"). Angry that he has been bested again, the Sheriff returns to the village and places a five-hundred-crown bounty on Robin Hood's head. In the next suggestively violent scene, the Sheriff's men seize the "hosts of Sherwood" and the Sheriff announces that he will "scour the jails of England" for any man equal to the outlaw; the Sheriff then kidnaps Maid Marian, threatening to hang her if Robin Hood refuses to surrender and return the stolen money.

Robin Hood demonstrates his benevolent nature and political loyalty in the next scene when he divides the bag of gold crowns taken from the Sheriff (indicated by the "clink" of coins) but keeps a reserve for the poor and for the usurped King Richard. As he explains, once the king returns from his holy Crusade, he will "sorely need funds to regain his throne" ("An Adventure"). Little John and the Merry Men plan to help the kidnapped Marian escape, but Robin Hood cautions them to "save thy loyalties for the people who shall need them when I'm gone" ("An Adventure"). The Merry Men disguise themselves as servants and crash the Sheriff's banquet, which is actually a trap for Robin Hood. O'Brien, the narrator, reassures listeners that Robin Hood is loyal to Maid Marian with the explanation that "a man without his loved one is like a ship without an anchor" ("An Adventure").

Maid Marian taunts the Sheriff, warning that Robin Hood will have his revenge. Appropriating Flynn's acrobatic athleticism as Robin Hood in the big-budget film *The Adventures of Robin Hood*, Robin Hood on radio enters the room using "curtains and chandeliers as other men use floors" ("An Adventure"). A short battle follows and the bandits of course escape with Marian in tow. Despite the Sheriff's treachery, this radio adaptation ends with a gallant Robin Hood showing goodwill toward the Sheriff and announcing his upcoming marriage to Maid Marian. Through their dialogue and actions, the rubric used to measure chivalry in these radio adaptations, Robin Hood and his Merry Men show themselves to be chivalric heroes. O'Brien concludes the story with an invitation to the audience to return to Sherwood Forest, as if the audience had actually been present during the past half hour, and inspires them to join in national prayer with the reminder that "The family that prays together stays together" ("An Adventure").

24. *Your Playhouse of Favorites*, "Robin Hood"

Your Playhouse of Favorites produced adaptations of literature that should have delighted even radio's harshest critics, who maligned radio programs as examples of "low-brow" culture. In addition to the episode "Robin Hood" broadcast one year earlier, the program aired adaptations of *The Three Musketeers* and *Treasure Island* in 1948, as well as a host of other novels. Though not as sophisticated a production as the *Family Theater* offering "An Adventure with Robin Hood" because of its lack of dramatic effect and the actors' subpar performance, "Robin Hood" is still a rather good adaptation. Moreover, this adaptation of Robin Hood's legend is the only one to attribute its storyline to a source.

The content of this radio dramatization and adaptation of Robin Hood's legend is attributed to a ballad collection printed by Wynken de Word in 1475. Wynken was a London printer and publisher of inexpensive books, who picked up the printing business where Caxton left off. Wynken's collection is known for its many errors, but it was a source for Joseph Ritson's eighteenth-century ballad collection (Knight and Ohlgren 80). Various ballads are woven together to create this action-packed drama, but one look at Pyle's *Merry Adventures of Robin Hood* is indicative of the episodes the writer for *Your Playhouse of Favorites* was attempting to capture. In this radio adaptation, Robin Hood disguises himself as a butcher, aids a disheartened knight, wins the golden arrow in the Sheriff of Nottingham's archery contest, and tricks the Sheriff into Sherwood Forest to buy a herd of horned "beasts," which are actually the king's deer;. the Merry Men also make an appearance, as does King Richard ("Robin Hood"). The radio audience is also treated to the love story of Robin Hood and Maid Marian.

The story opens with Robin Hood and his men enjoying a feast with Robin Hood's request for a dinner guest. A "sad and sorrowful" knight, Sir Richard of the Lea, makes a timely arrival and sets the story in motion when Robin Hood promises to "aideth" this "sorrowful knight" (Pyle, *The Merry Adventures* 158). The setting is Nottingham during the reign of

King Richard, and Robin Hood, the audience later finds out, is really the displaced nobleman Robert, Earl of Huntingdon. The type of sound effects the audience had come to expect in a story set in the Middle Ages are again used: hoof beats, crowd noises, and clashing metal. A bugle announces Robin Hood's entrances. A mix of background noise and music are used as transitional devices to better create a sense of the Middle Ages.

In an introduction that reflects a desire for intimacy with the radio audience, Robert Anthony Dean, the program's announcer, introduces the story as if his listeners are sitting in the same room, perhaps reading the legend, an "immortal romantic classic" of Robin Hood, along with him: "Our story today concerns a legendary hero, whose love of fair play and bold deeds have been written down in ballads since the time of Chaucer. His fame is equal to that of bluff King Hal or bonnie Prince Charlie.... While England shall be England, Robin Hood will be a well-loved name" ("Robin Hood"). Dean then invites the radio audience to travel with him to Sherwood Forest and to meet Robin Hood—a "champion of justice, an outlaw old and true who robbed the rich and readily helped the oppressed"—Robin Hood's Merry Men, Maid Marian Fitzwalter, the Sheriff of Nottingham, King Richard, and Guy of Gisborne. In radio adaptations of the legend, Guy of Gisborne is a bounty hunter disguised in horsehide, who is killed by Robin Hood. Cort Benson played Robin Hood.

This is a familiar but entertaining tale of Robin Hood's legend that incorporates the usual tropes borrowed for radio adaptations set in the Middle Ages, whether or not King Arthur or Robin Hood made an appearance: the trope of disguise, the lady as an object of exchange, and chivalric knighthood. Robin Hood, Maid Marian, and King Richard adopt various disguises in order to navigate Nottingham and to undermine Guy of Gisborne and his henchman, the Sheriff of Nottingham. Disguising himself as a deaf, old butcher, Robin Hood arrives in Nottingham, sells his meat at sharply reduced prices, and gives it away to widowed women. This is all part of a plan to lure the Sheriff into Sherwood Forest. In another disguise, this time as Reynald Greenleaf, Robin Hood trades his Lincoln-green costume for tattered red clothing and dyes his beard in order to enter and win the Sheriff of Nottingham's archery contest. Maid Marian also disguises herself as Sir Richard of the Lea's squire in order to gain entry into Sherwood Forest and ask Robin Hood to stop her forced marriage to Sir Guy. This is also an opportunity for the couple to declare their love for one another; this exchange also leads the audience to suspect that Robin Hood is actually Robert of Huntingdon.

King Richard disguises himself as an abbot, which "serve[s] to cover [his] countenance," in order to lure Robin Hood to him ("Robin Hood"). The king and his men arrive in an inn disguised as "fox" hunters. As the innkeeper warns the disguised king "simple gentry such as you could never find Robin Hood, but he will find you in the twink of an eye," if they are "clad" as men of the church and carry full pockets, the "bold Robin [will] smell [the] abbot a mile away" ("Robin Hood"). The king's ruse is a way to track down Robin Hood. The abbot-king and Robin Hood both share a love of justice and a love of a good fight, and the king praises the outlaw for maintaining justice in Sherwood Forest, noting that more justice exists "today in Sherwood than in Prince John's court" ("Robin Hood"). This segment clues the listener in to the abbot's identity. Robin Hood's chance to reveal his own identity as Robert of Huntingdon occurs at the church after he and the abbot-king stop Maid Marian's marriage. Realizing that she now loves two men, Robert of Huntingdon and Robin Hood, King Richard, now as himself, with a twist of humor announces that he will marry her to both men.

Robin Hood's willingness to help Sir Richard of the Lea raise ransom money for his son, a prisoner by Guy of Gisborne, is a further example of his chivalry. Sir Richard's son, a knight, is under arrest for accidentally killing Gisborne's squire during a tournament. Richard pledges his property to save his son, so he is now destitute and the money is due that evening. In *A Gest of Robyn Hode* and in Pyle's *Merry Adventures*, Sir Richard's son kills a knight of Lancaster and has a few days to pay his debt to Emmet Priory. For his part in helping the knight, Robin Hood gains Sir Richard as a friend for life.

An additional theme is the love story that follows the evolution of Robin Hood and Maid Marian's relationship. After meeting Maid Marian in Nottingham, Robin Hood, at that time disguised as a butcher, falls hopelessly in love with her. The meeting "greatly changed" Robin Hood, Little John suggests, and the yeoman spends months gazing longingly "into space" ("Robin Hood"). According to the lovesick Robin Hood, Maid Marian is "the freshness of morning dew, the sweetness of summer rose" ("Robin Hood"). Maid Marian in this version and in *Family Theater* is a spunky woman who is not afraid to argue with the menacing and violent Guy of Gisborne, the real antagonist in this episode.

In spite of this atypical depiction, Maid Marian is nonetheless an object of exchange between men. King Richard as her guardian betrothed her to the Earl of Huntingdon. With the king away fighting in the Crusades,

Marian became the ward of the Sheriff, who then betrothed her to Guy of Gisborne for an undisclosed amount of gold. Marian's marriage to the "black-hearted" Gisborne promises to be an unhappy one when he warns her that she will soon speak with a "more seemly tongue when [she is his] wife" ("Robin Hood"). During this half hour of action, adventure, and a little suspense, radio listeners are treated to a chivalric tale in which the story's heroic protagonist, Robin Hood, has all of the qualities of chivalry attributed to a knight, and even a cowboy, as discussed later: generosity, courtesy, loyalty, honor, justice, and prowess.

Before escaping into Sherwood Forest, Robin Hood was Robert, Earl of Huntingdon, banished by Sir John for distributing his revenue among the poor instead of contributing it to Sir John's "coffers" ("Robin Hood"). Sir Richard of the Lea shares his story with Robin Hood, who then goes out and finds the five hundred pounds needed to pay Richard's debt. The fact that Robin Hood takes the five hundred pounds and no more is indicative of his honor. In his transactions with Sir Richard, Maid Marian, and the disguised King Richard, Robin Hood's conduct, his courteousness and good sportsmanship, are above reproach. For instance, the king, disguised as an abbot, challenges the yeoman to a cudgel match and bests Robin Hood. While Robin Hood's Merry Men react in anger and intend to harm the abbot, Robin Hood, always the good sport in these radio productions, extends his hand in friendship. The abbot readily embraces this opportunity and assists Robin Hood in his plan to stop Maid Marian's marriage. Unbeknownst to Robin Hood, and perhaps the listener, the abbot is the king in disguise, so Robin Hood's courteousness pays off in the end.

Robin Hood's loyalty is to King Richard, not to Prince John and "his satellites" who have "caused much misery in England" ("Robin Hood"). Robin Hood swears to lay down his life for his king and is as good as his word. He promises to find the ransom money and to help Maid Marian escape the clutches of Guy of Gisborne. Robin Hood's sense of justice is obvious in the scene between the old butcher and the Sheriff of Nottingham as they enter Sherwood Forest for the "horns." Noting his hesitation, the butcher assures him that Robin Hood never hurt a "just man" ("Robin Hood"). During the "greatest" archery contest ever held in Nottingham, Robin Hood predictably exhibits his skill as an archer and as a strategist ("Robin Hood"). Standing seven yards away, Robin Hood aims his arrow at the bull's eye, splits his opponent's arrow in two, and beats Gilbert of the White Hand. Robin Hood wins the prize of the golden arrow and escapes into the forest. Safely hidden in the woods, Robin Hood shoots an arrow with a scroll, delivering a message to the Sheriff that while he "treasures" the arrow, he cannot wait to "plant it" in the Sheriff's "black heart" ("Robin Hood"). As a strategist, the yeoman easily maneuvers the unwitting Sheriff into a trap and plans the successful rescue of Maid Marian, with King Richard's help, though this is undisclosed at the time.

At the end of this radio play, the audience has no need to wonder if Robin Hood and Maid Marian ever married. Whereas in the *Let's Pretend* adaptation "Robin Hood," Robin Hood only promises to marry Maid Marian, an adaptation discussed next, in the *Your Playhouse of Favorites* version of events King Richard, with authority, arranges their wedding when he calls for the bishop to perform the ceremony.

25. *Let's Pretend*, "Robin Hood"

Let's Pretend, an award-winning children's Saturday morning radio series, aired an adaptation of Robin Hood's legend that, through Robin Hood, illustrates honor as an important character trait. "Robin Hood," written by Johanna Johnston and broadcast January 9, 1954, is based on material in Pyle's *Robin Hood* (1883), particularly the story "Robin Hood Turns Butcher," and the "Robin Hood and the Potter" ballad. Also following the traditional literary sources, the Sheriff of Nottingham jails Little John. Guy of Gisborne, a bounty hunter who in the ballad wraps himself in "odorous" skins, plays a significant role. Gisborne's clothing is described in terms somewhat similar to the horse-hide costume, his "capul-hide," worn in the fifteenth-century ballad and later described in Pyle's adaptation and chapter titled "Robin Hood and Guy of Gisborne" as "a horse's hide ... with the hair upon it," though he also wore a peculiar "cowl ... [with] ears ... stuck up like those of a rabbit" to hide his face (257). As in many Robin Hood adaptations, disguise is used to better aid the dispossessed. "Robin Hood" concludes with the marriage of Robin Hood and Maid Marian. Despite the serious undertone of this tale, the story is told in good fun.

Listeners of the radio episode are invited to hop on an imaginary motorcycle, an anachronistic device for time travel back to the Middle Ages. Host "Uncle" Bill Adams introduces the episode with the familiar phrase reserved for fairytales that quickly engages the attention of the young audience: "Once upon a time, many years ago there was a great green forest in England known as Sherwood Forest, and deep in the heart of this greenwood lived a band of outlaws and their leader" (Johnston, "Robin Hood"). As a loyal subject of King Richard, Robin Hood awaits the return of his monarch from the Third Crusade. Though he is an outlaw, Robin Hood speaks with confidence when he explains to his Merry Men that the king will pardon him and permit his marriage to Maid Marian, the "high-borne daughter" of the nobleman Sir Humphreys, a "cheat" (Johnston, "Robin Hood").

This adaptation has two storylines—the first of these is Robin Hood's attempts to prevent the corrupt Sheriff from repossessing a farmer's property. Paralleling Pyle's chapter "Robin Hood Turns Butcher" and the medieval ballad of "Robin Hood and the Potter," Robin Hood and Little John, disguised as butchers, travel to Nottingham to assist the farmer by setting up a market stall and undercutting market prices. As in most of the dialogue exchanges on radio between Robin Hood and the Sheriff or Robin Hood and Guy of Gisborne, the struggle between good and evil reinforces notions of chivalry and perhaps promotes certain ideals of American masculinity. The second storyline is Robin Hood's relationship with his love interest Maid Marian, whom he plans to marry.

Robin Hood tempts the crooked and greedy Sheriff with the promise that a stock of cattle waits in the greenwood. True to the conventions of radio drama, the Sheriff's interior monologue interrupts the action and permits the audience to hear his plan to steal the nonexistent herd, further emphasizing his corruption. Robin Hood's chivalric qualities and the Sheriff's corruption are juxtaposed to highlight the qualities the listener should adopt in the same type of situation. Maid Marian, a spirited young woman, arrives in Sherwood Forest to warn Robin Hood that the Sheriff hired the "cut throat" Guy of Gisborne to capture and to kill him (Johnston, "Robin Hood"). Ignoring her good intentions, and because Maid Marian is a woman trespassing in Sherwood Forest, a traditionally male-gendered space, Little John delivers a lecture to Maid Marian that the "greenwood is no place for a woman" (Johnston, "Robin Hood"). This comment reflects the gendered thinking reinforced in many radio productions. Just as the treatment of Maid Marian is indicative of assumptions about gender roles, this promotion of an idealistic masculinity was consistent with the treatment of the male hero in all of the radio adaptations of Robin Hood.

After stumbling over the sleeping Guy of Gisborne wrapped in animal skins, Robin Hood and the bounty hunter exchange insults and then cudgel blows. Guy of Gisborne accuses Robin Hood of being a "ninny" because he "never killed a man in his life" (Johnston, "Robin Hood"). Guy of Gisborne's bullying of Robin Hood is, for radio listeners, an example of how one should *not* behave. Because Robin Hood had so far illustrated the chivalric code through deeds and words, the audience would no doubt favor him as a hero. Unlike the ballads in which Robin Hood kills and then brutally defaces Guy of Gisborne, here the outlaw only knocks his opponent on the head. This alteration of the source's plot tones down the excessive violence of the early ballads and reinforces the importance of the chivalric qualities of fair play and compassion. Now dressed in Guy of Gisborne's "skins," Robin Hood rescues the jailed Little John, who is scheduled to hang on the "gallows tree at dawn" (Johnston, "Robin Hood"). This adaptation concludes with the medieval outlaw's anticipated defeat of the Sheriff and the narrator's promise that the Sherwood outlaw and Maid Marian will eventually marry. In the last scene, the audience is reassured that Maid Marian will finally have access to Sherwood, now that she is officially married to the outlaw.

In addition to radio scripts that embraced the medieval Robin Hood ballads, scriptwriters adapting the legend for radio also favored appropriating his persona and then attaching it to surprisingly different characters featured in various radio programs. Robin Hood is the focus of an adaptation featured on the crime drama *Casey, Crime Photographer*, the adventure anthology *Escape*, and the Western *Gunsmoke*.

25. *Casey, Crime Photographer*, "The Tobacco Pouch"

Robin Hood's reputation for stealing from the wealthy to give to the poor is the premise of an episode of *Casey, Crime Photographer*[4] titled "The Tobacco Pouch" that aired on September 18, 1947. This time, however, the perpetrator of the Robin Hood–like crime is a wealthy man who believes he really *is* Robin Hood incarnate.

Jack Casey, a hard-working, amateur detective and crime photographer, normally solves a crime using the crime scene photos he shoots for the *Morning Express*; however, in this episode Casey requires the help of a delusional kleptomaniac and modern-day Robin Hood. Starring in "The

Tobacco Pouch" are Staats Cotsworth as Jack Casey, Leslie Woods as Anne Williams, Casey's fellow reporter and girlfriend, and Jackson Beck as Capt. Bill Logan. Tony Marvin is the announcer. Alonzo Deen Cole, a busy radio writer and producer best known for his work on the radio horror program *The Witch's Tale* (1931–1938), wrote the script. John Dietz directed. The sponsors for the radio program were Anchor Hocking Glass from 1946 through 1948, Toni Home Permanents from 1948 through 1949, and Phillip Morris from 1949 through 1950.

Jack Casey was originally a character of pulp fiction created by writer George Harmon Coxe introduced in the magazine *Black Mask* in the 1930s. *Casey, Crime Photographer* aired on CBS radio from 1943 through 1955 under a few different titles with various stars playing the lead role. The program briefly aired on television from 1951 to 1952 on CBS. A fixture of the radio program was the music of a jazz piano played in the background of the Blue Note Cafe. Herman Chittison was the pianist.

"The Tobacco Pouch" opens in the Blue Note Cafe, Casey's favorite haunt, during a conversation with the establishment's erudite bartender, Ethelbert.[5] After a quick drink and passing introduction to the local heavy, Big Ben, the boss of Hook Ridge, Casey and Anne head to the local department store to do some shopping. The action gets underway when they see a well-dressed thief slip a bracelet into his umbrella and then pick Big Ben's pocket, stealing a nondescript tobacco pouch. However, before Casey can alert Big Ben to the crime, he suspiciously slips away, leaving Casey and the store detective to grab the unlikely thief. Anne is surprised that the "neatly dressed" man with a "nice face" who speaks with a cultured British accent is actually a thief: he "could be a college professor," she says (Cole). Casey warns her that looks are deceiving: "Not all crooks look like crooks" (Cole). Cole, like the early playwright John Skelton, took liberties with the British icon's image by gentrifying this "half pint" (Cole) Robin Hood and giving him a socialite for a sister.

The thief's full name is Mr. Wilmer Carrig, the brother of socialite Mrs. Clayton Westfield. Despite his obvious wealth and social standing, Carrig is an active "friend of the poor" (Cole). For anyone who might still be unfamiliar with the legend of the Sherwood outlaw, Capt. Logan provides a quick summary: Robin Hood is "the guy who stole from the rich and gave to the poor" (Cole). Logan's brief explanation also reflects the scriptwriter's assumption that the audience will determine Carrig is a "good" thief working for social justice rather than a run-of-the-mill criminal. However, if the audience was still unsure of what to make of Carrig's criminality, by the end of this episode, the pint-sized Robin Hood will have the opportunity to defend his actions.

Carrig's sister has managed to keep him out of jail because she pays for everything he steals by funding a "shoplifting charge account"; Carrig shows his sister what he stole, and then she pays for it (Cole). Casey is unable to understand why this "lousy little shop lifter is treated like he's a tin god" (Cole) and protected by the department store detective, who lets Carrig go after his shoplifting spree. In fact, Carrig manages to stay out of jail because of his family ties and, for the most part, he commits victimless crimes since he is a do-gooder who "gives the stuff to the people who he thinks need it" (Cole).

Casey discovers a hotel key in the stolen tobacco pouch, follows the clue, walks into a murder plot, is kidnapped, and almost killed. Just before Casey is shot, Carrig arrives on the scene, rescues Casey, insults the would-be murder calling him "varlet," and explains the events that led to his stealing the tobacco pouch. He assures Casey that all along his actions were driven by Robin Hood's same "mission in life," "to address wrongs" and to "defend right" (Cole). In response to Casey's pressing him to find out if he had a part in the conspiracy, Carrig is appalled that he would think such a thing: "Defenders of the right cannot be purchased" (Cole). As Carrig explains, he never disclosed his plan to take down Big Ben because he "retain[s] [his] old Robin Hood technique. I never tell everybody everything" (Cole).

26. *Escape*, Cold War Anxieties in Antony Ellis's "Robert of Huntingdon"

Antony Ellis's sinister, action-packed mid–1950s radio adaptation "Robert of Huntingdon" written for *Escape* was another example of how a radio scriptwriter engaged with medievalism and used the flexibility of Robin Hood's legend to address contemporary anxieties. "Robert of Huntingdon" aired during the early days of McCarthyism, a period marked by growing anxieties over a perceived Communist infiltration in the United States. In addition to playing to the audience's fears of espionage, this October 26, 1952, episode promoted anti–Russian sentiment typical of the era.

Broadcast on the CBS network from 1947 through 1954, *Escape* delivered on the promise to entertain its audience with stories of high drama and adventure. William Conrad introduced the program with the iconic opening lines: "Tired of the everyday grind? Ever dream of a life of romantic adventure? Want to get away from it all? We offer you, escape. *Escape*, designed to free you from the four walls of today for a half hour of high adventure" (Ellis). Conrad, at that time a hard-working radio and television actor and radio's most famous lawman, Marshal Matt Dillon of *Gunsmoke*, narrated part of the program and in this adaptation plays Robert of Huntingdon.

Robert of Huntingdon may be derived from the chivalric nobleman featured in adaptations from the sixteenth through the first half of the twentieth century and Munday's Robert of Huntington, a displaced nobleman and exemplary chivalric hero bent on serving justice. Ellis also borrows familiar characters and the more violent aspects of the ballads, such as the gruesome encounter between Robin Hood and Guy of Gisborne. The Sheriff recruits the bounty hunter here named Sir Martin of Matlock who presents himself to Robin Hood as Martin Greenleaf, "a wronged yeoman" (Ellis). Martin's surname Greenleaf is a modernization of the name Reynolde Grenelef, the *nom de guerre* used by Little John when he introduces himself to the Sheriff of Nottingham in *A Gest of Robyn Hode*. Greenleaf also describes for the audience Robin Hood as a "savior of the poor and the scourge of the rich" and alludes to earlier Robin Hood mythology with the comment that this "fairytale" is one "we've come to know pretty well" (Ellis).

Ellis's storyline is managed through fast-moving dialogue, contiguous and interwoven scenes, and vivid sound effects. Complex sound effects and period music, such as the early English folk tune "Greensleeves," aurally reproduce the Middle Ages. Since visuals that would normally connect scenes, as they do in films, are absent from radio dramatizations, realism is created via the multilayered sound effects. The trill of songbirds and the chirping of crickets turns day into night, and the sound of a bubbling brook and the voices and sounds evocative of a crowded marketplace transport the audience between forest and shire. The whiz of arrows and the clash of steel recreate a medieval skirmish.

"Robert of Huntingdon" opens with Conrad's invitation to listeners to imagine that they are the prey of a lone archer, though it is unclear whether this "prey" is Robin Hood or another fugitive. The scene is as follows: "You are hiding in the middle of a great forest, quiet as a shadow, while closing in on you, hunting you down like an animal, is a silent archer who will kill you with an arrow through the heart" (Ellis). As Conrad explains, Robin Hood's exile was the result of his pilfering the king's deer, and he is now considered a danger to Nottingham. The scene transitions from the forest to the shire. A male voice announces that a bounty has been placed on the heads of Robin Hood and his Merry Men: "Here ye! Here ye! Let it be known by all present that a sum of one hundred pounds is placed upon the head of the outlaw Robert of Huntingdon," with an additional "fifty pound reward" to be given to the man who "maims, kills, or captures" the "felons," a list that includes Little John, Will Scarlet and Friar Tuck (Ellis). Martin promises to "gather a force of men" to "exterminate Robin Hood once and for all" (Ellis). To trick Robin Hood into believing that he is an outlaw, a description meant to solicit his sympathy, Martin claims his lands were confiscated by the Sheriff after he was caught poaching the king's deer. Robin Hood commits this same crime in *A Gest of Robin Hood* and many later adaptations. However, the Sheriff doubts that Martin Greenleaf's plan will work and says as much when he states that he cannot "afford an army without a plan" since "most of [his] best men lie" dead in Sherwood Forest (Ellis).

Conrad introduces Robin Hood and Little John with a description of the men dressed in their traditional Lincoln-green garments, lazing by a brook in the greenwood. He does not specifically name Robin Hood, but leaves the audience to fill in the details based on their familiarity with the legend. One of these figures is a "tall, handsome" man with a "cap set carelessly at angle on his head" and the other man is at "least seven feet [tall]," "chew[ing] and suck[ing] at the marrow of an entire oxen thighbone" (Ellis). Little John plays the part of a skeptic who is quick to point out Robin Hood's faults. After Robin Hood ignores his warning that the yeoman Martin Greenleaf is dangerous, Little John points out an important character flaw: Robin Hood is an easy "mark for a sad story" (Ellis). The Sheriff of Nottingham, the corrupt and violent arm of Nottingham law, speaks in a stereotypical villainous foreign accent. Although his slightly affected accent is difficult to pin down, it is similar to the accent of Boris Badenov (bad enough), the Russian spy and villain featured in the cartoon *The Rocky and Bullwinkle Show*, also narrated by William Conrad, which aired much later on television in 1959. Though his voice comes off as cartoonish, the Sheriff's Russian accent presumably exploited the "horror of the disembodied voice" for the audience's benefit (McCracken 184). Even more so, the Sheriff's accent and violent behavior also represent a stereotype that might have played on the audience's anxieties about a Communist infiltration of the United States.

The 1950s was a period of paranoia that gave birth to patriotic programs such as the "espionage-thriller" *I Was a Communist for the FBI* that "capitalized on the Red Scare of the early 1950s" (Dunning 340). Matt Cvetic's book of his own supposed experiences as an undercover government operative was the source for this syndicated radio program and film. From 1952 to 1954, the Hollywood actor Dana Andrews voiced the part of the American spy who infiltrated the Communist Party. The radio drama *I Was a Communist for the FBI* stereotyped Communists and portrayed them as "cold and humorless, with their single goal to enslave the world" (Dunning 340). Voice on radio is a "sign system" that suggests the speaker's attributes, such as "gender, age, social, or regional background, [and] ... character traits. But it may also indicates a subjective perception or memory of a character's speech rather than representing the 'actual' speech of the character" (Huwiler, "Storytelling" 53).

The Sheriff's accented, disembodied voice would have affected the radio audience, causing listeners to be horrified, especially since theses voices were heard in their minds. The dark underpinnings of this episode and the horrors of Communist espionage—especially in the prison scene and the verbal exchange between the Sheriff and Little John—would have been hauntingly familiar. Although not affecting the same accent as the Sheriff, Martin Greenleaf's character is also an impersonation of a Russian spy in his ability to easily change identities and infiltrate the Merry Men. This deviant behavior surely mirrored the anxieties about Cold War spies on the loose in the United States. Robert of Huntington was an expert at disguise as well; however, the various identities he appropriated, such as that of a pasty maker, in contrast to Gisborne's more negative disguise, would be less threatening because his objective is supposedly honorable.

Martin Greenleaf successfully becomes a member of Robin Hood's band and earns his place among the men who travel to Nottingham to save Little John. Because of Robin Hood's inability to identify the bounty hunter early on, he risks the lives of his Merry Men. Robin Hood is blind to his deception; however, Little John suspects Greenleaf's motives and accuses Robin Hood of being gullible. Surprisingly Little John, not Robin Hood, risks his life to uncover the spy's identity when he disguises himself as a tailor and returns to Nottingham. Because of his towering figure, Little John is easy to identify and immediately captured by the Sheriff's men. In the suggestively violent prison scene between Little John and the Sheriff, the Sheriff's verbal abuse of his prisoner is superimposed over the sound of a physical scuffle between the two. Listeners may have been disturbed or even have "identif[ied] with either the psychotic murderer [here the Sheriff] or his/her intended victim [here Little John]" (McCracken 184). During this heated exchange, the Sheriff's accent is more pronounced and his anger even more obvious:

> SHERIFF: You naughty, naughty man. You're gonna pay for all these years you know.... Perhaps you thought I'd forgotten your treatment of me the last time I was forced to go with you into the forest ... [Ellis].

Little John's laugh briefly interrupts the Sheriff's speech. The Sheriff then vows that Little John will "pay, slowly, slowly," to which Little John replies that listening to this "nasty maggot" has been payment enough (Ellis). Pushed to the point of further violence by Little John's taunts, the Sheriff claims that he "won't have to bring" Robin Hood "out of hiding," rather "[h]e'll come to us" and "try to do something heroic" (Ellis). Little John's groans suggests the Sheriff is also torturing his victim. This scene concludes with the brief musical notes of the song "Greensleeves." As the tune slowly fades, listeners are treated to forest sounds, men's voices, and the sound of a blade being sharpened on a whetstone, sounds combined to suggest the setting has changed to Sherwood Forest.

Martin Greenleaf and the audience eavesdrop on Robin Hood's plan to free Little John; and the final action-packed scene opens on armed archers described as posted along the prison walls and stationed at the gates. Robin Hood, now disguised as a beggar, easily enters Nottingham and reaches the imprisoned Little John to free him. Robin Hood and Little John are spotted as they make their way along the courtyard walls, avoiding the crowd gathered to watch Little John's execution. A battle erupts between the Sheriff's men and Robin Hood's Merry Men. Robin Hood and Martin Greenleaf meet face-to-face during the melee, recreated for listeners through elaborate sound effects—whinnying horses, shouting men, and the clash of metal on metal. Greenleaf is killed. His death and the Sheriff's vengeance are enough to send Robin Hood back to the safety of Sherwood Forest. Robin Hood's horn signals his men, and they "escape." The Sheriff angrily threatens to bring Robin Hood to justice, a claim that promises further encounters between the two.

This mildly violent and well-acted radio adaptation of Robin Hood's legend as produced for *Escape* was a product of its time and is another example of radio medievalism. Solely through radio dialogue and sound effects, radio scriptwriters and sound effects men engineered a radio adaptation set in the Middle Ages that resonated with 1950s paranoia stoked by fears of Communist spies infiltrating the United States. This sense of paranoia was recreated in the Sheriff's villainous, Russian-inflected voice and in the allusions to intrigue, deception, and espionage woven through the episode.

"Robinhooding" the West: Robin Hood in the Radio Western

Folklorist Kent L. Steckmesser coined the phrase "Robinhooding" and refers to Robin Hood and "his American descendants ... [as] actors in a classic drama, the major theme of which is man's struggle against corruption and injustice" (350, 353). Robin Hood might have started out as an iconic *British* figure, but his ability to trigger the *American* twentieth-century imagination was based on his typology as a "mythic outlaw" (Mackie 38), a universal trickster figure who lived outside of the law. The "Robin Hood Principle" is based on the theory that "outlaw heroes are often related to powerful notions of national, ethnic, and regional identity" while "their legends" are adopted by groups who think themselves oppressed (Seal 69–70). Even though the early Robin Hood tradition exposed the hero as a true outlaw with violent tendencies, Robin Hood's image had undergone a transformation beginning in the sixteenth century. Some credit can be given to Howard Pyle for giving Robin Hood the qualities of a knight, qualities that are also attributed to the cowboy.

A cowboy's image was untarnished because he was, above all, acceptable as "completely good[,] ... completely bad, or as a Robin Hood who ... bend[s] the law to aid the unfortunate" (Frantz 71). Americans were familiar with the greenwood outlaw through ballads, garland collections, operas, and Robin Hood–themed fiction. Nineteenth-century Western dime novels kept Robin Hood in the public eye and linked him to the American cowboy, carrying tales about the still-living Jesse James, a popular hero at the time, who was characterized as both a violent villain and a benevolent Robin Hood figure (DeForest, *Storytelling* 18). Americans embraced the Old West and its heroes and villains just as they had British medieval legends and their heroes. Pyle had published his collection of

Robin Hood tales in 1883 and would be writing and illustrating his Arthuriad at the turn of the century, a fruitful period for medieval romance. American readers and theater-goers knew Robin Hood well. They read historical novels of medieval romance, such as Sir Walter Scott's "Waverley" novels (1814) and *Ivanhoe* (1819), and they saw Thomas Love Peacock's opera *Maid Marian* (1822), an adaptation of Robin Hood's legend touring American theaters, as well as the on-going productions of Harry B. Smith and Reginald DeKoven's *Robin Hood*, staged in 1890. Smith and DeKoven's operetta would be staged multiple times in 1891, 1900, 1912, 1919, 1929, 1932, and 1944, and Tennyson's Robin Hood play *The Foresters* was produced as an opera in 1892. Film and radio also assured that Robin Hood would remain fixed in the American imagination. Following Kinemacolor's *Robin Hood* in 1913, a film originally produced for British audiences, Douglas Fairbanks' *Robin Hood*, influenced by Scott's novel *Ivanhoe*, became a classic with its release in 1922; additionally, Errol Flynn would be forever remembered for his role as Robin Hood in the 1938 film *The Adventures of Robin Hood*. A number of other Robin Hood films would follow, assuring this British legend's place in American popular culture.

John Rollin Ridge, using his Indian name Yellow Bird, published *The Life and Adventures of Joaquin Murieta: Celebrated California Bandit* in 1854. Ridge, a Cherokee outlaw on the run for killing his father's murderer, fled to California during the Gold Rush and became a newspaper correspondent and writer. Ridge's pseudo-history fashioned Joaquin Murieta as a Mexican "Romantic Bandit," though history has failed to prove that this individual actually existed (Jackson xx)—the figure may actually have been a compilation of bandits wreaking havoc in California at that time. The cowboy is more often than not described as both a knight and Robin Hood. In Robin Hood fashion, Murieta was a defiant, "dashing" "outlaw" who "sprang ... to life whenever and wherever some people had much and others had nothing," taking from the rich and giving to the poor (Jackson xx). Ridge created Murieta as an American cult hero, but Walter Noble Burns "crystalli[zed] the Murieta story in the Minds of Americans" with his adaption of the Western's folk hero for his novel *The Robin Hood of El Dorado* in 1932, which was later adapted for film (Jackson xlv). Burns also wrote *The Saga of Billy the Kid* in 1926, during a decade that saw the birth of the ideal of the Old West. Burns depended upon the same popular story formula used by Ridge. Murieta's book was marketed as a history and biography of Billy the Kid, though it was not without literary embellishments. With Burns's help, the American outlaw/folk hero was, like Murieta, mythologized as a chivalric knight with Robin Hood qualities. Zorro, the rapier-wielding masked California nobleman (aka Don Diego de la Vega) was also a combination Robin Hood and the cowboy-knight and was a champion of the oppressed. Pulp fiction writer Johnston McCully based Zorro on Murieta and introduced his character in 1919. *The Adventures of Zorro* aired on radio in 1957, but fans are more familiar with the books and films featuring the dashing hero.

In the twentieth century, Robin Hood was part of the outlaw tradition that mythologized America's most notorious outlaws: Jesse James, Billy the Kid, Pretty Boy Floyd, and later Al Capone. Playwright Elizabeth Beall Ginty also contributed to the popularization of Jesse James and his identification with Robin Hood in her play *Missouri Legend* (1938) promoting James as the "Robin Hood of the Ozarks," who took from the rich to give to the poor. Outlaws and gangsters identified as the folkloric hero Robin Hood were, like Robin Hood, immortalized in ballads. Some might also add to this list of "outlaws" various political figures like Huey Long, who were "Robinhooded" for good or ill. In addition to the traditional period films set in the Middle Ages, Robin Hood also inspired Western films such as those produced by Republic Pictures: *Robin Hood of Texas* (1947), starring radio's Gene Autry, and *Robin Hood of the Pecos* (1941) and the *Trail of Robin Hood* (1950), starring another singing cowboy, Roy Rogers, who appeared on radio, television, and film.

From the Depression through the 1950s, novels and biographies trended toward reimagining notorious criminals, such as Pancho Villa, Jesse James, and Billy the Kid, as Robin Hoods of the West. Many Americans identified with Robin Hood. He too was a victim of oppression. Because Robin Hood was betrayed, the hero believed that "the law [was] corrupt" and that the innocent were persecuted, making him generous to the poor; Robin Hood was an unaggressive trickster figure who used disguise to outwit his opponents and recognized that "large classes of the population" are exempt from his revenge—as a result, he "never interfere[d]" with common people (Steckmesser 348, 350–52). Americans identified with this version of Robin Hood, making it easier for them to excuse Robin Hood's outlawry. The tradition of the Western tended to dress the outlawed cowboy as a "good bad guy," a "Robin Hood in a coat of tarnished tin" with the understanding that "debt's to one's friends must be paid" (Frantz and Choate 72). For instance, the Lone Ranger was a "hero of small boys and old women alike," and was described as a "Lochinvar and Robin Hood" (Wylie 279). He was a gentler version of Wister's cow-puncher.

George Trendle imagined his brainchild the Lone Ranger as a knight-errant and modern-day Robin Hood. *The Lone Ranger* radio program first aired on WXYZ in Detroit in 1933 and on various other radio stations as it grew in popularity. Mutual picked up the show in 1939, the Blue Network, later known as ABC, began airing the show from 1942 through 1954, and then the show aired through 1956 as a transcribed program. *The Lone Ranger* saturated American popular culture, featuring in comic books, Big Little Books, novels, a magazine, films, television, live performances in rodeos and state fairs, fan clubs, and organizations. The Lone Ranger is now firmly entrenched in American popular culture thanks to the program's signature introduction: an overlay of music, the *William Tell Overture*, and the famous and oft-quoted lines, "A fiery horse with the speed of light, a cloud of dust and a hearty 'Hi-Yo Silver! ... The Lone Ranger rides again!"

George Stenius originated the role of this masked cowboy-knight and played the earliest Lone Ranger in 1933, followed by Earle Graser from 1933 to 1941, and Brace Beemer from 1941 to 1954. John Todd played the masked man's Indian partner Tonto. Following Graser's death in an automobile accident in 1941, an editorial in the *New York Times* paid homage to the actor for his convincing portrayal of the Lone Ranger, a figure that the editorial describes as a composite of modern and medieval heroes. For writer and many others like him, the Lone Ranger was a combination of some of the greats: "Ulysses, William Tell, ... Robin Hood, Richard the Lion Hearted, Kit Carson, Daniel Boone, and Davey Crockett," a hero who was "truth and bravery" ("The Immortal Ranger"). Don Beattie, a scriptwriter for the radio program, saw similarities between the Lone Ranger and Robin Hood in their common emphasis on justice, but Beattie stopped short of romanticizing Robin Hood's image.

Beattie described Robin Hood a social bandit and more of a "rogue" (qtd. in Dorfman 64) than a chivalric hero. Unlike Robin Hood, the Lone Ranger did not begrudge the rich and powerful for what they had, as long as they did not trample "on the rights of the little people" (qtd. in Dorfman 64). James Gray, writing in 1954, described the Lone Ranger as a "Robin Hood of the frontier, minus 'merrie men, [who] operates a kind of one-man Community Chest, producing in his own rugged and romantic way, help for the needy and hard-pressed" (216). In wartime, and as part of the war effort, children had enlisted in the *Jack Armstrong* fan club; likewise, "hundreds of thousands of children" became members of The Lone Ranger Victory Corps, an organization "dedicated to victory, responsibility, citizenship, safety, and health" that enlisted members in the war effort (Waller 242). The Lone Ranger continued to be a cult figure in books, comic books and comic strips, on radio, on television, and in movies. Sponsorship came from regional bakeries and General Mills's Cheerios (Dunning 404). *The Lone Ranger* played simultaneously on television and radio from 1949 to 1957, with Clayton Moore as the Lone Ranger and Jay Silverheels as Tonto.

Westerns first aired on radio in the 1930s, but these programs failed to make an impact with adult listeners until the 1950s. Early radio Westerns were intended for younger listeners or followed the musical format popularized by the singing cowboys, Gene Autry and Roy Rogers. In the late 1940s and into the early 1950s, adult Westerns like *Gunsmoke* became grittier (MacDonald 216, 229). While radio Westerns were on the air, they provided "poignant reflections of American life ... and transmit[ed] societal standards" (MacDonald 208–09) in much the same way as children's radio programming had already been doing. Despite exhibiting a penchant for violence, knights and cowboys were readily adapted by scriptwriters for audiences who were willing to overlook lawless behavior. In the radio Western, the "good guy" cowboy could be a cowboy-knight with Robin Hood's gallantry as a hero of the oppressed. Using adjectives usually reserved for Robin Hood, Fred J. MacDonald describes the cowboy of radio as a champion of the oppressed and the weak, as well as a communicator of morality and a representative of society (209, 211, 214). Just as the Old West was a "soothing memory of the land that never was," adaptations of the legends of King Arthur and Robin Hood attempted to capture a unique "vision of a medieval world" (Rosenthal and Szarmach 8). As Bernard Rosenthal and Paul Szarmach suggest in *Medievalism in American Culture*, the familiar image of the "lone American cowboy riding into the sunset with the woman left behind, each ultimately too pure for any other outcome[,] ... is the juggling of America's paradoxical attractions for a country at once free from Europe and at the same time wedded to an Old World Medievalism" (7). While radio Westerns promoted the cowboy's chivalric qualities, such as his generosity, courtesy, and protection and championing of the weak and of the oppressed, storylines could also feature a Robin Hood–like cowboy, whose conduct bordered on the unlawful. The following section looks at how the popular radio Western *Gunsmoke* adapted Robin Hood's persona for a storyline that presents a civics lesson on good citizenship. "Robin Hood" parallels the way post-medieval medievalism was less about the medieval period and more about the century, or even the decade, in which the adaptation was produced.

27. *Gunsmoke*, "Robin Hood"

Radio Westerns of the 1950s could be overtly political and "product[s] of the realism in popular culture that developed during and after World War II" during a period of social and "economic inequalities" (MacDonald 217–18, 226). *Gunsmoke* was specifically written for "mature and intelligent individuals" and was a program that "demanded of its audience thoughtful reflection"; by doing so, the show "transcended mere entertainment and dealt with the stuff of life" in a world in which the "innocent are all too often victimized, and the guilty frequently escape earthly retribution" (Barabas and Barabas 4). *Gunsmoke* was CBS's most popular and longest running Western, airing on radio from 1952 to 1961 before moving to television and making history again with a twenty-year run that began in 1955. The radio program's multiple sponsors—Post Toasties, Ligget and Mauers Tobacco, Chesterfield and L&M Cigarettes—attested to the program's wide popularity. By choosing the contemporary and quite serious topics that they did, Norman Macdonnell and John Meston, the creators and writers of *Gunsmoke*, figured Dodge City, Kansas as a "metaphor for the world and the human condition" (Barabas and Barabas 5). Macdonnell and Meston use Robin Hood's medieval and post-medieval reputation to address contemporary issues significant for many Americans, despite the program's setting in a nineteenth-century frontier town.

Robin Hood's persona is appropriated by a violent thief in an episode of *Gunsmoke* that resonates with cynicism of civic institutions, corruption, and a lack of culpability. *Gunsmoke's* "Robin Hood" was broadcast on January 8, 1955, and this episode ranks among the better radio adaptations of the legend. This storyline was repeated twice on radio and later adopted for television. In "Robin Hood," Marshal Matt Dillon is no Sheriff of Nottingham and Teddy Bluefisher is no Robin Hood. The bandit who appropriates Robin Hood's myth is a criminal on the level of Jesse James, not the legend captured in the English ballad tradition and portrayed as a socio-political revolutionary in Ritson's eighteenth-century ballad collection, nor the easy-going benevolent hero adapted for children's literature and radio adaptations. Robin Hood comically bests the Sheriff of Nottingham in children's radio adaptations written for *Let's Pretend* and *Family Theater*; however, in *Gunsmoke*'s radio adaptation the law has the upper hand.

"Robin Hood" challenges the image of the legendary hero to distinguish for listeners the sometimes murky difference between a social bandit and criminal bandit. Eric Hobsbawn points out that the social bandit is a hero of the "marginal and outcast" who, like Robin Hood, operates within society and "could call on the goodwill of every man who [is] not a personal enemy or an agent of authority" (179).[6] On the contrary, criminal bandits are "heroes only among the marginal and outcast" and operate in the "underworld" (Hobsbawn 179). British highwaymen in the seventeenth and eighteenth centuries—like Dick Turpin and his fellow criminal bandits—became cult heroes, and their stories were sung about in broadside ballads and recorded in criminal biographies, even though they robbed and killed their victims and were hung for their crimes. In the *Gunsmoke* episode "Robin Hood," a criminal named Teddy Bluefisher appropriates Robin Hood's reputation. Marshal Dillon correctly judges the reaction Dodge City's residents will have on meeting Teddy Bluefisher. Instead of identifying him as the crook that he is, the townspeople are taken in by Robin Hood's reputation for helping the poor, and they protect him.

Bluefisher is a wolf in sheep's clothing, a Dick Turpin and Jesse James rolled into one, a rogue who will not hesitate to take what he wants at gunpoint, even from a poor farmer and his wife. The motif of disguise is adopted in this episode, as it is in most radio adaptations, but not by the benevolent hero of the Robin Hood tradition dressing as beggar or a merchant to get revenge on the evil Sheriff of Nottingham. Instead, under Bluefisher's flour sack and duster beats the heart of a violent criminal like Jesse James or Billy the Kid. When the Bowens, a hard-working couple, welcome Teddy Bluefisher into their home, they become his next victims. Teddy Bluefisher appropriates Robin Hood's legacy to illicit public sympathy during his crime spree. Meston sets his radio drama in the Old West, but incorporates medieval tropes to address contemporary issues, thereby engaging in medievalism. The Bowens' experience with Teddy Bluefisher suggests that their victimization is the risk people take when they adopt as a hero anyone who works contrary to civil authority. Thematically this episode suggests class warfare caused by economic inequality, though it also stresses the overriding importance of civil authority. A close reading of the radio script also suggests a link between economic disparity, as represented by the Bowens, and Robin Hood's persona as a celebrity criminal and champion of the poor. Marshal Dillon's remark that "banks make money even when their doors are closed" (Meston) is especially critical of the banking industry and American capitalism.

"Robin Hood" opens with Marshal Dillon meeting a stagecoach carrying Kitty, the owner of the Long Branch Saloon, and Mr. Botkin, a banker. Along their route, Kitty and Botkin were robbed by a man they describe for the Marshal as a gentleman "lone bandit," dressed in a "long linen duster," wearing a hood made from a flour sack (Meston 1–2). According to Marshal Dillon, who recognizes this description, the highwayman is Teddy Bluefisher, who supposedly has a reputation for robbing the rich and sparing the poor and "for being quite a gentleman about the whole business" (Meston 4). Deputy Chester Proudfoot's response to this description suggests that he is vaguely familiar with Robin Hood's legend. Chester associates the British legend with Native Americans, referring to Robin Hood as that "wild man" of the green wood but comically mispronouncing Hood as "Head," and describes the medieval hero of the downtrodden as "that green Indian they had over in one of them foreign lands one time" (Meston 5). Obviously the reference to this stranger's green garb is a reference to Robin Hood's Lincoln-green clothing. Undoubtedly this was enough of a description for the audience to associate with Teddy Bluefisher what they knew about Robin Hood as the easy-going, benevolent bandit who comically bests the Sheriff, a buffoon.

Marshal Dillon too is familiar with Robin Hood's myth, but when he comments that Teddy Bluefisher will steal from anyone, the listener is on unsteady ground. Marshal Dillon warns Chester that the residents of Dodge City will likely make the same dangerous association of Bluefisher with Robin Hood, as would the radio audience. Marshal Dillon assumes that the populace of the nineteenth-century frontier town would be familiar enough with the English legend that they might be sympathetic to a stranger acting the part, which might have been an accurate assumption considering the popularity of dime novels featuring the likes of Jesse James. To quell the potential disorder that might occur if he arrests Teddy Bluefisher, who might be seen by the residents of Dodge as a champion of the oppressed, Marshal Dillon acts quickly to reveal the man for what he is, a common thief who steals "from anybody … rich *or* poor" (Meston 7, emphasis added). He correctly suspects that Teddy Bluefisher's "whole game is based on" Robin Hood's legend and his reputation for "stealing from the rich," though the Marshal does not directly reference Robin Hood. Dillon organizes a fixed poker game in which Teddy Bluefisher loses his money and is forced to commit another crime.

Marshal Dillon correctly predicts that Teddy Bluefisher will embark on a crime spree to recoup his losses, and when he does, the lawman plans to be there. Bluefisher's first victims are the type of people Robin Hood would champion: farmers who live frugally and have something to show for their hard work. Marshal Dillon and Chester follow Bluefisher to the Bowens' farm, where they overhear a conversation in which the couple expresses their admiration for the thief and their distrust of banks. The Bowens share with Teddy Bluefisher their feelings of being cheated by the bank. The premise of the Bowen's argument is that the rich have too much while the poor have too little. Yet this couple does not appear to go without. Bluefisher is impressed by what he sees—"a nice house and some stock"—and compares what they have to "most folks" who "got nothing but a patch of corn and a sod hut" (Meston 15). Not everyone is so lucky, however. Times are tough, and that is why Dodge City needs a social bandit, someone like Robin Hood. As Mrs. Bowen voices her sympathy about her neighbors' harsh living conditions, Teddy Bluefisher promises to be like Robin Hood and make things right.

As Charlie Bowen explains, in times like these, "we kinda stand behind a man like you, Mr. Fisher," and not a wealthy man like Botkin, who apparently has more money than he needs and can afford to lose some of it (Meston 15). Bluefisher agrees with him and replies that "bankers don't have all the money in the world" (Meston 15). Unfortunately for the couple, Mrs. Bowen plays right into Bluefisher's hands when she tells him that neither Botkin nor the bank has their savings and "never will" (Meston 15). Teddy Bluefisher realizes the Bowens' savings is hidden somewhere on the homestead. Contrary to expectations about how Robin Hood would behave, Bluefisher draws his gun and robs the surprised couple. Unmoved by their shock and disappointment that he is no Robin Hood, Bluefisher boasts that he has robbed the poor before (Meston).

Marshal Dillon and Chester watch these events unfold and reveal themselves before anyone gets hurt. As the Marshal takes Teddy Bluefisher into custody, he delivers a coded warning to the criminal and to the radio audience: Teddy Bluefisher's capture is a warning to "other Robin Hoods like [you]" who will "be finished, too, when people hear what you're like when you think nobody's watching" (Meston 17). Here Marshal Dillon emphasizes the dangers of the criminal celebrity. Listeners would gather from the premise of this episode that assigning a criminal bandit such as Teddy Bluefisher, or anyone perceived to be a social bandit like Robin Hood, celebrity status under the rubric of "Robin Hood," seriously threatens civil authority.

8

Lighthearted Adaptations

Though long past its prime as a primary source for news and entertainment, radio was, and still is thanks to the Internet, a "vibrant and engaging form of storytelling" that can outdo "the best of motion pictures and television" (DeForest, *Radio* 228). Unlike these visual mediums, the aural medium of radio ignited the listening audience's imagination and encouraged imaginative play. During its heyday, radio was held in high regard and was expected to meet rather high expectations. Ideally, radio's goals were to turn a profit while delivering "educationally instructive" material (Bailey 1). For their part, scriptwriters were expected to produce quality programs for a mixed audience. According to critics and radio watchdogs, however, radio programs often fell short and failed to meet such lofty expectations. However, hardworking scriptwriters such as Norman Corwin, Arch Obler, and Orson Welles proved that writers could produce very good programs based on original content and on adaptations of classic novels, short stories, folk and fairy tales, films, and plays. Adaptations of Malory's *Le Morte Darthur*; the medieval romances of Scott, Tennyson, and Pyle, and adaptations of Robin Hood's legend based on Pyle; and medieval ballads were broadcast on many programs: *Let's Pretend, Family Theater, Smilin' Ed's Buster Brown Gang, Popeye, The Land of the Lost, The Adventures of Superman, Prince Valiant, Escape,* and the radio Westerns *Wild Bill Hickok, The Cisco Kid,* and *Gunsmoke*.

With the increase in the number of radio stations and the availability of affordable sets, critics and proponents of radio correctly predicted that the aural medium had the potential to significantly alter people's lives. Children were particularly vulnerable to what they heard on radio. Juvenile radio programming was therefore expected to follow the earlier example of children's literature and act as a "socializing agent" that imparted American values (MacDonald 46). This was especially true during wartime when young fans were encouraged to follow the example of characters like Jack Armstrong in *Jack Armstrong the All-American Boy*, an entertaining and educational program that emphasized respect for authority and adherence to moral living. Jack Armstrong exhibited the qualities young fans should practice in their daily lives in order to better their world.

Research into the children's book publishing industry and college textbooks published for aspiring radio scriptwriters suggest a correlation between the standards created at the turn of the century for children's literature and the 1930s "children's code," which was voluntarily adopted by the radio networks ABC, CBS, NBC, and Mutual. Juvenile literature and children's radio programs were charged with avoiding depictions of adult content and overt violence. In response to concerns about radio content in the 1930s, radio watchdogs—parents, educators, sociologists, and radio professionals—called for the regulation of content produced for children's radio programming. While children did enjoy tamer and perhaps more appropriate radio programs like *Let's Pretend* and *Family Theater*, they also listened to the same programs as their parents, mysteries and detective programs like *The Whistler* (1942–1955), *Suspense* (1942–1952), and *Dragnet* (1949–1957), and even horror anthologies such as *The Witch's Tale* (1931–1938) and *Inner Sanctum* (1941–1952).

The legends of King Arthur and Robin Hood were particularly easy for scriptwriters to adapt for radio. These legends were flexible, familiar, and could be made appropriate for an audience of all ages once the violent and sexual content was expurgated. Radio adaptations of these legends were soon found across radio genres, in children's programs such as *Popeye*, *Wild Bill Hickok*, and *The Cisco Kid*; in adult Westerns and dramas such as the well-acted classic *Gunsmoke* and the gripping adventure anthology *Escape*; and in *Crime Classics*, Martin Fine and David Friedkin's melodrama that dramatized the affair of Guinevere and Lancelot and King Arthur's death.

In the next section is a sample of radio programs not included in the overall analysis for two reasons: either the adaptation or appropriation of the King Arthur and Robin Hood legend was the material for a parody or gag, or the radio program aired after the 1950s. The following summaries offer an overview of skits based on the legends, as they were aired on Walt Disney's *Mickey Mouse Theater of the Air*, Red Skelton's *Avalon Time*, *Abbott and Costello*, *Sealtest Variety Theater*, *The Story Lady*, and *Crisis*. The only adaptations that even come close to mentioning chivalry were aired on *Abbott and Costello* and *Sealtest Variety Theater*. Thus the radio programs discussed in the following section were aired purely for entertainment.

28. *Mickey Mouse Theater of the Air*, "King Arthur"

King Arthur and Robin Hood were adapted and appropriated for a number of other radio programs. Unfortunately many of these are only searchable by title and are unavailable to hear online. In the 1930s, Walt Disney's half-hour children's program and musical variety series *Mickey Mouse Theater of the Air* produced an adaptation titled "King Arthur." No recording or script exists for this April 17 episode. Disney's program aired on NBC from January through May in 1938 and was sponsored by Pepsodent. The show featured thirty-minute adaptations of favorite children's tales such as *Snow White, Cinderella, The Old Woman in the Shoe,* and *Old MacDonald's Farm*. However, only twenty episodes were written for the program. John Hiestand was the announcer; Walt Disney hosted the program and voiced Mickey Mouse. The cast featured Disney cartoon characters Minnie Mouse and Donald Duck. The program was broadcast from the Disney Little Theater on the RKO lot. The program's originating broadcast coincided with the release of Disney's first feature-length animated film, *Snow White and the Seven Dwarfs* (458).

29. Red Skelton's *Avalon Time*, King Arthur and Robin Hood

King Arthur and Robin Hood were appropriated by the vaudeville actor and radio star Red Skelton in the 1930s. Skelton took liberties with the legends and history, claiming as Skelton ancestors King Arthur, Robin Hood, Napoleon Bonaparte and even Marco Polo in a series of skits produced for NBC's thirty-minute variety show *Avalon Time*. Sponsored by Avalon Cigarettes, *Avalon Time* was on the air from 1938 to 1940. Skelton's "Arthur Skelton aka The Thousand Dollars" and "Robin Hood aka Party at Red's House" do little with the legends other than borrow characters and tropes for a series of gags. "Arthur Skelton aka The Thousand Dollars" aired on March 18, 1939, and "Robin Hood aka Party at Red's House" aired

8. Lighthearted Adaptations

April 22, 1939. "Arthur Skelton aka The Thousand Dollars" is set in Britain, with Skelton playing King Arthur and Skelton's wife Edna Stillwell Skelton playing Guinevere. Red Foley, the country singer who with his band provided the music for the program, plays Sir Long Slot Foley, Guinevere's paramour. The title of the episode is misleading, given that lust, not money, drives this skit in which Edna Skelton's "lap-happy" Guinevere channels American sex symbol Mae West, neglecting her housekeeping and openly running around with Sir Long Foley (Lancelot) ("King Arthur"). The skit ends with a light-hearted duel between Arthur and Foley that ends in a draw. Skelton's "Robin Hood aka Party at Red's House" skit, set in Sherwood, depends on puns and treats as a joke Robin Hood's penchant for stealing gold and evading the Sheriff of Nottingham. Robin Hood Skelton's "yes men" are the feminized Alan of Drool who speaks with a lisp, Little John, Friar Tuck, and Robin Hood.

30. *Abbott and Costello*, "Knights in Shining Armor"

The comic duo of William "Bud" Abbott and Lou Costello also borrowed from Arthurian legend and the concept of the chivalric knight for a series of one-liners for a skit "Knights in Shining Armor," aired on the *Abbott and Costello* radio show. Abbott and Costello became partners in 1936, performing in vaudeville and burlesque shows before ending up on the radio program "The Kate Smith Hour." The *Abbott and Costello* radio program aired on NBC from 1940 to 1947, later transitioning to ABC, where it would remain until 1949. Camel cigarettes was the program's sponsor. Beginning in the 1940s, Abbott and Costello also made a series of films for Universal. American and British film actress Merle Oberon is the featured guest in "Knights in Shining Armor" a thirty-minute skit. Oberon plays Guinevere, Abbott is Sir Loin, and Costello is Sir Porterhouse. The cast includes Warner Brothers star Mel Blanc, who voices Botsford Twink, a character who suffers from severe hiccups induced by nerves, as well as Blanc's beloved cartoon characters Bugs Bunny and Porky Pig. The announcer is Ken Niles, an electric organ provides sound effects, and music for the program is provided by Leith Stevens and his orchestra, the Camel Five, along with singer Connie Haines.

This episode was broadcast live from Long Beach, California, on

November 19, 1942, for the Army Air Force Sixth Ferrying Group Air Transport. During wartime it was common practice for live radio programs to be broadcast as morale boosters on military bases stateside and overseas. The Air Corps Ferrying Command in Washington had been activated in June 1941; two months later, Long Beach Municipal Airport established the Western Division of the Ferrying Command in California. The Sixth Ferrying Group Air Transport Command was soon organized and quickly became identified as the "most versatile pilots in the world," ferrying trainers, fighters, bombers, and transports supplying air power to Allied forces (Sixth Ferrying Group 43–44). In February 1943, the WASPs, Women's Airforce Service Pilots, were activated to replace pilots sent overseas.[1] Many wartime radio programs would include references to wartime. This was a year of intense food rationing and a serious meat shortage, which probably inspired the episode's unusual surnames "Sir Loin" and "Sir Porterhouse." Women's wartime fashions, the "defense dress" and leg paint to substitute for stockings, are also mentioned in passing.

In a humorous attempt to lend a sense of authenticity to the skit "Knights in Shining Armor," Niles as the king speaks with an Americanized British accent with a heavy emphasis on rolling "Rs," but he fails to be convincing compared to Oberon's accent. Abbott and the squeaky voiced Costello, best-known for his attention getting line "Heyyyyy Abbott!" introduce the skit. Abbott is producing a film titled "The Brave Knight Cut off the Dragon's Tale, or the Dragon Isn't Waggin' Anymore" for the fictional Perfume Productions, Incorporated, and he needs a leading lady. One-liners drive this skit. Abbott and Costello are rehearsing for their new picture, a tale about the "knights of old." Costello plays the leading man, the brave Sir Loin. "Why Costello?" asks Oberon—"I thought knights were tall." To which Costello quips: "On account of daylight savings time, knights are getting shorter" (*Abbott and Costello*). Guinevere and the king await the arrival of "two brave knights, Sir Loin of the Bath from Saxony (Costello) and Sir Porterhouse (Abbott) from Constantinople," known for its Turkish baths (*Abbott and Costello*). Costello will save Guinevere and kill the dragon that burned the cornfields, an act that has left the now-angry villagers to starve (*Abbott and Costello*).

Sir Loin sneaks across the moat and climbs to Guinevere's balcony. Abbott directs Costello to look into her eyes and sets up the fall guy. Abbott delivers his line: "What will you say as you stand there in your iron suit" gazing into her eyes? Costello answers: "Hey, kid. You got a can opener?" (*Abbott and Costello*). Guinevere rivets Sir Loin's armor, a skill she acquired "work[ing] the swing shift on the side" and readies him for battle with the dragon (*Abbott and Costello*). Just as the audience would expect of Abbott and Costello, the last few minutes of the routine spiral into chaos and end in laughter. Costello threatens to cut off the nose of the dragon, who is played by the hiccupping Botsford Twink. Oberon's kiss cures him of hiccups.

31. *Proudly We Hail,* "Knights in Armor"

This next radio program did not air until 1957, but it is another good example of how medieval tropes, such as chivalric knighthood, can be incorporated into patriotic tales that identify the modern American soldier with the medieval chivalric knight. "Knights in Armor" is a thirty-minute drama about an American soldier searching for his sisters, who were left behind in Vicenzia, Italy, during World War II, and discovering more than he expected. As an Italian-American Army soldier, protagonist Enzio Cabrini is a blending of old world chivalry and modern maleness. "Knights in Armor" aired on *Proudly We Hail, the United States Army*[2] on April 7, 1957. *Proudly We Hail* was a public service program produced by the U.S. Army and Air Force Recruiting Publicity Department. The radio program presented a series of fiction and nonfiction dramas punctuated by a series of recruitment advertisements for the armed forces. The program initially aired for four months on CBS in 1941 and was back on the air from 1946 through 1957. The producer was C. P. MacGregor, and the program was broadcast from New York City.

Enzio is an army infantryman investigating the rumors that his sisters were Nazi sympathizers during the war: his quest is to prove the story false and to regain the Cabrini family honor. Enzio is the descendent of a long line of Cabrinis, "knights who sought to free their medieval world from tyranny," and as an American, he learned "to live by—honor and justice" ("Knights in Armor"). Here Enzio connects the medieval European knighthood and American ideals. These qualities also happen to be identified with Robin Hood. According to the unidentified narrator, this is a story in which "truth is victorious" ("Knights in Armor"); however, Enzio ultimately fails in his quest. He never shares his findings with the people of Vicenzia that would regain his family's honor, which he so desperately seeks.

Listeners are provided with a summary of the family history. The Cabrinis are descendants of a long line of well-respected knights, a point Enzio emphasizes a few times throughout the program. Enzio and his brothers are sent to the United States when fascist Benito Mussolini takes power of Italy in order to protect them from conscription into a fascist youth organization and war. Unfortunately, money and events prevent the boys' sisters, Marissa and Rosanna, from immigrating as well. The setting is Vicenza, Italy, on September 29, 1955. Enzio is among the soldiers in the First Battalion of the 350th Infantry Regiment of the United States Army, known as the Red Knights, and part of the Southern European Task Force (SETAF) that left Austria following the signing of the Austrian State Treaty on May 15, 1955.[3] The narrator soberly states that this is not the first trip to the area for the Red Knights. They "had been there before, or at least a few of them had. For many replacements had been made in the fighting units that thrashed its way up the boot of Italy to become the first American unit to reach the city in 1945 after breaching Hitler's gothic line" ("Knights in Armor").

In Act One, Enzio learns through a discussion with the Vicenzia town clerk that during the Nazi occupation, Marissa and Rosanna became too friendly with the occupying troops and were accused of colluding with the enemy. When the Allied forces arrived in 1945, the sisters were driven out of town and disappeared. Because of what was perceived to be their traitorous act, the entire Cabrini family history was stricken from the town registry. All along Enzio refuses to believe that his sisters collaborated with the enemy. Enzio and the audience are unaware that Marissa and Rosanna were actually spies feeding the Americans information about Nazi troop movements.

In Act Two, Enzio, with the help of Gina, a resident of Vicenza who knows the Cabrini family story and about the "day of shame" ("Knights in Armor"), tracks his sister Marissa to the Convent of the Sisters of San Marco; Rosanna has died years earlier. Despite being afraid to confront his sister with the truth, and the Mother Superior's explanation that "[it] was our shame that such things happened" and nothing can be gained from such a quest but to "bring pain to old wounds" ("Knights in Armor"), Enzio presses on. Marisssa, now a nun, has been in the convent all along and enters the scene to share her tale.

Marissa tells her story. No one in the town knew the sisters had been recruited to work for the Americans by Carlo Bertelli, who was, a little too conveniently, Enzio's former neighbor in the states. Bertelli knew about the Cabrini family from his friendly conversations with Enzio. When he was parachuted into the area, Bertelli tracked down the sisters and recruited them to the war effort. Just as the division of Red Knights approached, the Nazis ambushed and killed Carlo. Predictably, no one in Vicenza realized the girls were spies. Marissa and Rosanna were banished, sought shelter in the local convent, and took their vows. Ten years later, Marissa is content and believes nothing can be gained by now sharing her story. Considering how driven he was to uncover the truth and restore the Cabrini family honor, Enzio gives up his quest a little too easily. Despite the episode's title "Knight in Armor," which suggests that a man, or men, resolved the story's conflict, women are, in fact, the ones who behave valiantly when they risk their lives and reputations to help the village. Enzio's search for his family history is not part of his service as a soldier; furthermore, he even requires the help of another female helpmate, Gina, to lead him to his sister. Presumably the title is a reference to the Army soldier as the modern knight. The story concludes with Enzio satisfied that he has done his best for his family and the announcement that his next quest is to "win the fair lady" Gina ("Knights in Armor").

Enzio's last remark is punctuated by the notes of a trumpet to further emphasize the "medievalness" of this modern tale. In spite of the predictability of the plot, "Knights in Armor" is a well-acted story that incorporates sound effects to its advantage, creating a sense of realism for the radio audience through effects such as the engine noise made by Army jeeps, transport trucks struggling to climb a steep pass, and a blowing snowstorm.

32. *The Story Lady*, "King Arthur" and "Robin Hood"

The Story Lady is an example of the lengths to which a radio scriptwriter will go to adapt material to radio. As the Story Lady, Joan Gerber entertained radio listeners with adult versions of bowdlerized adaptations of fairy tales and literature with a unique twist. For example, The Story Lady's version of Shakespeare's *Romeo and Juliet*, which lasts about one minute and twenty seconds and concludes with the violent deaths of the young lovers, is written with a storybook happy ending. *The Story Lady* was a syndicated show out of Los Angeles with Byron Kane as the program's announcer. Gerber voiced a number of cartoon characters on television and in the movies. In this radio show Gerber narrates unique, parodic comic one-minute adaptations of classic folk and fairy tales that range from the legends of King Arthur and Robin Hood, Billy the Kid, and "Little Red Riding Hood," to literary classics such as Fyodor Dostoevsky's *The Brothers Karamasov*, Charlotte Brontë's *Jane Eyre*, and Cervantes' *Don Quixote*. Although *The Story Lady* was a product of the 1960s and is, therefore, beyond the scope of this study, Gerber's program illustrates the extremes to which radio scriptwriters would go to adapt King Arthur and Robin Hood to radio for a particular audience.

Kane introduces each brief tale with the standard line: "And now boys and girls, it's time for another story from the Story Lady." At one minute and twenty-three seconds, the story "King Arthur" only focuses on one now-familiar episode of the legend adapted *ad nauseam* in literature, on radio, and in film—Arthur pulling the sword from the stone. Disney released its animated musical and version of events as *The Sword in the Stone* in 1963, an adaptation of T. H. White's novel *The Once and Future King* (1938, 1958). Gerber's adaptation of "King Arthur" is undated.

The Story Lady sets up her tale with the stock phrase reserved for the fairy tale: "Once upon a time, a long time ago" (Gerber, "King Arthur"). As she explains, "merry old England" was without a king which "disturbed a lot people," but "mainly the French Canadians who had no body to holler at" (Gerber, "King Arthur"), a line inserted for laughs. Gerber sticks fairly close to the events as told originally, but makes a few interesting alterations. Missing from this version of Malory's tale is the archbishop, the anvil inscribed with letters of gold stating that the individual who succeeds pulling out the sword is Britain's rightful king, and Sir Kay's attempts to free the sword. Merlin appears to the people announcing that a "rock" with a "great" sword driven into it is located somewhere near London, and the person who pulls out the sword will become king (Gerber, "King Arthur"). Arthur, here of an indeterminate age, appears and sets to work, tugging and straining "for hours" before finally pulling the sword free (Gerber, "King Arthur"). Instead of concluding with the crowning of King Arthur, the Story Lady puts an interesting and humorous twist on events when the newly designated king is "rushed to the nearest hospital for a hernia operation" (Gerber, "King Arthur").

"Robin Hood" is another short radio narrative lasting only one minute and seventeen seconds that focuses on a familiar scene captured many times in adaptations of Robin Hood's legend. This tale is also set in "merry old England" and begins by introducing Robin Hood as someone known to run "around with ... outlaws in Sherwood Forest," who steals from the rich to give to the poor (Gerber, "Robin Hood"). The Story Lady's narrative focuses on Robin Hood winning the Sheriff of Nottingham's archery contest and concludes with a surprising and darkly humorous twist. In this version of events, Robin Hood enters the contest "cleverly disguise[d] ... as Errol Flynn," a jab at Flynn's iconic Robin Hood role in the 1938 Technicolor film, *The Adventures of Robin Hood*. After hitting the bullseye, Robin Hood proceeds to split his opponent's arrow in half while it was "still in its quiver" causing Sir Dwayne to bleed a lot and to die "quietly on the village green, leaving Robin Hood the undisputed winner" (Gerber, "Robin Hood").

33. *Crisis*, "The Robin Hood Heist"

As the 1960s syndicated *The Story Lady* attests, radio programs—comedies, dramas, and suspense anthologies, did not entirely disappear from the airwaves. Radio dramas continued to be written and aired well into the twentieth century. Another entertaining example of Robin Hood adapted for the air is found in 1975 on the syndicated radio program *Crisis*, a suspense anthology produced by Jim French. "The Robin Hood Heist Ep. 53," a twenty-minute broadcast on January 2, 1975, features actor Keenan Wynn in an adaptation that borrows the motif of disguise that is popular in so many adaptations of Robin Hood's legend. Joe Toledo narrates this story of the double-cross. Most of the action takes place on a train outside of Chicago. Vance, whose real names is Charles, disguises himself as an insurance agent and entices a retired thief to help with the recovery of a $350,000 diamond necklace. Toledo agrees to help steal the already stolen goods and split Vance's commission. Dressing as a Catholic priest and adopting an Irish accent, Toledo gains the confidence of the necklace's owner, who also happens to be Vince's girlfriend. During a mock arrest planned by one of his prison mates disguised as a police officer, Toledo tricks Vince in to giving him the necklace and the story ends.

* * * *

Medieval and post-medieval authors, including adapters writing twentieth-century radio episodes for programs such as those considered here, reworked and revised the legends of King Arthur and Robin Hood to suit the period in which they were writing, as well as to cater to their audience's taste. As had literary adapters, radio scriptwriters sometimes coded their adaptations of Arthurian romance and the legend of Robin Hood with contemporary subjects. Often the result was an entertaining, didactic tale of chivalry written specifically for a modern listener. Still other scriptwriters followed Red Skelton's lead, taking artistic liberties with the source text and creating skits that parodied the trope of medieval romance and the legends of King Arthur and Robin Hood.

While children's authors, youth organizations, and radio scriptwriters promoted the chivalric code as a model example of virtuous behavior and good citizenship, such as that practiced by Jack Armstrong, character-building organizations were also influenced by Arthurian myth. At the same time, fascist organizations such as the Ku Klux Klan and the Nazi Party subverted the idea of chivalry and appropriated Arthurian legend for an agenda that promoted racism and fascism. Radio scriptwriters practiced medievalism when they coded their radio plays with a modern context and addressed these and other timely, and quite serious, topics such as patriotism, war, McCarthyism, and economic disparity, all perceived threats to the stability of American society of the 1903s, 1940s and 1950s. For instance, ever alert to the current climate, radio writer and producer Robert Maxwell engaged with medievalism when he addressed bigotry in a post–Second World War storyline produced for *The Adventures of Superman*, and when he incorporated images and tropes identified with Arthurian legend for his modern allegory "Knights of the White Carnation."

Radio adaptations of medieval romance were an amalgam of complex sound effects, music, narratives that provided vivid descriptions of characters and events, and dialogue that created auditory time travel intended to play out in the listener's imagination. Listeners tuned their radio dials to hear *Let's Pretend, Family Theater, The Adventures of Superman*, or *Prince Valiant* and imagined that they traveled back to the Middle Ages to watch a medieval jousting tournament, rode alongside Sir Lancelot on his quest for the Holy Grail, slew a fire-breathing dragon, or championed the oppressed. The theater of the mind made this possible.

Chapter Notes

Prologue

1. Malory does not provide a title for his book but only refers to it as *The Hoole Book of Kyng Arthur and of His Noble Knyghtes of the Rounde Table* (Works 726). William Caxton, the early editor and printer of Malory's book, printed the Westminster edition in 1485 and titled it *Le Morte Darthur*, the correct title. Nevertheless, the common misspelling *D'Arthur* or *d'Arthur* plagues the work. A quick Internet search suggests that *D' Arthur* or *d' Arthur* has become standard usage with even the British Library referring to *Le Morte Darthur* as *Le Morte D'Arthur* (see https://www.bl.uk/collection-items/thomas-malorys-le-morte-darthur). A search for *"D'Arthur"* in the Robbins Library digital *Camelot Project*, a database of Arthurian resources, images, and texts and a project sponsored by the University of Rochester, lists Arthurian works—texts and art—titled *"d'Arthur"* or *"D' Arthure"* (http://d.lib.rochester.edu). Many of these books, poems, illustrations, and paintings were produced in the nineteenth-century during the medieval revival and in the early twentieth century. In this study of radio adaptations of Arthurian legend in the twentieth century, references to Malory's book follow Caxton's example and use the correct title *Le Morte Darthur*. Quotations from Eugène Vinaver's edition *The Works of Sir Thomas Malory* published by Oxford University Press, 1971 and are referenced using the book's full title *The Works of Sir Thomas Malory*, or, for brevity, Malory's *Works*.

Chapter 1

1. At the start of his radio career Welles, at twenty-two, played the mysterious detective Lamont Cranston from 1937 to 1938 in the long-running and popular crime melodrama *The Shadow*, broadcast on Mutual. The Shadow's identity remained a mystery. He solved crimes using his "hypnotic power to cloud men's minds."

2. Broadcasts by electrophone were being developed in the United States in 1891. Broadcasts were made by radio phone in the 1920s.

Chapter 2

1. Huey Long, a charismatic and controversial politician, adapted a popular radio icon for his own purpose. He called himself "Kingfish" after the "schemer" George "Kingfish" Stevens, a character in *Amos 'n' Andy*, one of the nation's most popular radio programs (MacDonald 133). Two white vaudeville actors, Southerner Freeman Fisher Gosden and Midwesterner Charles J. Corell, played the parts of Amos and Andy. Radio programs did feature programs that dramatized "minority-group life" (Barnouw, *A Tower*, 274), although African-American characters were for the most part played by white actors. *Amos 'n' Andy*, one of radio's most important and influential programs, was first broadcast as *Sam 'n' Henry* in Chicago on WGN in 1926 and had a presence on radio and television until 1960.

Chapter 3

1. For a comprehensive discussion of chivalric literature published in America and England for children, see Richmond's *Chivalric Stories as Children's Literature: Edwardian Retellings in Words and Pictures* (McFarland, 2014).
2. This last chapter was a direct response to and reflection of the Temperance Movement that encouraged Americans to limit their use of alcohol. The Temperance Movement was a nationwide effort organized by Protestant churches in the mid–1880s and was supported by female crusaders such as the Women's Christian Temperance Organization.
3. Nila Mack came to CBS radio in 1928 and later directed children's show *The Adventures of Helen and Mary*, the forerunner of *Let's Pretend* (Dunning 392). Following Mack's death in 1953, the program aired for another year under the direction of Jean Hight.
4. A direct transcript of this episode was not available, so I have relied on the version as quoted in Harmon.

Chapter 4

1. According to Eugene Vinaver, Caxton had Malory's *Morte* on his press on July 31, 1485 (*Works* vi).
2. Howard Deitz, publicity chief for M-G-M, in a short piece written in 1954 to coincide with the release of the picture, attempts to stir up interest in the film by highlighting Malory's past. Deitz describes Malory as the one who "wrote the bible of chivalry and knightly courtesy and in private was a rogue, a robber, a rapist—a triple threat": a production company's nightmare, had Malory been a screenwriter in the twentieth century.
3. "The film's plot reflects earlier attempts by Lord Robert Baden-Powell, the founder of scouting, to model his organization in part on the fellowship of the Round Table. The film is "also part of an attempt in America to link the story of Arthur to the issue of the proper eductation of young boys" (Harty 9).
4. Dorothy Lamour starred in the Bob Hope and Bing Crosby "Road" films of the 1940s. During wartime she actively promoted war bonds and became known as the "bond bombshell."
5. The debonair Ray Milland was a regular on radio and, like Lamour, was Paramount star with a long career.
6. The story is that two Glencoe, Illinois, children, five-year-old Margo Chinnock and her seven-year-old brother John, helped promote the campaign (Ossian 5). For an interesting study of how children functioned during wartime, see Ossian's *The Forgotten Generation: American Children and World War II* (New York: Columbia University Press, 2011).

Chapter 5

1. According to Barnouw, Coughlin was assigned to the Shrine of the Little Flower in Royal Oak, Detroit, in 1926. His original radio broadcasts were for children. Coughlin changed his format into a program for adult listeners, where he covered politics and the "perils of communism, the 'red serpent'" and spoke critically of wealth (*Golden Web*, 45). Coughlin was a supporter of Franklin D. Roosevelt through the 1930s.
2. While their children read Arthurian literature and comic books, played Arthurian-themed board games, or watched Arthurian—and Robin Hood—themed television programs from the 1930s through the 1950s, mothers and grandmothers baked with King Arthur flour and listened to the King Arthur Coffee Club. As Barbara Lupack points out, King Arthur was entrenched in American popular culture by at least the 1930s, when "radio audiences turned into the 'King Arthur Coffee Club' and "King Arthur Round Table of Song' and learned of new products like King Arthur Coffee, Tea, and Wheat Germ," products also "distributed to the poor through the Knights of King Arthur, as one of the charitable acts performed by the boys' clubs" (281).
3. I have only guessed at the spelling of the names Rozutti and Kelley as variants exist.

Chapter 6

1. "Varlet," used as an insult referring to someone as a rogue or rascal, is dated to the 1560s, according to the *OED*. The word specifically referred to a servant or groom.
2. The Middle Ages was in vogue in Britain and in the United States during the nineteenth and twentieth centuries, two eras that experienced medievalism. Girouard describes the Eglinton tournament staged in July 1838 at Eglinton Castle in Ayrshire as "the most obviously famous produce of nineteenth-century chivalry in Great Britain" (88). Southern "gentlemen" in post–Civil War Virgina took to the local meadows to participate in a joust, dressed in armor as medieval knights. A medieval tournament was recreated once again in the South during the summer of 1924.

Chapter 7

1. Literature on the history of Robin Hood abounds. Studies of Robin Hood include Stephen Knight's *Robin Hood: A Complete Study of The English Outlaw* (Oxford: Blackwell, 1994); *Robin Hood: A Mythic Biography* (Ithaca, NY: Cornell University, 2003); and Knight and Thomas Ohlgren's *Robin Hood and Other Outlaw Tales* (Kalamazoo, Mich.: Western Michigan University, 2000).
2. "Robin Hood and the Curtal Friar" was included in Thomas Percy's *Reliques*.
3. For more on the debate about dating the early ballads of Robin Hood titled *A Gest of Robyn Hood*, a collection divided into eight Fittes, see Knight and Ohlgren.
4. The program assumed various titles during its run on radio: *Casey, Crime Photographer* was one, but also *Flashgun Casey* (1943–44); *Casey, Press Photographer* (1944–1945); *Crime Photographer* (1945–1948, 1954–5); and *Casey, Crime Photographer* (1947–1950).
5. Ethlebert the bartender shares his name with the Anglo-Saxon and Christian king Ethlebert.
6. Hobsbawm's *Bandits*, an in-depth and entertaining study of the bandit tradition, explores banditry at length.

Chapter 8

1. For a history of the Air Corps Ferrying Command, see the yearbook produced for the Sixth Ferrying Group Yearbook by the AAF Air Transport Command Ferrying Division.
2. This program is not to be confused with the wartime film *So Proudly We Hail!* (1943) starring Claudette Colbert, Paulette Goddard, and Veronica Lake as nurses caught behind enemy lines in the Bataan Peninsula on the island of Corregidor, following the bombing of Pearl Harbor.
3. With the signing of this historic document, Austria was recognized as an independent state, and American forces were withdrawn. The Southern European Task Force was not active until October 25 of that year, and Camp Darby in Vicenza became its headquarters.

Bibliography

AAF Air Transport Command Ferrying Division. *Sixth Ferrying Group Yearbook. Archive. org*, https://archive.org/stream/SixthFerryingGroupYearbookLongBeach/Sixth FerryingGroupYearbook_LongBeach#page/n0/mode/2up.
"Acting in the Children's Classics." *New York Times*, 1948.
"An Adventure with Robin Hood." *Family Theater*. Narr. Edmond O'Brien. Perf. William Conrad, Ed Begley. 27 July 1949. Available at *Old Time Radio Downloads*, http://www.oldtimeradiodownloads.com/drama/family-theater/family-theater-49-07-27-128-robin-hood.
Agosta, Lucien L. *Howard Pyle*. Twayne, 1987.
Albrecht-Crane, Christa, and Dennis Ray Cutchins, eds. Introduction to *Adaptation Studies: New Approaches*, 11–24. Rosemont Press, 2010.
"America of the Future Is Dependent on Right Living Children of Today." *The Washington Post*, 2 March 1930, p. JP6.
"And to Think I Saw It on Mulberry Street." *Columbia Workshop*, 1 December 1940. Available at *Old Time Radio Downloads*, http://www.oldtimeradiodownloads.com/drama/columbia-workshop/columbia-workshop-40-12-01-056-and-to-think-i-saw-it-on-mulberry-street.
Anderson, Arthur. *Let's Pretend: A History of Radio's Best Loved Children's Show by a Longtime Cast Member*. McFarland, 1994.
Anderson, Benedict. *Imagined Communities: Reflections on the Origin and Spread of Nationalism*. Rev. ed. Verso, 2006.
Angell, Jams Rowland. Foreword to *Radio: The Fifth Estate*, by Judith C. Waller. The Houghton Mifflin Radio Broadcasting Series, edited by Albert Crews. Houghton Mifflin Co., 1946.
"Arliss Sees Radio Play as Great Dramatic Force: Says Broadcasting Gives Listeners Literature of the Theater, but Doubts That the Ether Can Coax Successful Actors from Stage." *New York Times*, 7 March 1926.
Baden-Powell, Robert. *Scouting for Boys: A Handbook for Instruction in Good Citizenship*. Edited by Elleke Boehmer. Oxford University Press, 2004.
Bailey, Norman, Romulus Linney, and Dominick Cascio. *Ten Plays for Radio*. N.p., 1954.
Banks, Louis Albert Reverend. *Twentieth Century Knighthood: A Series of Addresses to Young Men*. Funk & Wagnalls, 1900.
Barabas, Suzanne, and Gabor Barabas. *Gunsmoke: A Complete History and Analysis of the Legendary Broadcast Series with a Comprehensive Episode-by-Episode Guide to Both the Radio and Television Programs*. McFarland, 1990.
Barczewski, Stephanie L. *Myth and National Identity in Nineteenth-Century Britain: The Legends of King Arthur and Robin Hood*. Oxford University Press, 2000.

Barnouw, Erik. *The Golden Web: A History of Broadcasting in the United States, Vol. II— 1933 to 1953.* Oxford University Press, 1968.
_____. *The Image Empire: A History of Broadcasting in the United States, Vol. III, from 1953.* Oxford University Press, 1970.
_____. *A Tower in Babel: A History of Broadcasting in the United States, Vol. 1—to 1933.* Oxford University Press, 1966.
Bartlett, Kenneth. "How to Use Radio: An Outline of Practical Suggestions for the Teacher and the Radio Chairman." National Association of Broadcasters, 1938.
Blaisdell, Ruth W. "Chivalry Is Not Lost." *The Christian Science Monitor*, 1952.
Bloomfield, Morton W. "Reflections of a Medievalist: America, Medievalism, and the Middle Ages," in *Medievalism in American Culture: Papers of the Eighteenth Annual Conference of the Center for Medieval and Early Renaissance Studies*, edited by Bernard Rosenthal and Paul E. Szarmach, 13–29. Medieval & Renaissance Texts & Studies Press, 1989.
Blue, Howard. *Words at War: World War II Era Radio Drama and the Postwar Broadcasting Blacklist.* Scarecrow Press, 2002.
Bluestone, George. *Novels into Film: The Metamorphosis of Fiction into Cinema.* University of California Press, 1957.
Boemer, Marilyn Lawrence. *The Children's Hour: Radio Programs for Children, 1929–1956.* Scarecrow Press, 1989.
Boldrini, Lucia. "Translating the Middle Ages: Modernism and the Ideal of the Common Language." *Translation and Literature*, vol. 12, no. 1 (2003): 41–68.
"Book Needs of Scouts." *The Publishers' Weekly: The American Book Trade Journal*, vol. 101, no. 3 (1922): 117.
"Book Reviews Now Broadcast." *New York Times*, 12 October 1924.
Bowers, Rick. *Superman Versus the Ku Klux Klan.* National Geographic Society, 2012.
Boy Scouts of America. *The Official Handbook for Boys*, 4th ed. Edited by William D. Murray, George D. Pratt, and A. A. Jameson. Doubleday Page & Co., 1913.
Bryant, John. "Textual Identity and Adaptive Revision: Editing Adaptation as a Fluid Text," in *Adaptation Studies: New Challenges, New Directions*, edited by Jørgen Bruhn, Anne Gjelsvik, and Eirik Frisvold Hanssen, 47–67. Bloomsbury, 2013.
Bryden, Inga. *Reinventing King Arthur: The Arthurian Legends in Victorian Culture.* Ashgate, 2005.
Burke, Edmund. *Reflections on the Revolution in France.* Edited by L. G. Mitchell. Oxford University Press, 1993.
Callahan, Jennie Waugh. *Radio Workshop for Children.* McGraw-Hill, 1948.
Cantril, Hadley, and Gordon W. Allport. *The Psychology of Radio.* Harper & Brothers, 1935.
Caxton, William. Preface to *The Works of Sir Thomas Malory*, 2d ed. Sir Thomas Malory, edited by Eugène Vinaver, xiii-xv. Oxford University Press, 1971.
Chapman, James. "*The Adventures of Robin Hood* and the Origins of the Television Swashbuckler." *Media History*, vol. 17, no. 3 (2011): 273–287.
Chaucer, Geoffrey. *The Canterbury Tales. The Riverside Chaucer*, 3d ed. Edited by F. N. Robinson. Houghton Mifflin, 1987.
"Chivalry Is Dead aka Politeness Story." *The Life of Riley*, 31 March 1950. Available at *Old Time Radio Researchers Library*, www.otrrlibrary.org.
Cole, Alonzo Deen. "The Tobacco Pouch." *Casey Crime Photographer*, 18 September 1947. Available at *Internet Archive*, https://archive.org/details/OTRR_Casey_Crime_Photographer_Singles.
"Comic Books." Ep. 218. *The Life of Riley*, 5 November 1948. Available at *Old Time Radio Downloads*, http://www.oldtimeradiodownloads.com/comedy/the-life-of-riley/life-of-riley-48-11-05-218-comic-books.
Conrad, Peter. *Orson Welles: The Stories of His Life.* Faber and Faber, 2003.

Cook, Tim. *Radio Drama: Theory and Practice*. Routledge, 1999.
Cooney, Terry A. *Balancing Acts: American Thought and Culture in the 1930s*. Twayne, 1995.
Craig, Steve. "How America Adopted Radio." *Journal of Broadcasting and Electronic Media* 48 (2004): 179–195.
Crutchfield, Les. "Lochinvar." *Gunsmoke*, 17 October 1952. Available at http://www.oldtimeradiodownloads.com/western/gunsmoke/lochinvar-1952-10-17.
"Curb Is Urged on Crime Programs on Radio: Appeal Is Made Probiems [sic] of Youth." *Christian Science Monitor*, 19 August 1938.
Dann, Sam, adapt. "The Connecticut Yankee in King Arthur's Court." Ep. 411. *CBS Mystery Theater*, 8 January 1976. Available at http://www.cbsrmt.com/episode-411-a-connecticut-yankee-in-king-arthurs-court.html.
Davidson, Roberta A. "Reading Like a Woman in Sir Thomas Malory's *Morte Darthur*." *Arthuriana*, vol. 16, no. 1 (2006): 21–33.
Davis, Arthur. "With a Grain of Salt: The Funny Book: Blessing or Menace?" *New Journal and Guide*, 20 March 1943.
de Charny, Geoffroi. *A Knight's Own Book of Chivalry*. Translated by Richard W. Kaeuper and Elspeth Kennedy. University of Pennsylvania Press, 2005.
de Lorris, Guillaume, and Jean de Meun. *The Romance of the Rose*, 3d ed. Translated by Charles Dahlberg. Princeton University Press, 1995.
DeForest, Tim. *Radio by the Book: Adaptations of Literature and Fiction on the Airwaves*. McFarland, 2008.
_____. *Storytelling in the Pulps, Comics, and Radio: How Technology Changed Popular Fiction in America*. McFarland, 2004.
Dierks, Margaret. "If Chivalry Is Dead, Women Killed It: They Expect Courtesy but Fail to Return It." *Chicago Daily Tribune*, 14 August 1955.
Dietz, Howard. "The Anomalous Sir Thomas Malory." *New York Times*, 10 January 1954.
Dobson, R. B., and J. Taylor. Introduction to *Rymes of Robin Hood: An Introduction to the English* Outlaw, 1–64. Heinemann, 1976.
Dorfman, Ariel. *The Empire's Old Clothes: What the Lone Ranger, Babar, and Other Innocent Heroes Do to Our Minds*. Duke University Press, 2009.
Douglas, Susan J. *Listening In: Radio and the American Imagination, from Amos 'n' Andy and Edward R. Morrow to Wolfman Jack and Howard Stern*. Random House Books, 1999.
Driver, Martha W. "Kid Crusaders: Heroic Children on Film." *The Medieval Hero on Screen: Representations from Beowulf to Buffy*. Edited by Martha W. Driver and Sid Ray. McFarland, 2004.
Dryer, Sherman H. *Radio in Wartime*. Greenberg, 1942.
Duff, David. *Romance and Revolution: Shelley and the Politics of a Genre*. Cambridge University Press, 1994.
Dunning, John. *On the Air: The Encyclopedia of Old-Time Radio*. Oxford University Press, 1998.
Eco, Umberto. *Travels in Hyperreality*. Harcourt Brace Jovanovich, 1986.
Ellis, Antony. "Robert of Huntingdon." *Escape*, 26 October 1952. Available at *Escape and Suspense!*, http://www.escape-suspense.com/2009/11/escape-robert-of-huntington.html.
"Exploits of Robin Hood Ok'd by Indiana's Educational Chief." *Chicago Daily Tribune*, 1953.
Fine, Morton, and David Friedkin. "The Triangle on the Round Table." *Crime Classics*, 18 November 1953. Available at *Old Time Radio Downloads*, http://www.oldtimeradiodownloads.com/crime/crime-classics/triangle-on-the-round-table-1953-11-18.
Finke, Laurie A., and Martin B. Shichtman. *King Arthur and the Myth of History*. University of Florida Press, 2004.

Foertsch, Jacqueline. *American Culture in the 1940s*. Edinburgh University Press, 2008.
Forbush, William Byron, and Dascomb Forbush. *The Queens of Avalon*, 3d ed. The Knights of King Arthur, 1915.
_____. *The Queens of Avalon or Ladies of the Court of King Arthur*. Frank Lincoln Masseck, 1908.
_____, and Frank Lincoln Masseck. *The Boys' Round Table, a Manual of the International Order of the Knights of King Arthur*, 6th ed. Frank Lincoln Masseck, 1909. Available at *HathiTrust*, https://catalog.hathitrust.org/Record/000569424.
Frantz, Joe B., and Julian Ernest Choate, Jr. *The American Cowboy: The Myth and the Reality*. University of Oklahoma Press, 1955.
Fraser, John. *America and the Patterns of Chivalry*. Cambridge University Press, 1982.
Fulton, Helen, ed. Introduction to *A Companion to Arthurian Literature. Blackwell Companions to Literature and Culture*, 1–11. Wiley-Blackwell, 2012.
"Gene Gets Discovered: Promo for Doublemint Gum Dealers." *Melody Ranch*. Perf. Gene Autry. Available at *Old Time Radio Researchers Group*, https://archive.org/details/OTRR_Melody_Ranch_Singles.
Gerber, Joan. "King Arthur." Ep. 136, *The Story Lady*. N.d. Available at Dumbwww, http://www.dumb.com/oldtimeradio/listen/8199/Comedy/The_Story_Lady/136_King_Arthur.html.
_____. "Robin Hood." Ep. 70, *The Story Lady*. N.d. Available at Dumbwww, http://www.dumb.com/oldtimeradio/listen/8132/Comedy/The_Story_Lady/070_Robin_Hood.html.
Giles, P. "Afterword: The Limits of Appropriation." *American Literary History*, vol. 22 no. 4 (2010): 951–960.
Girouard, Mark. *The Return to Camelot: Chivalry and the English Gentleman*. Yale University Press, 1981.
Godfrey, Donald G., and Frederic A. Leigh, eds. *Historical Dictionary of American Radio*. Greenwood, 1998.
Godwin, William. *Life of Geoffrey Chaucer, the Early English Poet: Including Memoirs of His Near Friend and Kinsman, John of Gaunt, Duke of Lancaster: With Sketches of the Manners, Opinions, Arts and Literature of England in the Fourteenth Century*. 1803. Nabu Public Domain Reprints, 2013.
Goebbels, Joseph. "Radio as the Eighth Great Power." *German Propaganda Archive*, edited by Randall Bytwerk. Calvin College, available at http://research.calvin.edu/german-propaganda-archive/goeb56.htm.
Gould, Jack. "On Rewriting Twain: Ford Theatre's 'Connecticut Yankee' Proves a Disappointment." *New York Times*, 12 October 1947.
"Governor Silent in 'Red Robin' Tale." *New York Times*, 1953.
Gray, James. *Business Without Boundary: The Story of General Mills*. University of Minnesota Press, 1954.
Harmon, Jim. *Radio Mystery and Adventure and Its Appearances in Film, Television, and Other Media*. McFarland, 1992.
Harty, Kevin J. "The Knights of the Square Table: The Boys Scouts and Thomas Edison Make an Arthurian Film." *King Arthur in America*, vol. 4, no. 4 (1994): 313–323.
Haworth, Mary. "Much Neurotic Tension Today is Caused by Individuals Trying to Adhere to Behavior-Ideals of King Arthur's Time, Despite Different Demands of the Modern World." "Mary Haworth's Mail," *The Washington Post*, 12 February 1952.
Heckert, Robert, adap. "Fifty-first Dragon." 12 April 1950. Available at *Old Time Radio Downloads*, http://www.oldtimeradiodownloads.com/drama/family-theater/family-theater-50-04-12-165-the-fifty-first-dragon.
Henthorne, Tom. "Boys to Men: Medievalism and Masculinity in *Star Wars* and *E. T.: The Extra-Terrestrial*." *The Medieval Hero on Screen: Representations from Beowulf to Buffy*. Edited by Martha W. Driver and Sid Ray, 73–85. McFarland, 2004.

Hilmes, Michele. *Radio Voices: American Broadcasting, 1922–1952*. University of Minnesota Press, 1997.
Hobsbawm, Eric. *Bandits*. The New Press, 2000.
Hutcheon, Linda. *A Theory of Adaptation*. Routledge, 2006.
Huwiler, Elke. "Engaging the Ear: Teaching Radio Drama Adaptations." *Redefining Adaptation Studies*. Edited by Dennis Cutchins, Laurence Raw, and James M. Welsh, Lanham, 133–145. Scarecrow Press, 2010.
_____. "Storytelling by Sound: A Theoretical Frame for Radio Drama Analysis." *The Radio Journal—International Studies in Broadcast and Audio Media*, vol. 3, no. 1 (2005): 45–59.
"The Immortal Ranger." *New York Times*, 10 April 1941.
Jackson, Joseph Henry. Introduction to *The Life and Adventures of Joaquin Murieta: The Celebrated California Bandit*, xi-l. Yellow Bird (John Rollin Ridge). University of Oklahoma Press, 1955.
Johnston, Johanna, adapt. "King Arthur and How He Won His Sword." *Let's Pretend*, 2 October 1954. Available at *Old Time Radio Downloads*, www.oldtimeradiodownloads.com/kids/lets-pretend/lets-pretend-54–10-02-king-arthur-rebroadcast.
_____. "Robin Hood." *Let's Pretend*, 9 January 1954. Available at *Old Time Radio Downloads*, www.oldtimeradiodownloads.com/kids/lets-pretend/lets-pretend-54–01-09-robin-hood.
Jones, William B., Jr. *Classics Illustrated: A Cultural History*, 2d ed. McFarland, 2011.
Jones, Winfield. *Story of the Ku Klux Klan*. American Newspaper Syndicate, 1921.
Kaueper, Richard W. Introduction to *A Knight's Own Book of Chivalry*. Geoffroi de Charny. Translated by Elspeth Kennedy. University of Pennsylvania Press, 2005.
Kaufman, Amy S. "The Law of the Lake: Sir Thomas Malory's Sovereign Lady." *Arthuriana*, vol. 17, no. 3 (2007): 56–73.
_____. "Medieval Unmoored." *Studies in Medievalism XIX*. Edited by Karl Fugeso, 1–11. D. S. Brewer, 2010.
"King Arthur aka The Thousand Dollars." *Avalon Time*, 18 March 1939. Available at *The Internet Archive*, https://archive.org/details/AvalonTimeRedSkelton.
Knight, Stephen. *Robin Hood: A Mythic Biography*. Cornell University Press, 2003.
Knight, Stephen, and Thomas Ohlgren, eds. Introduction to *Robin Hood and Other Outlaw Tales*. TEAMS: Middle English Texts Series. Western Michigan University, 2000.
Knights in Armor." *Proudly We Hail*, 7 April 1957. Available at *Old Radio Programs*, https://oldradioprograms.us/My%20Old%20Radio%20Shows/P/Proudly%20We%20Hail/Proudly-We-Hail-1957–04-07-AFRS-444-Knights-in-Armor.mp3.
"Knights in Shining Armor." *The Abbott and Costello Show*, 19 November 1942. Available at *Archive.org*, https://archive.org/details/AbbottAndCostello421119KnightsInShiningArmorWithMerleOberon.
"Knights [Knives] of the Square Table." *The Land of the Lost*, 28 October 1945. Available at *Old Time Radio Downloads*, http://www.oldtimeradiodownloads.com/adventure/the-land-of-the-lost/knights-of-the-square-table-1945–10-28.
"Knights of the White Carnation." *The Adventures of Superman*, 26 February 1947. Available at *Old Time Radio Fan*, http://www.otrfan.com/otr/superman/kwc.php.
Lanier, Sidney. *The Boy's King Arthur: Being Sir Thomas Sir Thomas Malory's History of King Arthur and His Knights of the Round Table Edited for Boys with an Introduction*. Charles Scribner's Sons, 1880. Available at *HathiTrust*, https://catalog.hathitrust.org/Record/007666517.
Lazarsfeld, Paul. *Radio and the Printed Page: An Introduction to the Study of Radio and Its Role in the Communication of Ideas*. Duell, Sloan and Pierce, 1940.
Lawrence, Jerome, and Robert Lee, adapts. "A Connecticut Yankee in King Arthur's Court." *Favorite Story*, 11 October 1947. Available at *Old Time Radio Downloads*,

http://www.oldtimeradiodownloads.com/drama/favorite-story/favorite-story-471011–005-connecticut-yankee-in-king-arthurs-court.

____. "A Connecticut Yankee in King Arthur's Court." *The Railroad Hour*, 27 November 1950. Available at *Old Time Radio Downloads*, http://www.oldtimeradiodownloads.com/variety/railroad-hour/railroad-hour-50–11-27–113-a-connecticut-yankee.

Lejeune, Anthony. "The Rise and Fall of the Western." *National Review*, vol. 41, no. 25 (1989): 23.

Leuchtenburg, W. E. *Franklin D. Roosevelt and the New Deal, 1932–1940*. Harper-Perennial, 2009.

Lewis, William B. "Reformers Challenged by Superman." *Broadcasting, Telecasting*, vol. 30, no. 19 (1946): 75.

Leyerle, John. "Conclusion: The Major Themes of Chivalric Literature." *Chivalric Literature: Essays on Relations between Literature and Life in the Later Middle Ages*. Edited by Larry D. Benson and John Leyerle, 131–146. University of Toronto Press, 1980.

Long, Huey P. "Share Our Wealth: Every Man a King." *Huey Long: The Man, His Mission, and Legacy*. Available at http://www.hueylong.com/programs/share-our-wealth.php.

Loewenthal, Max. "Report of the Washington Radio Conference." *Radio*, vol. 4. no. 4 (1922): 10–50.

Lull, Ramon. *The Book of the Ordre of Chyualry or Knyghthode by Ramon Lull, Translated by William Caxton with, L'Ordene de Chevalerie, an anonymous French Poem, translated by William Morris as; The Ordination of Knighthood, with a frontpiece by Edward Burne-Jones and edited by F.S. Ellis*. 1893. Edited by F. S. Ellis. Sovereign Press Canada, 2009.

Lupack, Alan. "Arthurian Youth Groups in America." *Adapting the Arthurian Legends for Children: Essays on Arthurian Juvenalia*. Edited by Barbara Tepa Lupack, 197–216. Palgrave MacMillan, 2004.

____, and Barbara Tepa Lupack. *King Arthur in America*. D. S. Brewer, 1999.

Lynch, Andrew. "*Le Morte Darthur* for Children: Sir Thomas Malory's Third Tradition." *Adapting the Arthurian Legends for Children: Essays on Arthurian Juvenalia*. Ed. Barbara Tepa Lupack. New York: Palgrave MacMillan, 2004. 1–49.

MacDonald, J. Fred. *Don't Touch That Dial! Radio Programming in American Life, 1920–1960*. Nelson-Hall, 1991.

MacLeod, Anne Scott. *American Childhood: Essays on Children's Literature of the Nineteenth and Twentieth Centuries*. University of Georgia Press, 1994.

____. "Howard Pyle's Robin Hood: The Middle Ages for Americans." *Children's Literature Association Quarterly*, vol. 25, no. 1 (2000): 44–48.

Malory, Thomas. *The Works of Sir Thomas Malory*, 2d ed. Edited by Eugène Vinaver. Oxford University Press, 1971.

Maltin, Leonard. *The Great American Broadcast: A Celebration of Radio's Golden Age*. New American Library, 1997.

Mancoff, Debra A., ed. Introduction to *The Arthurian Revival: Essays on Form, Tradition, and Transformation*. Garland, 1992.

Marshall, Sidney. "The Valiant Lady." *Family Theater*, 26 April 1950. Available at *Old Time Radio Downloads*, http://www.oldtimeradiodownloads.com/drama/family-theater/family-theater-50–04-26–167-the-valiant-lady.

Marianne. "News of Interest to Women: Tete-a-Tete." *The China Press*, 8 July 1932.

Match, Richard. "Scram Cinderella." *New York Times*, 1942.

Mathis, Andrew E. *The King Arthur Myth in Modern American Literature*. McFarland, 2002.

McConnell, Ed. "Knights and Tournaments." *The Buster Brown Gang*, 26 July 1946. Available at *Old Time Radio Downloads*, http://www.oldtimeradiodownloads.com/kids/buster-brown-gang/knights-and-tournaments-1946–07-27.

McCracken, Allison. "Scary Women and Scarred Men: *Suspense*, Gender Trouble, and

Postwar Change, 1942–1950." *Essays in the Cultural History of Radio: Radio Reader*. Edited by Michelle Hilmes and Jason Loviglio, 183–208. Routledge, 2002.

McFarlane, Brian. *Novel to Film: An Introduction to the Theory of Adaptation*. Oxford University Press, 1996.

McGillis, Roderick. *He Was Some Kind of a Man: Masculinities in the B Western*. Wilfrid Laurier University Press, 2009.

Meston, John. "Robin Hood." Ep. 28, *Gunsmoke*. 8 January 1955. Available at *Old Time Radio Researchers Group*, https://archive.org/details/OTRR_Gunsmoke_Singles.

Milligan, Harold Vincent Mrs. "Women's Radio Committee Clarifies." *Variety*, 22 May 1935.

Mott, Robert L. *Sound Effects: Radio, TV, and Film*. Focal Press, 1990.

"Nazis Declare Intention to Build Race of Supermen." *The China Press*, 1932.

Nicklas, Pascal, and Olive Lindner, eds. *Spectrum Literaturwissenschaft/Spectrum Literature: Adaptation and Cultural Appropriation: Literature, Film, and the Arts*. De Gruyter, 2012

O'Brien, Mae. *Children's Reactions to Radio Adaptations of Juvenile Books*. King's Crown, 1950.

Ossian, Lisa L. *The Forgotten Generation: American Children and World War II*. Columbia University Press, 2011.

Painter, Sidney. *French Chivalry: Chivalric Ideas and Practices in Mediaeval France*. John Hopkins University Press, 1957.

"Parents Will Find Knighthood of Youth Great Assistance in Home Training." *The Washington Post*, 22 December 1929.

Phalen, Patrick F. "Profound Sound: Family Theater Radio, 1947–1970." *Journal of Radio Studies*, vol. 11, no. 1 (2004): 116–130.

"Popeye Meets Robin Hood." *Popeye the Sailor*, 1930. Available at *Old Time Radio Downloads*, Radiohttp://www.oldtimeradiodownloads.com/kids/popeye-the-sailor/popeye-the-sailor-36-xx-xx-popeye-meets-robin-hood.

"Pupils Voice Views on Radio Programs." *New York Times*, 22 December 1946.

Pyle, Howard. *The Merry Adventures of Robin Hood of Great Renown, in Nottinghamshire*. 1883. Dover, 1968.

_____. *The Story of King Arthur and His Knights*. New American Library, 1986.

"Radio as Modern Story-teller Seen as No Menace to Books and Reading." *New York Times*, 16 February 1936.

"Radio: Plan 'Superman' Roadshows in Combo Hype for Program, Juve shows and Tolerance." *The Billboard (Archive: 1894–1960)*, vol. 58, no. 47 (1946): 7.

"Radio Talk Tells Parents and Children Fundamentals of Knighthood of Youth." *The Washington Post*, 15 December 1929.

"Radiotorial Comment." *Radio*, vol. 4. no. 4 (1922): 9.

Richmond, Velma Bourgeois. *Chivalric Stories as Children's Literature: Edwardian Retellings in Words and Pictures*. McFarland, 2014.

Ritson, Joseph. *Robin Hood: A Collection of All the Ancient Poems, Songs, and Ballads, Now Extant, Relative to That Celebrated English Outlaw: To Which Are Prefixed Historical Anecdotes of His Life in Two Volumes*. Vol. 1. London, Printed for T. Egerton, Whitehall, and J. Johnson, St. Pauls-Church-Yard. Available at *Eighteenth Century Collections Online*.

"Robin Hood." *Your Playhouse of Favorites*, 1949. Available at Dumbwww, http://www.dumb.com/oldtimeradio/listen/67697/Drama/Your_Playhouse_of_Favorites/xxxxxx_49_Robin_Hood.html.

Rosenthal, Bernard, and Paul E. Szarmach, eds. Introduction to *Medievalism in American Culture: Papers of the Eighteenth Annual Conference of the Center for Medieval and Early Renaissance Studies*, 1–12. State University of New York at Binghamton, 1989.

Sanders, Julie. *Adaptation and Appropriation*. Routledge, 2006.

Saul, Nigel. *Chivalry in Medieval England*. Harvard University Press, 2011.
Savage, Barbara Dianne. *Broadcasting Freedom: Radio, War, and the Politics of Race, 1938–1948*. University of North Carolina Press, 1999.
Savage, William W., Jr. *The Cowboy Hero: His Image in American History and Culture*. University of Oklahoma Press, 1979.
Scala, Elizabeth. "Disarming Lancelot." *Studies in Philology* 99.4 (Autumn 2002): 380–403. *JSTOR*.
Schoen, Lillian, adapt. "A Connecticut Yankee in King Arthur's Court." *The Ford Theater*, 5 October 1947. Available at *Old TimeRadio Downloads*, http://www.oldtimeradiodownloads.com/drama/the-ford-theater/connecticut-yankee-in-king-arthurs-court-1947-10-05.
Scott, Sir Walter. *Sir Walter Scott's Marmion*. Longman's English Classics. Edited by Robert Morss Lovett. Longmans, Green, and Co., 1896. Available at *Hathitrust*, https://hdl.handle.net/2027/loc.ark:/13960/t6j10nh86.
Seal, Graham. "The Robin Hood Principle: Folklore, History, and the Social Bandit." *Journal of Folklore Research*, vol. 46, no. 1 (2009): 67–89.
"Sir Cisco, Knight of the Round Table." Ep. 616. *The Cisco Kid*, 5 June 1958. Available at *Old Time Radio Downloads*, http://www.oldtimeradiodownloads.com/western/cisco-kid-the/cisco-kid-58-06-05-616-sir-cisco-knight-of-the-round-table.
"Sir Lancelot of the Lake." *Family Theater*, 28 June 1950. Available at *Old Time Radio Downloads*, http://www.oldtimeradiodownloads.com/drama/family-theater/family-theater-50-06-28-176-sir-lancelot-of-the-lake.
"Sir Lancelot of the Lake." *Sealtest Variety*, 16 September 1948. Available at *Archive.org*, https://archive.org/details/SealtestVarietyTheater.
"Sir Tommy, the Silver Knight." Ep. 39, *Wild Bill Hickok*, 24 December 1951. Available at *Old Time Radio Westerns*, http://www.otrwesterns.com/membership/adventures-of-wild-bill-hickok/.
Sklar, Elizabeth S. "The Case of the Disappearing Text: *Connecticut Yankee* for Kids." *Adapting the Arthurian Legends for Children: Essays on Arthurian Juvenalia*. Edited by Barbara Tepa Lupack, 73–105. Palgrave MacMillan, 2004.
Smith, Katherine. "Survey of Children's Programs on the Radio Finds Marked Improvement." *The Washington Post*, 1935.
Steckmesser, Kent L. "Robin Hood and the American Outlaw: A Note on History and Folklore." *The Journal of American Folklore*, vol. 79, no. 312 (1966): 348–355.
Stein, Sonia. "It's Parents, Not Kids, That Worry Radio." *The Washington Post*, 20 April 1947.
"Superman Combats Race Intolerance." *Atlanta Daily World*, 1946.
Tennyson, Alfred Lord. *Idylls of the King and a Selection of Poems*. Signet Classic, 1961.
Tondro, Jason. "Camelot in Comics." *King Arthur in Popular Culture*. Edited by Elizabeth Sklar and Donald L. Hoffman, 169–181. McFarland, 2002.
Tuchman, Barbara. *A Distant Mirror: The Calamitous 14th Century*. Ballantine Books, 1978.
Twain, Mark. "A Word of Explanation." *A Connecticut Yankee in King Arthur's Court: An Authoritative Text, Backgrounds and Sources, Composition and Publication, Criticism*. Edited by Allison R. Ensor, 5–10. W. W. Norton & Co., 1982.
Tye, Larry. *Superman: The High-flying History of America's Most Enduring Hero*. Random House, 2012.
United States Office of War Information. *American Handbook*. Prepared by the Office of War Information, 1945. Available at *HathiTrust*, https://catalog.hathitrust.org/Record/000246869.
"Val Becomes a Knight." *Prince Valiant*, n.d., MP3.
"varlet, n." *OED Online*. Oxford University Press, 2017.
Venuti, Lawrence. "Adaptation, Translation, Critique." *Film and Literature: An Introduction and Reader*, 2d ed. Edited by Timothy Corrigan, 89–103. Routledge, 2012.

Verma, Neil. *Theater of the Mind: Imagination, Aesthetics, and American Radio Drama.* University of Chicago Press, 2012.
Waller, Judith. *Radio: The Fifth Estate.* The Riverside Press, 1946.
Weaver, Luther. *The Technique of Radio Writing.* Prentice-Hall, 1948.
Whitaker, Alma. "The Last Word: Is Chivalry Still Dead?" *Los Angeles Times*, 27 December 1926.
Williams, David. "Medieval Movies." *The Yearbook of English Studies*, 20 (1990): 1–32.
"Winged Words." *National Radio News* 1.7 (January 1929). Available at *Old Time Radio Researchers.* http://www.otrr.org/FILES/Magz_pdf/National%20Radio%20News/NRN_V01_(07)_Jan29.pdf.
Wister, Owen. "The Evolution of the Cow-Puncher." *Harper's New Monthly Magazine.* September 1895. Available at *HathiTrust*, https://babel.hathitrust.org/cgi/pt?id=njp.32101074885466;view=2up;seq=2;skin=mobile
Wylie, Max. *Radio Writing.* Farrar and Rinehart, 1939.
Zeliff, Jane Seely. "When Is a Lady?" *Los Angeles Times*, 11 September 1955.
Zylstra, Maryon. "Do You Think Chivalry Is Dead?" "Inquiring Camera Girl: The Question," *Chicago Daily Tribune*, 5 January 1946.

Index

Abbott and Costello (radio) 10; "Knights in Shining Armor" 181–183; *see also* Abbott, Bud; Costello, Lou
Adaptation and Appropriation 6
"An Adventure with Robin Hood" 152; *see also Family Theater*; O'Brien, Edmond
The Adventures of Robin Hood (television) 58; film 154
The Adventures of Sir Galahad (film) 87
The Adventures of Superman (radio) 2, 8, 20, 29, 33, 57, 59, 116, 119, 188; *see also* "Knights of the White Carnation" (radio) 120–129; Maxwell, Robert; medievalism
The Air Corps Ferrying Command 182, 191*n*1
Albrecht-Crane, Christa 46
Allport, Gordon W. 5, 12, 27–29, 120
American Culture in the 1940s 30
American Handbook 14
Amos 'n' Andy (radio) 1, 189*n*1
And to Think That I Saw It on Mulberry Street 32
Anderson, Arthur 51–52, 81; *see also Let's Pretend*
Anderson, Benedict 5, 6, 28
Angell, James Rowland 12
"Arthur Skelton aka The Thousand Dollars" *see Avalon Time*; Skelton, Red
Arthurian youth groups 60, 63, 67; *see also* Forbush, William Bryan
Astarita, Rafael (*New Comics, Detective Comics*) 47
Autry, Gene 4, 75–76, 83, 136–137, 170, 172; "Cowboy Code" or "Cowboy Commandments" 138
Avalon Time 9, 10; "Robin Hood aka Party at Red's House" 180–181; Skelton, Red 180–181

Baden-Powell, Robert 75, 190*ch*3*n*3
Bakhtin, Mikhail 46
banditry *see* Billy the Kid; Hobsbawm, Eric; James, Jesse; Robin Hood
Banks, Louis Albert 71, 73
Barczewski, Stephanie 56
Barnouw, Erik 1, 3, 5, 190*ch*5*n*1
Barthes, Roland 46
Bendix, William 49
Berg, Gertrude 1
Billy the Kid 169–170
The Black Knight (film) 87
Blue, Howard 119
Bluestone, George 34
Boemer, Marilyn Lawrence 6
Bowers, Rick 123
Brand, Max 5, 9, 134
Broun, Heywood 36, 37, 99
Bryden, Inga 86
Bulfinch, Thomas 47
Burke, Edmund 65, 76
Burns, Walter Noble 169–170
Buster Brown 20

The Campbell Playhouse see *The Mercury Theater*
The Canterbury Tales 33
Cantril, Hadley 5, 12, 27–29, 120
Casey, Crime Photographer 9, 191*ch*7*n*4; "The Tobacco Pouch" 161–163
Cassidy, Hopalong (character) 135–136
Caxton, William 23, 63–64, 140
CBS Mystery Theater 40
Cervantes, Miguel de *(Don Quixote)* 5, 81, 84, 140, 142
Charny, Geoffroi de 25, 63

201

Index

Chaucer, Geoffrey 8, 33–34, 47, 143–144, 156; *see also* chivalry in *The Canterbury Tales* 62
The Children's Hour: Radio Programs for Children, 1929–1956 6
children's radio programming: anti-fascism campaign 119; negative influence 29; network standards 34, 87; socializing agent 29, 146
chivalry 2–4, 36, 59, 123–124, 188; American national identity 71–74, 79; Arthurian knighthood trait 70; Arthurian youth groups influence on 60, 63, 75, 138; Burke, Edmund 65; chivalric code 61, 88, 138, 152, 188; chivalric cowboy 3, 9, 136, 171–172; chivalric revival 86, 142, 191*ch*6*n*2; gender 3, 8, 60, 62, 72–77, 160, 183; Lanier, Sidney 67–68, 71; *Le Morte Darthur* 23, 61–62; *Prince Valiant* (radio) 133; Pyle, Howard 69–70; racism 120; radio episodes in 100, 104–108, 100, 111, 114, 116, 127, 129, 188; Robin Hood trait of 21, 70, 148, 156, 160; scouting movement 4, 75, 82; "The Valiant Lady" 99–102
"Chivalry Is Dead" *see Life of Riley*
Chrétien de Troyes 86
Cisco Kid (radio) 2, 5, 9, 20, 83, 136–137, 139, 178; chivalry 3; "Sir Cisco, Knight of the Round Table" 139–142; *see also* medievalism
Classics Illustrated (*Comics Illustrated*) *see* comic books; Kanter, Albert
"Clean Your Plate" Club 22, 190*ch*4*n*6
Cole, Alonzo Deen 162; *see also The Witch's Tale*
Collyer, Clayton "Bud" 121; *see also* Superman
Colman, Ronald 102
Columbia Workshop *see* "The Fall of the City"; MacLeish, Archibald
"Comic Books" *see The Life of Riley*
comic books 47–48; *see also* Astarita, Rafael (*New Comics*, *Detective Comics*); Kanter, Albert (*Classics Illustrated* or *Comics Illustrated*) 47–48
Communism 22, 30, 57–59, 163, 166, 168; *see also* Ellis, Anthony; *Escape*; "Robert of Huntingdon"
A Connecticut Yankee (musical) 40; *see also* Fields, Herbert
"A Connecticut Yankee in King Arthur's Court" *see The Ford Theater*; *The Railroad Hour*; *Favorite Story*; Twain, Mark
Conrad, Peter 28; *see also* Welles, Orson
Conrad, William (radio work) 100, 110, 164–165
Cooper, James Fenimore 5, 9, 27, 134
Corell, Charles J. 1; *see also Amos 'n' Andy* (radio); Freeman, Fisher Gosden
Corwin, Norman 59, 178
Coughlin, Charles E. 118, 122, 190*ch*5*n*1; *see also* fascism
The Count of Monte Cristo 27
courtly love 111–112; *see also* chivalry
Cowboy Commandments 4, 138; *see also* Autry, Gene; chivalric cowboy; chivalry; scouting movement
Crime Classics 8, 20, 57, 87–88, 179; "Triangle on the Round Table" 110–115; *see also* Fine, Morton; Friedkin, David
Crisis 10; "The Robin Hood Heist" 187; *see also* French, Jim;
Crump, Irving (*Boys' Life*) 82; *see also Jack Armstrong, All American Boy*; Strong, Paschal
Crutchfield, Les 107; *see also Gunsmoke* (radio)
Cutchins, Dennis Ray 46
Cvetic, Matt (*I Was a Communist for the FBI*) 166

DeForest, Tim 6, 52, 130
Deitz, Howard 190*ch*4*n*2
DeKoven, Reginald 169
de Pizan, Christine 25, 63–64; *see also* chivalry
Detective Comics 48; *see also* comic books
Devin, Andy 143; *see also Wild Bill Hickok* (radio)
Dickens, Charles 7
Dillon, Matt 83, 108–110, 136; *see also Gunsmoke* (radio)
Disney, Walt 179–180
Dr. Seuss 13, 32
Don't Touch That Dial! Radio Programming in American Life from 1920–1960 5
Douglas, Susan J. 5, 34, 52
Dracula 27, 32
Driver, Martha W. 56
Dryer, Sherman Harvard (radio in wartime) 12

Index

Dumas, Alexander 27
Dunning, John 5, 33, 41–42, 49, 51

Eco, Umberto 20, 122–123
Edison, Thomas: *The Knights of the Square Table* (film) 89
Eisenhower, Dwight D. 112
Ellis, Antony 9, 58; *see also Escape*; "Robert of Huntingdon"
Escape 2, 9, 20, 110, 161, 179; "Robert of Huntingdon" 163–173
E.T.: The Extra-Terrestrial 21

Fairbanks, Douglas 169; *see also Robin Hood* (film)
"The Fall of the City" (radio) 33; *see also Columbia Workshop*; MacLeish, Archibald
Family Theater 2, 7–9, 19, 20, 36, 54, 80–81, 98–100, 111–112, 157, 179, 188; "An Adventure with Robin Hood" 152–155; "Fifty-first Dragon" (radio) 36–41; "In Shining Armor" 91–92; "Sir Lancelot of the Lake" (radio) 96–99; "The Valiant Lady" 99–102; *see also*; Peyton, Father Patrick
fascism: America in 119; fight against 121; radio on 118, 128–129; Superman fights 123–124; *see also* Coughlin, Charles E.
Favorite Story: "A Connecticut Yankee in King Arthur's Court" (radio) 40, 45–49
"Fifty-first Dragon" (radio) 36–37, 99; *see also* Broun, Heywood; *Family Theater*
Fine, Morton 110–112; *see also Crime Classics*; "The Triangle on the Round Table"
Finke, Laurie 120
Fischlin, Daniel 38
Flynn, Errol 39, 152, 169, 187; *The Adventures of Robin Hood* (film) 154
Foertsch, Jacqueline 30
Forbush, William Bryan 72–73, 75; *see also* Arthurian Youth Groups
Ford Theater (radio) 7; "A Connecticut Yankee in King Arthur's Court" (radio) 40–42; *see also* Gould, Jack; Schoen, Lillian
Fortier, Mark 38
Foster, Hal 116, 129–130; *see also Prince Valiant*
Franklin, Benjamin 17, 147–148

French, Jim *see Crisis*; "The Robin Hood Heist"
Friedkin, David 110–112, 179; *see also Crime Classics*; "The Triangle on the Round Table"

Geisel, Theodore *v* 32; *see also* Dr. Seuss
gender: Arthurian radio adaptations 88–89, 92
Gerber, Joan: *The Story Lady* 38–39, 185
Gest of Robyn Hood 9, 18
Ginty, Elizabeth Beall 170
Girouard, Mark 124, 191n2; *see also* chivalry
Godwin, William: Chaucer, Geoffrey biography 66; chivalry 65; medievalism 66
Goebbels, Joseph 120
The Goldbergs 1
The Golden Web 5
Gosden, Freeman Fisher 1; *see also Amos 'n' Andy*; Correll, Charles J.
Gould, Jack (*New York Times*) 41–42; *see also* "A Connecticut Yankee in King Arthur's Court" (radio); *The Ford Theater*; Schoen, Lillian
Gray, James 171
Grey, Zane 9, 134
Gunsmoke (radio) 2, 4–5, 8–10, 13, 20, 83, 161, 172, 179; "Lochinvar" 107–110; "Robin Hood" 173–177; *see also* Scott, Sir Walter

Hamlet 32
Harte, Bret 5, 9, 99, 134
Have Gun Will Travel (radio) 136
Hawthorn, Mary (*Washington Post*) 4
Henthorne, Tom 21
Hickok, Bill "Wild" 5, 140, 142
Hilmes, Michele 5
Hitler, Adolf 13–14, 117–118, 120, 123, 184–185; Nazi Party 120
Hobsbawm, Eric 174
Hoole Book 20
Hoover, Herbert 11, 30, 105, 118
Hoover, J. Edgar 30
Houseman, John *see* "War of the Worlds" (radio); Welles, Orson; Wells, H.G.
Huckleberry Finn 17
Hurd, Richard 65–67
Hutcheon, Linda 6, 38–40, 44, 46
Huwiler, Elke 34, 39

Index

The Image Empire 5
Imagined Communities 5
"In Shining Armor" 88; *see also Family Theater*
Inner Sanctum 13, 32, 179

Jack Armstrong, the All-American Boy 17, 29, 75, 80, 82–84, 126, 128, 171, 178–179, 188; *see also* Crump, Irving; Munday, Talbot; Strong, Paschal
James, Jesse 170
James, G.P.R. 100
Johnston, Johanna 93–94, 159
Jonson, Ben 147

Kanter, Albert (*Classics Illustrated* or *Comics Illustrated*) 47–48
Kennedy, Jacqueline 20–21
King Arthur: historical persona 86
"King Arthur" (radio) *see Mickey Mouse Theater of the Air*; *The Story Lady*
"King Arthur and How He Won His Sword" 51, 89, 98; *see also Let's Pretend*
Knight, Stephen 22, 191*ch7n*1
"Knights and Tournaments" *see Smilin' Ed's Buster Brown Gang*
"Knights in Armor" *see Proudly We Hail*
"Knights in Shining Armor" *see Abbott and Costello*
Knights of the Round Table (film) 87, 97
"Knights of the White Carnation" 9, 59, 86, 116; *see also The Adventures of Superman*; Ku Klux Klan; Maxwell, Robert
A Knight's Own Book of Chivalry 25
"Knives of the Square Table" *see The Land of the Lost*
Kristeva, Julia 46
Ku Klux Klan 8, 59, 86, 116–118, 122, 124–125, 128, 188; *see also The Adventures of Superman*; "Knights of the White Carnation" (radio)

Lambert, Mark 98
Lamour, Dorothy 102; *see also* "Knives of the Square Table"; *Sealtest Variety Theatre*; "Sir Lancelot of the Lake" (radio)
The Land of the Lost 8, 57; "Knives of the Square Table" 89–91
Langland, William 146; *see also* dream vision
Lanier, Sidney (*The Boy's Froissart*) 67–68; *see also* chivalry
Lawrence, Jerome 44; *see also The Railroad Hour* (radio)
Lee, Robert 44; *see also The Railroad Hour* (radio)
Let's Pretend (radio) 2, 8–9, 19, 51, 57, 80–81, 93, 96, 111–112, 115, 179, 188; "King Arthur and How He Won His Sword" 93–96; "Robin Hood" 159–161; *see also* Anderson, Arthur; Mack, Nila
Lewis, Elliott 110; *see also Crime Classics*; "The Triangle on the Round Table"
The Life of Riley 7; "Chivalry Is Dead" 77–82; "Comic Books" 49–55; *see also* Bendix, William
Lindner, Oliver 39
Lindsay, Howard 42
Listening In: Radio and the American Imagination from Amos 'n' Andy and Edward R. Murrow to Wolfman Jack and Howard Stern 5
"Lochinvar" (radio) *see Gunsmoke*; Scott, Sir Walter
Lolita 38
The Lone Ranger 13, 83, 135, 137, 170–172, 189*ch2n*1
Long, Huey 54–55, 58, 118, 122, 170, 189*n*1
Lull, Raymond 25, 63; *see also* chivalry
Lupack, Alan 41, 67, 74, 87
Lupack, Barbara Tepa 41, 67, 74, 87, 190*ch5n*2

Mabie, Hamilton Wright 71
MacDonald, J. Fred 5, 82, 172
Macdonnell, Norman 173
Mack, Nila 80, 93, 190*ch3n*3; *see also Let's Pretend*
MacLeish, Archibald *see Columbia Workshop*; "The Fall of the City"
MacLeod, Anne Scott 31, 69, 136
Madison, Guy 143; *see also Wild Bill Hickok* (radio)
Malmesbury, William of 86
Malory, Sir Thomas 2, 7, 8, 13, 23–24, 37, 85, 94, 110, 112–115, 132, 135, 146; *Le Morte Darthur* 3, 36, 86, 111, 126, 131, 137, 178, 189*prologuen*1; *see also* Vinaver, Eugene
Mancoff, Debra 85, 124
Marshall, Sidney 100; *see also Family Theater*; "The Valiant Lady"

Index

Match, Richard (*New York Times*) 19
Maxwell, Robert 33, 59, 86, 116–117, 121–126, 128, 188; *see also The Adventures of Superman*; "Knights of the White Carnation"
McCarthy, Joseph 59; *see also* Communism
McConnell, Ed 54, 104–106, 111, 150–152; *see also Smilin' Ed's Buster Brown Gang*
McCully, Johnston 170; *see also* Zorro
McFarlane, Brian 46, 53
medieval dream vision 28, 143, 149; *see also* Langland, William
medieval romance 132
medievalism 2, 7, 20, 21, 56, 59, 68, 83, 117, 119, 121–122, 135, 163, 168, 172–174, 188; chivalric revival 63; revival 57, 86; Old West 172; twentieth-century America in 87; *see also Cisco Kid* (radio); "Knights of the White Carnation"
Melville, Herman 13
The Mercury Theater on the Air 27
Merrill, Lou 110
The Merry Adventures of Robin Hood of Great Renown, in Nottinghamshire 10, 40
Meston, John 173–174
Mickey Mouse Theater of the Air 10; "King Arthur" 180; *see also* Disney, Walt
Milland, Ray 102; *see also Sealtest Variety Theater*; "Sir Lancelot of the Lake" (radio)
Monmouth, Geoffrey of 86
Moore, Clayton *see The Lone Ranger*
Le Morte Darthur 3, 7, 8, 18, 19, 23, 36, 61, 63–65, 69–70, 85–115, 126, 131, 137, 178, 189*prologuen*.1
Mott, Robert L. 130–131
Mulford, Clarence Edward 135; *see also The Lone Ranger*
Munday, Anthony 146–147
Munday, Talbot 82
Murrow, Edward R. 14

National Association of Broadcasters Code 30; *see also* children's radio programming; radio
Nazi Party 120, 183, 188; *see also* Hitler, Adolf
Nicklas, Pascal 39
Novels into Film 34

Oberon, Merle 181–182; *see also* Abbott and Costello
Obler, Arch 178
O'Brien, Edmond 153; *see also* "An Adventure with Robin Hood"; *Family Theater*
Ohlgren, Thomas 191*n*3
On the Air: The Encyclopedia of Old-Time Radio 5
"Operation Toleration" ("Operation Tolerance") 116, 121, 124; *see also The Adventures of Superman* (radio); Maxwell, Robert
Ossian, Lisa 190*ch*4*n*6

paladin 136
Peacock, Thomas 169
Percy, Thomas 86, 134; Robin Hood ballads 147, 191*ch*7*n*2
Peyton, Father Patrick 36, 81, 152; *see also Family Theater*
The Picture of Dorian Gray 38
Piers Plowman 22; *see also* Langland, William
Poe, Edgar Allan 13
Poe, Elizabeth 76
"Popeye Meets Robin Hood" *see Popeye the Sailor*
Popeye the Sailor (radio) 2, 9, 20, 178; "Popeye Meets Robin Hood" 148–150
Porter, William Sydney 139
Prince Valiant (comic) 20, 129; character 130; film 87; radio 2, 8, 19, 57, 116, 129–133
Proudly We Hail, the United States Army 10; "Knights in Armor" 183–185
The Psychology of Radio 5, 27
Pyle, Howard 3, 5, 10, 19, 75, 129, 149, 151, 168, 178; chivalry opinion 70; *Merry Adventures of Robin Hood* (book) 3, 40, 155, 157; radio adaptation 69, 159–160; *The Story of King Arthur and His Knights* 131

radio: American culture influence 6, 12–13; children influence 29, 146, 178; network "children's ode" 15–17, 31, 179; standardization of English 15
Radio by the Book: Adaptations of Literature and Fiction on the Airwaves 6
Radio Voices 5
The Railroad Hour 40; "A Connecticut Yankee in King Arthur's Court 44–

45; *see also* Lawrence, Jerome; Lee, Robert
Richmond, Velma Bourgeois 30, 68, 190*ch*3*n*1
Ridge, Rollin John (Murieta, Joaquin character) 169–170
Ritson, Joesph 5, 9, 148, 150, 173
"Robert of Huntingdon" 9, 51, 58, 110; *see also Escape*
Robin Hood: 134–135; ballads 20, 81, 132, 146–147, 149, 151, 154, 159–160, 164–165, 173; chivalry 62, 88; cowboy characteristics 137, 169–170; Communism 22; *Gunsmoke* (radio) 176–177; social bandit 170–171
Robin Hood (film) 169; *see also* Fairbanks, Douglas
"Robin Hood" (radio) 38, 39; *Cisco Kid* 139; *see also Gunsmoke; Let's Pretend; Smilin' Ed's Buster Brown Gang; The Story Lady; Your Playhouse of Favorites*
Robin Hood: A Collection of All the Ancient Poems, Songs, and Ballads, Now Extant, Relative to That Celebrated English Outlaw: To Which Are Prefixed Historical Anecdotes of His Life in Two Volumes 9
Robin Hood: A Mythic 22
"Robin Hood aka Party at Red's House" *see Avalon Time*; Skelton, Red
"The Robin Hood Heist" *see Crisis*; French, Jim
Romeo and Juliet 35
Roosevelt, Theodore 134
Rose, Ralph 18
Rosenthal, Bernard 172

Sanders, Julie 6
Savage, Barbara 117
Savage, William 136
Schoen, Lillian 41; *see also* "A Connecticut Yankee in King Arthur's Court" (radio); *The Ford Theater*
Scott, Sir Walter 7–8, 13, 69, 81, 169, 178; works adaptation 83, 107, 109; *see also Gunsmoke* (radio)
Sealtest Variety Theater 8, 102; "Sir Lancelot of the Lake" 102–104
Seeing Things at Night 36
Shakespeare, William 13, 27, 32, 35–37, 99, 147, 185
Shelley, Mary 13
Shichtman, Martin 120

Shirer, William L. 13
Shuster, Joe: Superman 120; *see also* Siegel, Jerry
Siegel, Jerry: Superman 120; *see also* Shuster, Joe
Silverheels, Jay *see The Lone Ranger*
Simmons, Joseph William 117; *see also* Ku Klux Klan
"Sir Cisco, Knight of the Round Table" 84; *see also Cisco Kid*
Sir Gawain and the Green Knight 24, 36, 131
"Sir Lancelot of the Lake" (radio) 54, 98–99; *see also Family Theater; Sealtest Variety Theater*
"Sir Tommy, the Silver Knight" *see Wild Bill Hickok*
Skelton, John 147
Skelton, Red 180–181; *see also Avalon Time*
Sklar, Elizabeth S. 41
Smilin' Ed's Buster Brown Gang (radio) 2, 8–9, 20, 22, 54, 57, 111; "Knights and Tournaments" 104–107; "Robin Hood" (radio) 150–152
Smith, Harry B. 169
sound effects (radio) 32, 52–54, 93, 164
Star Wars 21
Steckmesser, Kent L. 168
Stevenson, Robert Louis (radio adaptations of works) 13, 17, 27, 32, 81, 99
Stoker, Bram 27, 32
The Story Lady (radio) 10, 38; "King Arthur" (radio) 185–187; "Robin Hood" (radio) 185–187; *see also* Gerber, Joan
Storytelling in the Pulps, Comics, and Radio: How Technology Changed Popular Fiction in America 6
Strong, Paschal (*Boys' Life*) 82; *see also* Crump, Irving; *Jack Armstrong, All American Boy*; Munday, Talbot
Superman 120, 124, 127; *see also* Collyer, Clayton "Bud"; Shuster, Joe; Siegel, Jerry
Suspense 179
Szarmach, Paul 172

Tales from Far and Near 40
Tennyson, Alfred Lord: *The Foresters* 169; *Idylls of the King* 68, 82, 98, 178; radio adaptations 69, 103; "The Valiant Lady" 88, 99; *see also Family Theater*
Theater of the Mind 5

A Theory of Adaptation 6, 38
Trendle, George 171; *see also* Lone Ranger
"The Tobacco Pouch" *see Casey, Crime Photographer*
A Tower in Babel 5
Treasure Island 17, 27, 32
"Triangle on the Round Table" 88; *see also Crime Classics*; Fine, Morton; Friedkin, David
Truman, Harry 105
Tuchman, Barbara 111
Turner, Frederick Jackson 134
Twain, Mark 7, 17, 42; *A Connecticut Yankee in King Arthur's Court* (novel) 40, 141; medievalism 71; radio adaptations 40–41, 46, 99; *see also* Ford Theatre
Tye, Larry 1, 121, 123

"Valiant Becomes a Knight" 129; *see also* Foster, Hal; *Prince Valiant* (radio)
"The Valiant Lady" *see Family Theater*
Van Nostrand, Jack 91
Venuti, Lawrence 46
Verma, Neil 5, 52–53
Vinaver, Eugene 18, 23, 87, 93, 96, 99, 190*ch4n*1

WABC–New York 33
Wace 86
Waller, Judith 17, 34

The War of the Worlds 27–28, 33
"War of the Worlds" (radio) *see also* Welles, Orson; Wells, H.G.
Warton, Thomas 86
WDRC–Connecticut 4
Welles, Orson 28, 33, 37, 120, 178; *see also* "War of the Worlds" (radio)
Wells, H.G. (*The War of the Worlds*) (novel) 27–28; *see also* Welles, Orson
West, Mae 181
WGY–New York 16, 35
The Whistler (radio) 179
White, T.H. 87, 186
Wild Bill Hickok (radio) 3, 9, 20, 136–137, 178; "Sir Tommy, the Silver Knight" 142–145
Wister, Owen 5, 9, 134–135
The Witch's Tale (radio) 130, 179
The Wizard of Oz 38
WLW–Cincinnati 35
The Works of Sir Thomas Malory 23
WXYZ–Detroit 171; *see also The Lone Ranger*
Wylie, Max 32, 37–39
Wynken de Worde 155

Your Playhouse of Favorites (radio) 152; "Robin Hood" 155–159

Zorro 170; *see also* chivalric cowboy; chivalry

www.ingramcontent.com/pod-product-compliance
Ingram Content Group UK Ltd.
Pitfield, Milton Keynes, MK11 3LW, UK
UKHW042002140426
5217IPUK00015B/942

9 781476 667041